PRAISE FOR *COSTLY LOVE*

Love is the best thing we have—and yet we struggle to describe it, let alone live into it. That's because love is a cross and an empty tomb; loving is knitting the church back together and saving the world. John Armstrong is perfectly placed to write about love—with evangelical zeal, catholic wisdom, and erudition without obscurity.

Dr. Jason Byassee
Butler Chair in Homiletics at Vancouver School of Theology
Fellow in theology and leadership at Duke Divinity School

Christian unity is not found in academic papers or sacred doctrines and practices. True unity is only found in sharing together in the costly love God has poured out upon us. John Armstrong has boldly called us to get out of the way to become open vessels of divine love to others, indeed to the whole world. He gives us hope, and a clear road map, for *how* costly love transforms us into Jesus' unity.

Doug Haugen
Executive Director, Lutheran Men in Mission

As a pastor who deals with both with people who are hurting and national issues that bring division, I cannot think of a remedy more important than "the unity of love." John Armstrong makes this central concept of God's identity and command both clear and applicable in our lives. This book is helping me do what I thought I knew!

Dr. Joel C. Hunter
Senior Pastor Northland,
A Church Distributed

John Armstrong loves his friends, loves Christ's church, and loves the Lord. He personally knows the *cost* of love. Rooted deeply in John's personal experience of costly love, this book is timely and meets a serious need in these days of deep division. Like John's life and ministry, *Costly Love* is a gift to us all.

Dr. Craig R. Higgins
Founding and Senior Pastor
Trinity Presbyterian Church
Rye, New York
(member of the Redeemer Network of churches)

If only for an introduction to some of the church's greatest fans, you should read this book. But I'm not one of them and I'm not because of the facts John Armstrong lays out in this critically important book. Here's a taste: "From the apostolic era to the present, it seems to me, love has always been the greatest struggle inside the church. The real struggle has not been about evangelism, heresy, money, or programs—not even discipleship, at least as it is commonly understood. Love has been our constant problem." He continues: "If you read a newspaper (especially the "Letters to the Editor"), blogs, and Facebook posts, listen to your neighbors (especially younger ones), and observe the most basic data from any serious polling, you can readily see the world does not believe that Christians are people of love." Then try to grasp this: "Without doubt, schism and disunity have thwarted the mission of Christ, perhaps *more than any other catastrophe* in all of Christian history."

When I said yes to Jesus 49 years ago I had no idea I was also saying yes to the church, the bible or Christianity. I thought following Jesus actually meant devoting oneself to the practice John Armstrong calls *Costly Love*. I was quickly disabused of that idealism as a result of my introduction to church and how many interpreted the bible. It would take 32 years before I realized that Christians had taken advantage of my spiritual enthusiasm, my lack of historical knowledge and my biblical naiveté to get me to buy into their actual agenda which Paul the Apostle so astutely spelled out in I Corinthians 13: "now remain these three, faith, hope and love" *but the greatest of these is truth.*

Was it all bad? No, of course not. Jesus is still able to get through to us in spite of the church. Maybe if more people read this book they might be able to turn this thing around. I know that's what John is hoping for and I for one am cheering him on.

Jim Henderson
Author, *Jim and Casper Go To Church*
Executive Producer, Jim Henderson Presents

Discipleship is all about falling in love with Jesus, and John Armstrong's *Costly Love* beautifully details what this really means. I commend it.

James P Danaher, Ph.D.
Professor of Philosophy, Nyack College
Author, *Jesus' Copernican Revolution:*
The Revelation of Divine Mercy.

When I began to read *Costly Love* I intended to read a couple of chapters each day but then I couldn't put it down. John reveals deep, carefully developed insights into the heart of our shared life. *Costly Love* puts things into proper perspective and offers possibilities for renewing the church. The reader will discover a history that has often been forgotten as well as some surprises regarding how love has transformed the lives of people through two thousand years of Christian history.

Rev. Donald McCoid
Executive for Ecumenical and
Inter-Religious Affairs (Retired)
Evangelical Lutheran Church in America

Costly Love is a passionate, scripturally-rich, experientially-based, faith-sharing book which posits that we are not merely disconnected individuals but whole persons designed for communion and love. Other virtues are vital, but all of them flow from an every-moment, Spirit-given sacrifice that allows us to die to ourselves and give up our desires and comforts for the sake of others. John Armstrong insightfully develops the inherent connection between costly love and Christian unity, which provides the real-life context in which people can see God's love in action. An inspiring and motivating read that can deepen your personal engagement with other members and parts of the whole Christian family.

Fr. Thomas Ryan, CSP
Director, Paulist North American Office for
Ecumenical and Interfaith Relations

Good books make you think, great books provoke you to change. John Armstrong has given us a great book that has the potential to transform churches and leaders. *Costly Love* presents a vision of life that is biblically faithful and consistently congruent with reality. This is as timely a work on this subject as any I have read. This is surely a book we all need for our divided times.

Rev. Tyler Johnson
Lead Pastor, Redemption Church
Phoenix, Arizona

John Armstrong has discovered the transforming power of love. His heart beats to its rhythms. In this new book, he invites us all to discover and practice "love without limits" toward both God and our neighbors, regardless of the personal price. *Costly Love* gives a thoroughly biblical examination of love and each page is chock-full of wisdom. This book can change your life!

R. Alan Streett, PhD
Senior Research Professor of Biblical Theology
Criswell College, Dallas, Texas

Never has a book strummed so many resonant strings in my own heart than John Armstrong's *Costly Love*. It is as if he has walked through the chambers of my own habitation in Christ and captured, in enviably readable prose, my deepest convictions of the supreme need of the body of Christ in this hour. *Costly Love* is as timely a book as I have ever read. At the risk of premature hyperbole, *Costly Love* has the potential to become a timeless Christian classic. Saying "you must read this book" is to me inadequate understatement—but what else can I say?

Stephen R. Crosby, D. Min.
Stephanos Ministries
www.stevecrosby.com
www.stevecrosby.org

If you are satisfied with your present understanding of scripture and the church and believe that the fulfillment of Jesus' prayer that we may "all be one" can be met by others coming into agreement with your personal understanding of both, then do not waste your time on this book. It will likely convict you, down in your bones, that unity in Christ is something quite other than agreement about principles, doctrines, theologies, or traditions. Attaining unity in Jesus requires deep humility and a willingness of spirit well beyond our staked-out positions.

So be ready to excuse the sin of disunity when The Day arrives. Or read John Armstrong now, and begin a rigorous, humbling and challenging journey to discover that Jesus prayed for a unity formed by the presence of Christ and His love in us, not by assent to ideas or methods. Too radical? Then don't read the book.

But get that excuse good and ready.

Rev. George Byron Koch
Pastor, New Jerusalem House of Prayer,
West Chicago, IL

In his latest book, John Armstrong challenges all Christians with a simple and demanding insight—*unity has its origin in God's nature as love*. The insight is also a prescription for what truly ails Christianity. For Christian churches to express faithfulness to Jesus' prayer in John 17, they must dwell with each other in the unity of God-Love.

The Very Rev. Thomas A. Baima
Vicar for Ecumenical and Interreligious Affairs,
Archdiocese of Chicago, IL

Has there been a time in history when this message was more needed, more vital, than right now? John Armstrong's insight into a topic that has been written about for centuries is both deeply historic and refreshingly current. His words clear the fog from the mountain top and point us in a deeply needed trajectory. I cannot recommend this book enough.

Rev. Ian Simkins
Pastor, Community Christian Church, Naperville, IL
Founder, Beauty in the Common

Costly Love constitutes an interesting and valuable reflection on the mystery of God as love. The implications of this mystery are explained here in terms of the costly love Jesus had for his disciples and the deep ecumenism he desires for each one of us. *Costly Love* should be welcomed by theologians and ecumenists of different Christian traditions as a loving gift from the evangelical tradition. The book has a powerful narrative and organizes theological matters (especially given a topic so central to the Christian faith) in a most insightful way. The book witnesses the author's personal commitment to the cause of the unity of the Body of Christ, as well as his attention to the "signs of the times," the prompting of the Spirit to the world, the needs of all the people of God.

Dr. Teresa Francesca Rossi
Centro Pro Unione
Rome

John Armstrong is one of my heroes, a rare evangelical leader who cares deeply about ecumenism and lives a deep passion for fostering real unity within the body of Christ (John 17). In this thorough, and at times complex, study we see why. He cares because God cares, indeed because God *is* love. We sometimes say this so glibly that too few have plumbed the depths and ruminated on the implications of love as thoroughly as John has in this remarkable work. Who of us doesn't want more love in our lives and our modern world? This book may not be all we need, but need it we surely do. *Costly Love* guides us towards entering into love and unity more fully.

Byron Borger
Hearts & Minds Books
Dallastown, PA

You may surmise that the topic of love has been both analyzed and overly sentimentalized, thus concluding that this book might be redundant or irrelevant. It is neither. *Costly Love* is a daring challenge to receive God's love again; to live out his love in our 24/7 experience. *Costly Love* is a cry for the church, and all who know Christ's love personally, to radically reset love as the *core apologetic* to a culture adrift in search of truth. Read John's message as if the future of the church depends upon it. I think it does!

Rev. Phil Miglioratti
LOVE2020.com
Pray.Network
Cityreaching.com

My friend John Armstrong speaks with passion, conviction and a profound understanding of what is needed in the global church today. Never has there been a time when followers of Jesus needed to be more united than today. John provides us with a clear and effective framework for this vision. Every church leader, indeed every follower of Jesus, needs to read this timely and important work. But be warned, the result may be costly love.

Dr. Geoff Tunicliffe
Former Secretary General, World Evangelical Alliance
Global Media Strategist
Vancouver, BC

Jesus has revealed that God is love, but what does God's love actually mean for the church? John Armstrong approaches this question as a missional-ecumenist who longs to see divine love not only engage human souls personally but he longs to see us united by love in a bond of Christian communion. In pursuit of this vision, John presents insights from a stunning array of sources, illustrating the prominence of such love through the centuries. Regardless of your views about ecumenism, this book will nevertheless challenge and inspire you to pursue the costly radical love that God offers his people.

Chris Castaldo, PhD.
Lead Pastor, New Covenant Church, Naperville, IL
Author of *Talking with Catholics about the Gospel*

John Armstrong's *Costly Love* echoes the cry of God's heart. Our lack of costly, sacrificial love is at the root of myriad divisions in the church and among Christians. If we live out the premises of this book, the church and the world will be transformed.

Rev. Carlos L. Malavé
Executive Director
Christian Churches Together

John Armstrong loves the body of Christ and possesses a passion for the world to see the church as a family communion of the One Father's children who have come to Him through His One Son, and through the life-giving One Holy Spirit. This Trinitarian love takes us to depths beyond our shattered surfaces, away from the rocks of our human shortcuts to unity. He explains the urgency of *Costly Love* with this simple observation: Jesus is not (commonly) apprehended by direct sight. God's power and grace is made known through love. Who can argue with that?

Fr. Wilbur Ellsworth
Pastor, Holy Transfiguration Orthodox Church
Warrenville, IL

Costly Love: John Armstrong has been on a lifelong journey to transcend his background where theological and propositional truth and argument trumped generous and costly love. At last we have reached the summit of his journey in this, his latest work. With clear, profound biblical engagement, John argues for the priority of sacrificial love as the culminating quality in the being of God and the life of the church. More and more, John reminds me of his mentor, Lesslie Newbigin. I could not recommend this book more.

Dr. Rick Richardson
Professor and Author
Wheaton College and the
Billy Graham Center for Evangelism

The concept of love has received short notice in Western culture. Mired in emotion, our words of love lack the substance and depth the term so desperately deserves. Fortunately, John Armstrong offers us a pathway toward recovery from the "relational breakdowns" that for too long have plagued the witness of the church. By situating our response toward others in the central act of love that God showed us in Christ Jesus, we find a way not only to maintain our unity as believers in the face of the differences that exist among us, we also discover the secret to extending such love to those around us who crave a community of acceptance and grace. For that reason, *Costly Love* is a must read for pastors and congregational leaders who are laboring to keep their churches together in a day of enormous forces seeking to pull them apart, and also for those believers who simply want to delve deeper into the essence of Christian discipleship, which is to love one another in the same way that Jesus has loved us.

Doug Dortch
Senior Minister, Mountain Brook Baptist Church
Birmingham, AL
Moderator, Cooperative Baptist Fellowship (2017)

Costly Love

The Way to True Unity
for All the Followers of Jesus

John H. Armstrong

Foreword by
Cardinal Joseph W. Tobin

New City Press
of the Focolare
Hyde Park, NY

Published by New City Press of the Focolare
202 Comforter Blvd.,
Hyde Park, NY 12538
www.newcitypress.com

Cover design by Timothy R. Botts

Book design and layout by Steven Cordiviola

Electronic versions of this book are also available.

Library of Congress Control Number: 2017934973

ISBN: 978-1-56548-616-4

Printed in the United States of America

"Love, to be real, must cost—it must hurt—it must empty us of self."

Mother Teresa of Calcutta

DEDICATION

For the advancement of the missional mandate of Jesus Christ in the third millennium and the renewal of biblical ecumenism through the witness of Holy Scripture and the wisdom of the Christian tradition.

And for my late friend and pastor, and the former chairman of our ACT3 board, Reverend Gregory C. Moser. Greg was an incredible blessing to many and a profound joy to me.

And for the current board members of the ACT3 Network: George B. Koch, Thomas Masters, Richard Johnson, Susan Taylor, Robert Miller, Alice Sopala, Pat Gerber Bornholt, Richard McDaniel, Ian Simkins, and Scott Brill. Each of these servants of God has helped me to discern the Spirit's leading as we move ACT3 from being a mission toward being a covenant community centered on our call to missional-ecumenism.

CONTENTS

FOREWORD

WHEN JOHN ARMSTRONG FIRST told me his personal story, I realized I'd heard something similar before. While I was Superior General of the order, one of my fellow Redemptorists, Fr. Gerry Reynolds, was intimately involved in the Northern Ireland peace process. Our house, Clonard, was located just off the Falls Road fault line between Catholic and Protestant factions. One of Fr. Reynolds's principal collaborators was Rev. Ken Newell, of the Fitzroy Presbyterian Church. They participated in the Fitzroy-Clonard Fellowship, which was awarded the Pax Christi International Peace Award in 1999 for "its exemplary grass-roots peacemaking work in Belfast."* The process that led to the Good Friday Agreement of 1998 could not have happened without Ken's active participation. But that peace came at great personal cost. Rev. Newell, at one time chaplain for the Orange Order, was shunned by many members of his Fitzroy Church, even threatened for betraying his community. Indeed his love was costly, a kind of love I see reflected in John Armstrong's experience.

We first met one another at a Chicago meeting of the United States Conference of Catholic Bishops' Committee on Ecumenical and Interreligious Affairs. John had been invited to share the story of his ecumenical journey, which took him from the peak of a highly successful national ministry to the depths of rejection because he too sought to talk across fault lines—in his case, between Protestants and Catholics. In chapter 5 of this book, he describes his experience: "I only entered into the love I write about after thirteen years in my

---

*   http://www.fitzroy.org.uk/Articles/125832/Fitzroy_Presbyterian_Church/About_Us/Ministries/Fitzroy_Clonard_Fellowship.aspx 'ministry desert.' In calling me to a unique life-changing experience God took away almost everything I treasured about my public ministry. He placed me in a quiet place where I learned just how much he loved me."

John explains, "Unless we are prepared to get 'outside the box' of our common ways of thinking we will settle for conventional wisdom. But to experience costly love we must die. There is no other way to be raised to new life. The old ways of the world will never fulfill the desire for love God has planted in us."

Of course, that "new life" is the fulfillment of what Jesus prayed for: "That they may all be one. As you, Father, are in me and I am in you, may they also be in us, so that the world may believe that you have sent me" (Jn 17:21). Armstrong explains, "His prayer is that our becoming one will be the catalyst for people to come to know God's love. ... Christian unity in relationships is clearly the divine design for showing the world that God loves them."

Pope Francis proposes that Christians work for unity by building up a "culture of encounter" in which they work as Jesus did—"not just hearing, but listening; not just passing people by, but stopping with them; not just saying 'what a shame, poor people!', but allowing yourself to be moved with compassion; and then to draw near, to touch and to say, 'Do not weep' and to give at least a drop of life."* Such gestures come at a cost, but if we do not touch, if we do not speak, we cannot help create a culture of encounter, a culture of profound relationships among all of us, who need Jesus' words, Jesus' caress.

John Armstrong describes this call as "missional-ecumenism," which means building up Christian unity by loving deeply, a love that is, as he puts it, "both relational and inclusive." But, he notes, "I could not pursue unity until I learned to pursue and live God-Love." He uses Chiara Lubich's words to unpack that dense term: "God-Love [re-

---

veals to us] not a God who is distant, immovable and inaccessible to people. God-Love … meet[s] every person in thousands of ways. … [God is] love in himself, love for all his creation." When we work for missional-ecumenism, when we work for unity as Pope Francis urges us through building up a culture of encounter and dialogue, we work as Jesus did. The crucified and forsaken Jesus, in whose total sacrifice we see love totally revealed, has to be our center. "If we learn how much Jesus really loves us, we can love God—and one another—with a love that will never be cheap or diluted."

Few of us will have to pay a price like Ken Newell or John Armstrong did, but every Christian is called to expend what is necessary to build unity by establishing a culture of encounter wherever we find ourselves—in our families, in our churches, in our neighborhoods, in our nation. In a world that has become accustomed to what Pope Francis calls "a culture of indifference," we can offer our own small reflection of God's costly love, confident that our actions can return to each person their dignity as children of a God who is love.

Cardinal Joseph W. Tobin, C.SS.R
Archbishop of Newark, New Jersey

ACKNOWLEDGMENTS

I HAVE ALWAYS FOUND AUTHORING books to be a profound burden and an incredible joy. The burden is known by most authors. There are restless moments, those times when you give up because of the sheer inner turmoil in your mind and heart. Then there is the hard work of trying to make your words carefully serve your purpose. These struggles are common to serious authors. But joy eventually comes when you have finished the book and feel as if you completed what you hoped you might accomplish. In fact, in this case the end result is far more than I could have imagined when I began. I now realize I had to live sixty-eight years, struggle through many years of study and writing (including my full recovery from open heart surgery in 2016), and then pray more than I ever have before so this book would become a reality.

I began forming my ideas for this book many years ago. Back in 2013 I expected I could finish a book within eighteen months. So much for plans. The wise writer expresses what I learned day-after-day: "The human mind plans the way, but the Lord directs the steps" (Proverbs 16:9). Never have I felt this to be more true than now. I undertook a task I soon realized I was woefully unable to complete. I wanted to write a serious book, yet one readable to non-specialists. *Yet my topic may be the most overworked subject in the English language.* I hoped and prayed, through this painfully long process, that I could explore love in a way that all Christians could agree with my central thesis, namely that costly love is God's will for us. Such love is the very core of what God has revealed about his character and our life's purpose. If this is true how then could I avoid being trite, on the one hand, and overly obtuse on the other? I found this to be no easy task.

I owe more to my wife Anita than I can express. She read many early drafts, saw me in agony as I struggled to finish, and offered profound support at every turn. I am especially grateful to Sue Taylor, a professional editor with incredible skill and deep love for me as her brother in Christ. She read the "first" finished draft and made amazing suggestions. Thanks to George August Koch, who edited my "second" finished draft late in the process and made it feel far more polished and clear. Tom Masters then went beyond the bounds of any editor I have ever worked with to complete this book. For all of you, including those who read the text and endorsed the book, and for the input you gave that helped me better share my message, thank you. I had a "dream team" standing with me all the way!

Soli Deo Gloria.

INTRODUCTION

> It is the shortcoming of Protestantism that it
> never has sufficiently described the place of
> love in the whole of Christianity.
>
> Paul Tillich,
> *The Protestant Era*

THEOLOGIAN J. I. PACKER called the thesis of my earlier book *Your Church Is Too Small* a "corrective vision." That book identified a serious defect in our Christian practice—a defect that has led us to embrace countless new divisions within Christianity. We value our personal views and opinions above all else, including the fellowship of our brothers and sisters, whom God the Father loves and whom Christ redeemed. In America we have clothed democratic individualism in "God words" and embraced an agenda of perpetual separation. We have chosen ideology over the Carpenter of Nazareth. We seem to have forgotten the inheritance Jesus left us: our God-given oneness (John 17:20–24).

The breakdown of unity has undermined modern life, especially our communities: marriages, families, local churches, neighborhoods, workplaces. Borrowing the words of a friend, I call this relational breakdown an "unholy separation." The causes of this separation are too numerous to elaborate but I believe we are living through a culture-wide breakdown of virtue that has resulted in *profound indifference*. This *indifference* results in a lack of love toward those who differ from us. This "unholy separation" has caused a persistent, painful wound in the Christian church, especially since the sixteenth century. It now threatens to keep us from

1

making a true difference in our broken and divided world (John 17:21). Recall Jesus' warning in Matthew 5:13: "You are the salt of the earth; but if the salt has lost its taste, how can its saltiness be restored? It is no longer good for anything, but is thrown out and trampled under foot."

At a similar time in human history, during the first two decades of the thirteenth century, God raised up an Italian reformer named Giovanni de Pietro di Bernardone. We know Giovanni today as Francis of Assisi (1182–1226). Perhaps no one (at least since the early centuries of the church) has sought more *intentionally to imitate the life and love of Christ* as did Francis. Bishop Robert Barron recently said, "Francis represents a back to basics evangelicalism, a return to the radicality of the gospel."[1] In this book I propose the same "return to the radicality of the gospel." Although hundreds of modern Christian authors have sought the same goal, we still have not achieved "a back to basics evangelicalism."

Globalization has shrunk distance within the human family, yet our bonds with those closest to us are being weakened. Our children hope for a better tomorrow, yet multitudes of young adults are leaving the church. The next generation dreams of making a positive difference in a world marked by so much negativity. They aim high, creating courageous projects and embracing a vision of partnership that promotes love and community. But the church doesn't heed the young. We focus on our ritual and church-based internal programs, rather than engage in the hands-on love of Jesus with one another and our neighbors. In truth, our biggest problems are not doctrinal but relational. To address the breakdown of unity we must bridge this "unholy separation" by naming it and then repenting of it.

Many of us in Western culture sense a fresh call to co-create with the mystery of the universe. After all, even though we have rejected many traditional ideas about God, we remain an inherently religious people. We recognize the rampant breakdown of common sense. We long to heal the many families wounded by divorce. We hunger for better earthly cities modeled on transcendence. We grasp for something—or Someone—more. We wonder: What can sustain us politically, ethically, economically, and socially?

Religious leader Chiara Lubich (1920–2008), founder of a Catholic movement that seeks the recovery of spiritual oneness, gave her life to pursuing loving relational unity. "A world immersed in secularism, materialism and indifference," she once observed, "has brought us so many sharp divisions, to such poverty and crises! [But] things go backwards, [initially] in order to advance. The world returns to the unity of the human family as God intended it to be."[2] I have written *Costly Love* because I believe our need for "advance" is far more evident now than at any time since World War II. I also wrote it because I am convinced God is already leading us toward greater unity. There is growing evidence of this unity around the world developing through many diverse movements of faithful people.

Since the publication of *Your Church Is Too Small*, I've been stunned by the way ideas about unity have caught fire (my book being only a small spark, I am sure). In remarkable ways the Holy Spirit seems to be bringing more and more of us into unity, calling people, churches, and movements into a *kairos* moment.[3] In our broken and divided world, God is calling people into circles (little communities) of love where spiritual relationships bridge division. Almost all forms of Christian spirituality agree that all of nature feels itself in accord because all life has a divine unity rooted in the life of our Creator. Martin Luther King, Jr. said, "All men are caught in an inescapable network of mutuality." I am convinced that this "network of mutuality" is central to God's design at the dawning of a new age of social media. Will our individualistic expressions of Christianity further divide the world and the church, or will we advance this "network of mutuality" for Christian unity?

I now believe the growing movement of unity I have witnessed among followers of Jesus from all our Christian traditions will change our world as this new century unfolds. In the foreword to my earlier book, J. I. Packer wrote:

Embracing this vision will mean that our ongoing inter- and intra-church debates will look, and feel, less like trench warfare, in which both sides are firmly dug in to defend the territory that each sees as its heritage, and more like emigrants' discussions on shipboard that are colored by the awareness that soon they will be confronted by new tasks in an environment not identical with what they knew before.[4]

"This vision," which I call *missional-ecumenism*, is *directly* rooted in the nature of God. *Your Church Is Too Small* anticipated the central question I address in this book: "What does it mean to believe that God is love and, more particularly, what does it mean for the church of Jesus Christ to live out this divine love?"

Pursuing unity as an end in itself will *not* heal our divisions. We must reconsider our view of God's divine nature. We must return to the central truth that God is a merciful Father revealed in the person of Jesus Christ, who incarnates holy love (1 John 4:8, 16). For Christians, there is no separation between God's holiness and God's love. But this does not mean we try to *balance* God's holiness and wrath with his divine love and grace in order to form a *composite view of God's nature*. In his epistles, John clearly says love *is* God's character, while holiness and wrath are what one modern theologian calls his "dispositions." Such dispositions become active on particular occasions but love *alone* is eternal.[5] Love constitutes God's essence in a way that wrath does not because love alone is *adequately Christocentric*. If our experience and understanding of God are merely philosophical, then our love for one another will be philosophical too, which means it may become rigid and cautious. Unless we *experience* the depths of divine love, no effort for unity will ever become a deep work of the Spirit. The true knowledge of God is expressed in communion with others where mutuality and love are perfected in us at great cost.

Jesus' words in John 13:34–35 demonstrate my point:

> I give you a new commandment, that you love one another. Just as I have loved you, you also should love one

another. By this everyone will know that you are my disciples, if you have love for one another.

Jesus gives us a "new commandment." But what is "new" about this command? The command to "love" is not "new." What then is "new"? Jesus answers, "*Just as I have loved you, you also should love one another.*" The centrality of love's pattern is now the life and actions of Jesus, a life which becomes the *basis* of our love. We are to love *as* Jesus loved!

In his new commandment Jesus expresses clearly his will for *all his people throughout this present age.* Yet by the late second century the church began to lose sight of the centrality of this commandment to faith and practice. The church did not move so far from Christ that she lost the new commandment entirely, but something slowly developed that was not healthy. We cannot restore this truth of love in the present by tearing down the past. But I *do* believe that theological debates *within* the church have distracted the faithful from the centrality of the new commandment. These debates are often essential to the teaching of the church, at least on one level. Yet because of *how* such battles have been waged the new commandment has often been lost. How did this happen? The church lost sight of the Jewishness of the Messiah and embraced a Greek and Latin paradigm, especially after the first-century Jewish community rejected the early church in large numbers after AD 70.[6] This non- or anti-Jewish paradigm has never served the church well. Cut off from its central story, a story clearly rooted in Israel's history, the church was left with serious problems for both theology and practice. Large elements of this unfortunate split continue still in church history. As a result, the church is sometimes defined by agreement with doctrinal conclusions rather than by our obedience to Jesus' expressed will in the new commandment.

In graduate school, one of my mentors, Dr. H. Wilbert Norton, began each class with meditations on John 13–17. His insights into these last words of Jesus shaped me. Reflecting on this period in my life, I now realize how Dr. Norton's teaching prepared me for what has become my lifelong passion—promoting the unity of the whole church in the mission of Christ by *rooting all that we do in the triune love of God in Jesus Christ*. In my early twenties my passion was the Great Commission (Matthew 28:18–20). It was also Dr. Norton's. He helped launch the famous Urbana Missionary Conference, served as a missionary in Africa, and started a number of mission teaching institutions in the U.S. and Africa. He desired to take the gospel to all the nations. But Dr. Norton showed me that the Great Commission *without* the Great Commandment would amount to a form of activism that uses people as a means to a religious end *without* the love of Christ. As a zealous young evangelical minister I learned the hard way that pragmatism *without* love was a formula for catastrophe.

My first full-time pastoral ministry was a new church plant in a fast-growing suburb of Chicago. My youthful activism expressed itself in reaching and baptizing new Christians. "Church-growth" thinking shaped my ministry, but something was missing. I began to seek a better understanding of God and the gospel. By my late twenties and early thirties, I had become a more precise doctrinal preacher, which is not a bad thing at all. But in the process, I had "lost my first love" (Revelation 2:4). By my late thirties I was *starving* for the love of Christ I had known in my childhood and college years. I had lost my burning fire of intense love for Christ and his kingdom.

In 1981 I began a regular gathering for Protestant ministers in Wheaton, Illinois. Those meetings focused upon reformation and revival. After leading these meetings for more than a decade, I was thrust into a wider ministry that I have served since 1991, ACT3 (Advancing the Christian Tradition in the Third Millennium). Its vision is clear: "ACT3 seeks to empower leaders and churches for unity in Christ's mission." But initially this interdenominational ministry was shaped by the angular theological perspective I embraced in my reaction to decision-based evangelism. As my ministry grew wider, I discovered that certain tendencies in my own theological perspective were undermining what God was doing in my soul. I hungered for love and relational one-ness. I longed to *experience* the eternal love of God and then to share this love through deep friendship. I now see this longing reflected in Paul's affirmation: "God's love has been poured into our hearts through the Holy Spirit that has been given to us" (Romans 5:5).

After writing *Your Church Is Too Small*, I realized well-intentioned Christians settle for divisions and schism because they have not experienced the fullness of God's love. (It is also rooted in the busy rituals, programs and activities that can fill church life.) Settling for theological concepts—and not pursuing the *experience* of a loving and gracious God revealed in Jesus Christ—surely makes love die. Thus this book was birthed through my active work for the unity of the entire church.

I continue to treasure my academic work and read widely. I love to teach and write. I also love theology, philosophy, and discussing the big issues of our day. I joyfully embrace the intellectual ability God gave me; Jesus said to love God "with all your mind." *But the mind can be divorced from the spirit.* The famous French thinker René Descartes (1596–1650), called the father of modern philosophy, believed we should clear our minds of everything we know and start fresh. Accordingly, he concluded then our most basic certainty is of our own existence, thus his famous dictum: "I think; therefore I am." But it is not thinking that lies at the core of our human existence. What most shapes our identity, who we really are, is love. *What we ultimately love gives us our sense of purpose and fills our life with meaning.* That is, *We think because we are loved.* To be fully human, our deep thinking must prompt deeper love. If we continue to pursue thinking as our primary purpose in life we will lose our way (Philippians 1:9–11).[7]

The vocabulary and resources of *formal* theology can lead into abstractions if theology settles for thinking as its *ultimate* goal. These abstractions chill the soul. When we cease to grow in divine love, we miss the central truth of Jesus' life and mission. Few of us realize this—those driven by thinking about great ideas rather than by great love. I didn't come to this realization during my first twenty years in ministry. I often spoke in large churches and conferences all across North America and overseas, yet I was missing one of the clearest truths in all of Scripture: *"Little children, let us love, not in word or speech, but in truth and action"* (1 John 3:18). God had gifted me to teach and preach, but I was failing to love deeply. Slowly, I grew to understand the intimate relationship between the mind and the heart. I learned to build bridges between them; true wisdom lies on these bridges.

The Way Ahead

Costly Love is divided into five parts. Part one (chapters 1 through 3) considers the nature, or character, of God. By understanding that "God *is* love" we come to see who God is and how his costly love can mark our daily life. Part two (chapters 4 and 5) asks: "Why should we love with God's love?" Can we actually "fall in love" with God? Can we really enter into God *as* love within the hard reality of living among broken people and communities? How does this love show us the way to treat others, even our enemies? Part three (chapters 6 through 8) develops how the church can make love its goal and why love is at the heart of Christian discipleship. In my reading on discipleship (within my evangelical Protestant background), I have almost never seen love rightly connected with discipleship. I seek to make that connection. Part four (chapters 9 through 11) considers Jesus' "new commandment." The majority of Christians today are not *astounded* by this commandment. Finally, part five (chapters 12 through 15) unfolds what makes love *costly* in the fullest sense of the word. By rediscovering "God-Love" we can experience fully the grace and mercy God has poured out upon the whole world. And the world around us will see this love when we truly love one another, just as Jesus prayed in John 17. What we shall see throughout this book, in many different ways, is that we must enter into the gift of unity in the Spirit by being filled with God's gift of costly love.

My goal is simple: to explain what I call "God-Love," a compound word that I believe will help us adopt a vision of unity that is immensely empowering and genuinely transforming. I wish to do this in such a way that you will *truly* love God and your neighbor. Then I shall lead you into a discovery of the power of the new commandment (John 13:34–35) so that with your heart and soul you can learn how to love your brothers and sisters as Jesus commanded. By this way you can learn to practice the love of Jesus as a daily pattern of life. Through the lens of this divine love, this *costly love*, you can see how unity then becomes a shared reality that transcends our divisions.

A Fresh Interpretation of Love

The quotation that begins this introduction says, "It is the shortcoming of Protestantism that it never has sufficiently described the place of love in the whole of Christianity." Both Catholicism and Orthodoxy have a rich theology of divine love, especially because of their deeply Trinitarian understanding of God. In seeking a more-robust place for *faith* the Protestant Reformation tended to create a theology that distanced itself from *experiential love*. For this reason theologian Paul Tillich concluded, "A fresh interpretation of love is needed in all sections of Protestantism, an interpretation that shows that love is basically not an emotional but an ontological power, that it is the essence of life itself, namely, the dynamic reunion of that which is separated."[8] *Costly Love* attempts to offer a "fresh interpretation of love" that will, I humbly pray, appeal to all Christians everywhere.

Behind Tillich's thought lies the sad reality that millions of Christians (and not just Protestants) have *replaced* love with faith, or church doctrine. Moreover, multitudes have replaced love with religion and ended up teaching Christianity *as* doctrine and theology. Active faith is reduced to knowing dogma or propositions. People are urged to pursue a better understanding of sound teaching, as if this itself is *living* faith. In the end, faith and knowledge are celebrated as if these were Christianity's highest ideals! A century ago a new kind of Protestant "theological warfare" divided liberals and conservatives. (Catholics would come to experience the consequences of these battles decades later in different ways.) Sadly, this division continues. Many conservative Protestants have divided the church even further, separating from their fellow conservative Protestants *over how to define and explain the faith in precise ways.* Now more conservative Protestants are dividing yet again, this time over moral and political issues that weren't even on the table when I was a young pastor.

Yet Paul, the apostle of faith, says the love of Christ must *become* "the very spring of our actions" (2 Corinthians 5:14, *J. B. Phillips New Testament*). This great apostle of the Christian faith also said, "In Christ Jesus neither circumcision nor uncircumcision counts for anything; *the only thing that counts is faith working through love*" (Galatians 5:6, italics added). If this is God's truth, then how does faith *working through love* shape who I am *and* what I do? How does this faith working through love empower the church? Ultimately, my central premise is rooted in these words: "For right now, until that completeness, we have three things to do to lead us toward that consummation: Trust steadily in God, hope, love. And the best of the three is love" (1 Corinthians 13:13, *The Message*). *I hope extravagant love describes what you desire for your life and church.* I understand *extravagant* love as the kind of love that goes beyond reason, beyond what we call common sense. This leads me to my title: *Costly Love.* God's extravagant love was ultimately poured out at a great price: Christ's total sacrifice. Such love is extravagant because it cost God everything. Such love has value beyond words.

PART ONE

WHO IS GOD?

God is love, and those who abide in love abide
in God, and God abides in them.

(1 John 4:16)

CHAPTER ONE

THE STEADFAST LOVE OF THE LORD

> May the loving and compassionate God, Who is truth itself, grant to me, and to all who are to read this book an inward awareness of truth.
>
> Meister Eckhart

THE BIBLE SAYS "GOD is love." But what *is* love? What do these three words tell us about God's nature? And what do they mean in terms of how we live as Christians?

What we believe and how we choose to live depends on how we understand these three words. This revealed truth—"God is love"—explains *eternal* love. And unlike the "love, sweet love" in popular music, *eternal* love does not pass away.

Since the moment of creation, God has been engaged in a loving relationship with the human beings he made in his image and likeness. In our hearts God planted the desire to be united with him in his love. The centrality of God's love permeates the biblical story. From the creation account through the call of Abraham and Moses and the giving of the law, God displays his love. Its mystical dimension emerges in the erotic poetry of the Song of Songs. Even the prophets' call to repentance reveals God's love. Speaking of a day when the exiles would be rescued, God says to Israel, "I have loved you with an everlasting love; therefore I have continued my faithfulness to you" (Jeremiah 31:3). The perfection of divine love was revealed in the life, death, and resurrection of Jesus

Christ. God's love reaches a glorious crescendo in the most famous text in the Bible: "For God so loved the world" (John 3:16). Salvation is rooted in this love, which sustained the Chosen People in the darkness of fear and terror and can sustain us, too, in the modern world.

Why We Think About God

How then should we think about the heart of God? How can we get our minds around who God *is* and what it means to believe that God loves us? In the Introduction I noted that at the core of the Christian doctrine of God is a fundamental belief—he exists as eternal love. But before pondering how we understand God, we should consider why we believe in God at all.

In every age, in every culture, people have developed religious rituals and beliefs that are held together by faith in gods, or God. Different religions have different interpretations of the power or person that exists beyond our physical perception. But human beings are drawn toward transcendence. When we see the starry host on a glorious evening or a majestic vista like the Grand Canyon, we "know" and "feel" that there is something more. Our inborn sense tells us that life has purpose and meaning. We also have a profound awareness of mortality, as evidenced by the burial mounds and markers that every civilization has left. Such experiences call out, "What is our life? Why do we matter?"

But beyond these moments of wonder at the transcendent, many believe in God because we have experienced love. We sense the real mystery of our lives is rooted in love. Maybe we first discovered this in a deep friendship or in our parents' sacrificial care for us. Such deep reflection prompts this experience of love. These experiences give our lives deep pleasure.

Many have concluded that life does not make sense *unless* there is a personal God who loves the world. We reason that the alternative—the universe and our lives being mere *accidents*—does not make sense. We believe we are more than complex machines. In other words, at our core we believe in an active, caring, and personal mystery; and we call that mystery "God." Desiring *and* loving God defines us because love alone has the power to shape us and to form our vision of life. All our actions and decisions, even our simple daily habits, are connected with our desire to love and be loved.[1]

God and Religion

Religion, which involves outward signs of faith, is expressed in different forms—celebrations, statements, codes of behavior, and visible signs. But faith and religion are not the same. A person can be deeply religious and not have true faith. And he or she can practice religion and not believe that God is love. Religious beliefs vary, but all seek to express what faith means through particular social practices.[2]

Perhaps the world contains so many religions because people have so many ways of expressing how they understand their experience. According to the biblical tradition there are many "gods," but there is *only one true* God (Exodus 18:11; 20:3; 23:24, etc.). This distinction, which is called *monotheism,* made the Hebrew faith unique in the ancient Middle East. God revealed himself by the unspoken name of YHWH. (Since Hebrew has no vowels, this name is sometimes written "Jehovah" in English.) God is presented as the Lord who reigns over all. Moses asks, "Who is like you, O LORD, among the gods? Who is like you, majestic in holiness, awesome in splendor, wonders?" (Exodus 15:11). Moses, and even God for that matter, never denies that there are other man-made gods. But he affirms that YHWH is *the* Lord, the one who is "majestic in holiness, awesome in splendor, doing wonders," the true and living God. This is the God that Jews and Christians believe "has the whole world in his hands."

Religion has its rightful place (see James 1:27), but only through divine revelation can we truly know God's character. How can I know that love guides the universe? Abundant evidence suggests otherwise when we consider the evil we see in the world. And if God *is* love, how then should

I respond to this core truth? *What constitutes an authentic expression of faith in a healthy religious context?* Is faith only a private "hope," or does it make a difference in how I treat others? Given what many people see done in the name of religion, some popular atheists now suggest that all religion is *inherently* evil.

What Does God Reveal to Us?

A comprehensive discussion of what God has revealed would require many volumes. For our purposes, I will address only a few critical matters regarding divine love before we consider why our love must be costly.

I am concerned first and foremost with the meaning and practice of love. Is love only a dimension of God's identity, or is love God's actual response to the world? In light of immense and complicated tragedies and profound evil, what does it mean to say that "God is love"? Explanations have offered only limited help. In the end, the Christian response proclaims that God created the world out of infinite love and allowed it to fall into a state of sin and death. But the story does not end here.

At least for Christians, any discussion of what God has revealed has to begin with what he has made known in and through Jesus Christ. This is true for several reasons, but the central one may surprise you. What Jesus said about God, and how the earliest Christians understood what he said, is the only solid basis for a *Christian* answer. The right response to sin and death is found in the redemptive life and suffering of Jesus. Because the God who "is love" expressed himself and suffered in the person of Jesus, he truly suffers with all people in a uniquely human way. While we rightly work to alleviate suffering, we remain mindful that our suffering ultimately has *meaning* precisely because God *is* love.

Perhaps Jesus' most remarkable claims are these: "Whoever has seen me has seen the Father" (John 14:9), and "[No one] has seen the Father except the one who is from God; he has seen the Father" (John 6:46). Jesus is saying, "If you want to know what God is really like, look at me!" Time and time again he claimed to share an eternally intimate relationship with the Father: "Do you not believe that I am in the Father and the Father is in me? The words that I say to you I do not speak on my own; but the Father who dwells in me does his works" (John 14:10).

Divine revelation implies there is a God who loves us enough to take the initiative to *explain* himself openly. But he did far more than that. He became one with our humanity in the incarnation of Jesus. The Sacred Mystery became what Leslie Newbigin calls the "open secret." And now God has given those who follow him the Holy Spirit so they can know what is necessary for true life and godliness: "I have said these things to you while I am still with you. But the Advocate, the Holy Spirit, whom the Father will send in my name, will teach you everything, and remind you of all that I have said to you" (John 14:25–26).

The Christian religion clearly reveals that *faith is a gift of God.* We can experience God only when we have been initiated into divine love through God's grace. True religion is *not* us working our way to God but rather God *giving* us the gift of his love. True religion is thus rooted not in our keen intellect or special religious status, but in this gift.

But *Is* God Love?

Most religions emphasize what is believed about who God is, how we know him, what he expects of us, etc. But religion also includes mysteries that cannot be explained. These mysteries call us to growing devotion. This is what Pius X meant when he said, "Our life is a mystery to be lived, not a problem to be solved." In the Christian tradition these mysteries are central to theology. Divine revelation, and subsequent faith, cannot be explained by philosophy or rational comprehension. Christian theologians have argued, from the earliest stages of the church, that the incomprehensible God has come to us as mystery. This is how the Apostle Paul understood what he calls "the mystery of Christ" (Ephesians

3:4; see also Romans 16:25; 1 Corinthians 2:1; Ephesians 1:9; Colossians 1:27, 2:2, 4:3)

It is heartbreaking when religious devotion is rooted in fear. This should never be true of the Christianity, but unfortunately this has happened all too often. When Christianity is reduced to formal propositions, especially propositions that have little to do with human experience, the "mystery of Christ" is lost. As a result fear often replaces the experience of grace. Devotion based on such fear contradicts Scripture's clear teaching: "There is no fear in love, but perfect love casts out fear; for fear has to do with punishment, and whoever fears has not reached perfection in love" (1 John 4:18).

Some ministers and teachers say that God is *equally* love and wrath. Such thinking is a consequence of what philosophers and theologians call the "divine attributes." To form a more systematic idea of God's being, and to hold to the implications of the revealed biblical truth, we must conclude that God is an all-perfect being. But be careful with this word *perfect*. It becomes problematic when God's divine *characteristics* (called attributes) are said to make up the perfection of his one simple being. Although true, a focus on God's perfection can lead believers into the weeds of a faith *not* rooted in divine love.

Some Christians argue that the perfection of God requires that words such as *love* and *wrath* be placed side-by-side in our theological consideration. For some, what they believe about God comes down to this: God has many attributes yet he is one simple, perfect being. This means he must be *equal parts* love, kindness, and mercy mixed with equal parts anger, judgment and wrath. These divine attributes are even said to be "the contents of our idea of God." Such contents are then laid out in a systematic and philosophical way. Some Christians act as if this content provides an "exhaustive statement" about God. Such thinking owes more to Greek philosophy than biblical revelation.[3] But this is not the only problem. This notion about how various pieces of the Bible can provide an "exhaustive statement" of God's Being has profoundly negative spiritual and emotional consequences. Listing biblical attributes in this way surely leads us to conclude that God is a complex Being. But I have found it impossible to love a complex Being, a God whose nature is rationally rooted in philosophical propositions. Presenting the Holy One in this manner has caused the mistaken notion that at the center of God's heart is a *multiphasic* personality. This leaves God loving me one moment and resenting me the next. Approaching the heart of God like this discourages healthy belief and practice. How can I genuinely love such a God?

Life's Central Reality

Does our understanding of God prompt deep, love-filled awe or irrational fear? John does not say God is *half* love and *half* wrath. Coming to understand God by combining love and wrath *equally* in one simple divine being, I believe, leads to the unfortunate, deeply mistaken result of a bipolar deity.

"God is love, and those who abide in love abide in God, and God abides in them" (1 John 4:16b). We should *first* understand that God is love. And apart from grace, God's love remains hidden. Karl Barth famously said, "God is known through God, and through God alone."[4] God is revealed in the Incarnation. Jesus has revealed that God is love. Therefore, abiding in God's love is the *essence* of personal faith in Christ.

Love is life's central reality because God is love. Love alone gives real purpose to every other attribute of God's holy nature. Love determines the selfless actions of God and explains everything he does, including his justice and judgment.

The Modern Dilemma

Years of study and personal observation have convinced me that modern men and women are increasingly cut off from the experience of God's personal and relational love. The result is a deep, lingering sickness. Our view of God has unleashed a spiritual virus that has become a Western pandemic. It is also polarizing the Christian church and defacing its public witness. This isolation from God's love has generated a growing dislike for the church. Increasingly, people find Christians offensive and loveless because they have seen how many Christians lack mercy and compassion. To be truthful, they don't even find most Christians "likable." Thus the most indicting modern critique against the church is our failure to follow Jesus in love! Many people do not desire God because Christians demonstrate, in word and in deed, that God must be angry at them. They watch us and conclude, "God must not like me or care deeply about me." This response emerges in daily life but especially in our debates about morality, culture, and politics. This growing perception of Christianity should alarm us because people really do feel rejected; they see that Christians do not like them, much less love them.

This book will lead you on a personal journey into the question, "What does love mean for true Christianity?" I hope to demonstrate that the character of a personal, loving God is the only matrix within which we can rightly understand our personhood. Nothing may be more important for the collective future of the West than a healthy understanding of human persons and their significance. Modern humanity has accepted a truncated and impoverished definition of life focused almost entirely on material realities. Are we merely disconnected individuals, made up of parts like a complex machine, or are we whole human persons designed for communion and love? It is true love that defines personhood, because *love is God's identity.* Love is God's power, purpose, and will.

In this journey I hope you will seek the source of your own personal significance. What does your life *really* mean? Answering this requires you to go deep into the fabric of your daily life. Are you prepared to just get by, or do you really want to discover the *life principle* of God's holy, triune love? Until we recover this understanding of God and love, our view of everything will remain distorted. The eternal Word (Christ), born in time, came into our world in human flesh. This is not abstract metaphysics or mere ideology.[5] Our hearts cry out for a personal engagement with passionate love. Love without a costly love for persons cannot last. Why? The true object of life's deepest desire is Jesus, a fully human person like us. He is the Word who reveals that God's eternal nature is love. He is the lover and we are the objects of his love.

The problem we face is clear—it is related to the idea of true possession. All creation speaks of the glory and infinity of God. God's beauty transcends all symbols, or created things. In a sense, everything in creation is a picture, or an icon (window). Through these pictures, or icons, we *see* something of God's beauty. But if we try to *possess* God *in the way* we possess material things, we remain slaves. Ernesto Cardenal captures the paradox of this point: "Possessing God means becoming detached from things. Becoming detached from things is embracing God." [6]

Nevertheless, possessing God requires detachment, or intentional separation, since the only thing we can *truly* possess is God! We cannot even possess those we love: our spouses, children, or dearest friends. God can enter into our deepest self and possesses us, allowing us to *partake of him in an eternal union*. This is the greatest mystery of earthly life. When we partake of God in the eternal union of holy love we overcome our separation. And this union lies at the heart of true salvation, because true salvation consists in knowing God and entering into eternal love. We thus become followers not of mammon and material goods, but of the true and living God. But this following comes at a price to us, and to God. This price is high, but it is entirely voluntary. God, in Christ, is the true and eternal lover who desires only our best!

So, do we possess anything? *Yes, only what we have in God. Thus what we possess is only within his love.* When we truly possess God we possess everything else because God possesses all. All things come from God and all things return to God. "The mystery of our religion is great" (1 Timothy 3:16). But the greatest paradox is that we can possess something only when we renounce it, when we truly give it up. *We truly live only when we first die* (John 12:24). John of the Cross expressed what I believe Jesus meant by dying; the saint said that the true way to possess all things is to be dispossessed of all. This is a great mystery, but it has been revealed in such a way that it shines brightly through the radiance of Christ's burning love for us.

The Modern Response

The philosopher Bertrand Russell (1872–1970) said, "I don't think it is certain that there is no such thing as God. I think it is on exactly the same level as the Olympic gods, or the Norwegian gods; they also may exist. I can't prove that they don't. I think they are a *bare* possibility."[7] Whether an atheist or merely agnostic, Russell *clearly* repudiated belief in God as understood in the Judeo-Christian sense. Yet Russell realized that a universe *without love or compassion* was a dreary and dangerous place:

> What stands in the way? Not physical or technical obstacles, but only the evil passions in human minds; suspicion, fear, lust for power, intolerance.
>
> The root of the matter is a very simple and old-fashioned thing, a thing so simple that I am almost ashamed to mention it, for fear of the derisive smile with which wise cynics will greet my words. The thing I mean—please forgive me for mentioning it—*is love, Christian love, or compassion* [italics added].[8]

Remarkably, Russell understood that amid the massive evils that have defined our modern world, what we really need is "love, Christian love, or compassion." I agree. Mother Teresa of Calcutta did as well:

> The biggest disease today is not leprosy or tuberculosis, but rather the feeling of being unwanted, uncared for and deserted by everybody. *The greatest evil is the lack of love and charity*, the terrible indifference towards one's neighbor who lives at the roadside assaulted by exploitation, corruption, poverty and disease [italics added].[9]

Conclusion

This book is my deeply personal and prayerful invitation that you submit your mind and heart to the love that is perfectly revealed in Jesus Christ. My premise is simple but profound: *Love is true life.* True life and light have been revealed in Jesus Christ. Therefore, *to know Jesus Christ is to experience eternal love.* And to embrace him in his love is to possess uninterrupted love forever. To love him, as he has revealed himself in his love, is the only truth that will lead you to true religion. "Religion that is pure and undefiled before God, the Father: to care for orphans and widows in the distress, and to keep oneself unstained by the world" (James 1:17).

Once I began to research and write on love, I discovered the endless questions we have about love. Theologian Carter Lindberg asks the questions we all should ask:

> Is love a feeling? Is love an act? Is love an art? Is love voluntary or involuntary, or both? How is self-love related to love of neighbor? Does love extend to enemies? What is the relation of love to sexuality? Can love be commanded? Is love redemptive? Is love divine? Is divinity love? How does love form and inform our existence?[10]

Indeed, *what is love?* The answer is complex and encyclopedic. I will not attempt to answer all of the above questions.[11] My concern is highly selective. What I want you to understand is this: *Because "God is love," we can embrace the costly divine love that will lead us to genuinely "love one another"* (1 John 4:7–8).

The book of Lamentations was composed in a time of incredible human suffering. One scholar says, "The reader is invited to ground zero of the destruction, there to stand dumbfounded by the enormity of the collapse of this once glorious city [Jerusalem]."[12] The author (likely Jeremiah) faces immense pain head-on and laments what has transpired. The prophet does not promote a feel-good, self-centered religious experience called love. Yet he writes confidently, "The steadfast love of the LORD never ceases, his mercies never come to an end" (Lamentations 3:22). Amid the challenges of a complex and confusing modern age, what our hearts long for is God's steadfast love. This love cannot be sentimental. It is not romantic. And it is much more than being nice.

Only through the revelation of God's costly love given to us in Christ can we turn back the deadly virus that is destroying our Christian witness to the world. When Christ's costly love empowers us, we will once again experience deep transformation. John concludes, "We love because he first loved us" (1 John 4:19). If you enter the mystery of eternal love then you will learn to die daily to yourself and, with others, live in the resurrection power of costly love.

writer for *New Scientist*, concluded, "This kind of linguistic exuberance should come as no surprise…since languages evolve to suit the ideas and needs that are most crucial to the lives of their speakers."[4]

The same is true for "love." Our understanding of the word and its meaning is conditioned by our social experience. We tend to conceive of love as generic kindness, a positive emotion or the good will that seeks harmony. For example, Christians often say that their church is loving because they greet guests warmly and make people feel welcome. We talk about love a great deal. We often quote Bible verses to remind ourselves of love. But none of this encompasses what I mean by *costly* love.

To live "costly love" we must pay a prodigious price: total sacrifice! *Jesus told us that we must die in order to live in his love.* But discussing death is easier than choosing to die. Defining love will *not* cause us to love, but the more we understand the nature of costly love, the less likely we are to confuse our conventional understanding with the demanding, life-changing love that Jesus demonstrated and revealed by his teaching.

Krista Tippett has captured something of what I mean about recovering the meaning of love in our modern age:

> I long to make this word echo differently in hearts and ears—not less complicated, but differently so. Love as muscular, resilient. Love as social—not just about how we are intimately, but how we are together, in public. I want to aspire to a carnal practical love—*eros* become civic, not sexual and yet passionate, full-bodied. Because it is the best of which we are capable, loving is also supremely exacting, not always but again and again. Love is something we master only in moments. It crosses the chasms between us, and likewise brings them into relief.[5]

Modern usage has drained the word "love" of its meaning. Many of us find ourselves yearning, "I wish the word meant something to me."

The Biblical Reality of Love

Even though the Bible, especially the Old Testament, rarely mentions love, biblical writings contain the only meaningful description of love in all of ancient literature. In 1 Corinthians 13 Paul tells us what love *actually looks like.* (By substituting the name of Christ in place of the word *love* in this text, you can better see its portrayal of costly love.)

> Love is patient; love is kind; love is not envious or boastful or arrogant or rude. It does not insist on its own way; it is not irritable or resentful; it does not rejoice in wrongdoing, but rejoices in the truth. It bears all things, believes all things, hopes all things, endures all things (1 Corinthians 13:4–7).

Biblical love always seeks the highest and best for the other person. We long to receive this love, but have a hard time giving it. The only love that seeks your highest good at all times and in all circumstances is that which comes from God. Why? Because God *is* love, and that love is *fully revealed* in Jesus Christ. At the core of the biblical story is the Holy Trinity—Father, Son, and Holy Spirit in whom love is *perfectly* revealed. *In the Trinity, love is both eternal and relational.*[6]

Dictionaries contain multiple definitions of *love*—one includes 21! Moreover, multiple faith traditions use the word *love.* Almost every religion has ideas about love, but these ideas differ significantly. Most also profess the equivalent of The Golden Rule: "Do to others as you would have them do to you" (Luke 6:31). From this common ground, interreligious dialogue with non-Christians can proceed. The Golden Rule is rooted in love, but costly love is much, much more!

People of faith speak about loving God. The core teaching and practice of most religions is based on divine love. But the deeper you go into those teachings and practices, the more these religions diverge from the biblical story. In the Christian story there is this central difference: The Christian understanding of love is perfectly revealed in the incarnation of Jesus Christ. Jesus shows us the loving heart of God and reveals the nature of relational love. So, then, what does *love* really mean in Holy Scripture?

In his classic book *The Four Loves*, C. S. Lewis begins with the biblical text "God is love." He says he wanted to draw a contrast between "need-love" (such as the love of a child for its mother) and "gift-love" (God's love for humanity).[7] But Lewis reveals the complicated nature of these basic categories. His observations warn us of a danger I call *simplistic distinctions*. Such *simplistic distinctions* are often built on a cursory knowledge of the three common Greek words used for love in the New Testament era. Christians hear these three words, opt to pour divine love into the meaning of only one of them (*agape*), and thereby create *simplistic* (even false) *distinctions*. For example, Lewis says a child's need for parental comfort is a necessity, not a *selfish indulgence*. Conversely, excessive parental gift-love can easily be perverted.[8]

Lewis's observations lead us to ask: Does love express a *multiplicity* of realities, or is it a *simple, single* reality? The answer will appear as we move into a deeper understanding of the nature of costly love.

In the New Testament the most frequently used word for love is agape. Unfortunately, the actual meaning of this Greek word has become muddled, if not completely mistaken. Yet the word remains critical in understanding God's identity, and in our own misperceptions of what love means. And these misunderstandings resist change.

Love in the Old Testament

Throughout the Old Testament powerful images communicate the meaning of love, images like parenthood, marriage, weddings, adultery, and betrayal. When we scrutinize God's love in the Old Testament, some things seem out of focus. Is God *really* love? Old Testament professor Travis Bott suggests that Psalm 136 provides a corrective lens. There are several different Hebrew words for God's love, but Psalm 136, which uses the word twenty-six times ("The steadfast love of the Lord endures forever"), is the best place to start.

Modern readers of the Old Testament can make several major mistakes. The first is to think that God is *not* fundamentally love but anger or wrath. The corollary to this view is that God is revealed as loving *only* in Jesus Christ. This creates a bipolar understanding of God that in the second century was condemned when it first appeared.

When we view God in this manner, we risk thinking of him in terms of our own mood swings. Bott says, "We suppose that the angry pole [side] was really *Israel's mistaken perception of God*, but now we know better: the loving pole is our more accurate understanding of God's true nature" (italics added). But the glorious expression of praise and worship in Psalm 136 denies this. The psalmist says God made the world, delivered his people from Egypt, and gave them the Promised Land, and "[he did all of this] from a single, continuous movement... of love." Bott concludes, "Although Christians today live under a different covenant than ancient Israel, God's character has not changed." The reason, the psalmist says, is that "the steadfast love of the Lord endures forever."[9]

But Psalm 136 reveals still more. Even if we believe God's nature is fundamentally loving, we can easily fall into a second misconception: "the idea that God loves us in a [purely] emotional or sentimental way." This error produces a wounded god, a codependent deity, an understanding often reflected in popular Christian preaching and music. Travis Bott adds, "We may make a mess of our lives and this world, but God will still be there, waiting in the wings, to help us clean up. God desires us; God needs us." God does *desire* us, but does not *need* us, at least not in the way we generally use the word "need." Desire is *not* the same as need. Only when we see that God *freely* loves us can we understand that he makes the ultimate sacrifice in order to reveal costly love.

Psalm 136 says YHWH is the God of gods, the Lord of lords, the majestic God of heaven (136:1–3, 26). He is not a *passive presence* who dotes on us. That is not divine love! Divine love is robust and bold. Psalm 136 uses sixteen different

Hebrew verbs to refer to *divine deeds.* "Over half of these verbs are participles that express God's character through activity," Bott writes. "By contrast, humans never act in this amazing psalm. In addition God's fearsome power is not opposed to his love but precisely the means by which God expresses his love." This psalm says that God brings Israel out of Egypt because of his great love. And because of love, God strikes down and kills mighty kings (Psalm 136:17–18). Psalm 136 depicts God's love as "covenant fidelity not romantic infatuation."[10] Note that covenant love always involved sacrifice and death. This sacrifice was not intended to appease God, as if he were a capricious deity like the gods of the ancient Near East. *The sacrifice reveals the depth and cost of his* covenantal love.

Without question, understanding the Old Testament is a challenge for twenty-first century readers. Its customs and practices are foreign. Contemporary readers need to understand that the patriarchs were really a lot like their pagan neighbors, who kept multiple wives and held unformed and inaccurate ideas about God. To grasp the meaning of the great love stories of the Old Testament requires a deeper covenantal understanding. Examining some key Hebrew words terms can open up such understanding.

The most important Hebrew word for our consideration here is *hesed.* It is translated as "mercy" (149 times), "kindness" (40 times) or "loving-kindness" (39 times), as well as "unfailing love" and "loyalty." *The word clearly carries the idea of a positive display of deep affection and sacrificial mercy.* It occurs in the Psalms more in any other part of the Old Testament (Psalms 25:10; 36:10; 86:5, 15). The Old Testament depicts God as full of *hesed.*

Of the other Hebrew words for love, one of the most interesting, at least for my purpose, is *rahamim.* This word denotes the deep parental love of a mother (*rehem* is the Hebrew word for "womb") for her child. Such love *cannot* be earned. *Rahamim* conveys a wide range of *intense feelings,* such as goodness and tenderness, as well as patience and understanding. It also communicates a readiness to forgive and restore.

Such words demonstrate that God's love speaks to human experience in sacrificial ways. God's love seeks our best interest, always going beyond the requirements of justice. His love for Israel was deep and life-changing![11]

If Love Is the Answer, What Is the Question?

In the Old Testament the English word *love,* or other forms of it, occurs over 200 times. The rich range of the Hebrew words prepares us to move into the full sunlight of God's revelation of love in Jesus Christ. Remember, Christianity is founded on the truth that God became flesh and revealed his love in the person of Christ. But this was not the first time that God revealed his love, just the fullest revelation of his eternal love.

Our common cultural understandings of love do not convey the depth of these various biblical words. This is never more true than in the word agape, which takes on a distinctly Christian meaning in the writings of the apostles and prophets.

Krista Tippett rightly says love is the "superstar virtue of virtues."[12] She is also correct in saying that love has to be "the most watered down word in the English language."[13] This is why we must *define* love better before proceeding to deeper reflection upon the meaning of "costly love." And to do so, we must get past the conventional definitions of love, such as a term of endearment, a feeling of strong attachment or deep affection, sexual passion, or the beloved who is the object of such feelings.

Once we grasp the biblical meaning of love, however, we can begin to rephrase the entire question. By doing so, we begin to understand why *love is the one word that matters most in terms of how we understand God and one another.*

Love in the New Testament

Greek has five words that signify "love." But our focus here should be on the single word that the New Testament writers used almost exclusively: agape.

In the New Testament, agape names selfless, sacrificial, unconditional (costly) love. C. S. Lewis defined agape as *gift-love*. (Surprisingly, in his book he never used the word agape.) Lewis believed agape was the *only* word that fully revealed deep care and costly sacrifice. Grace, mercy, and goodness all flow from the divine energy of agape. As do almost all other Christian writers and theologians, Lewis recognized that this one word represents the highest expression of love. And he saw this virtue as *uniquely* Christian.

Agape describes love perfectly because it explains what is revealed in the Incarnation. We see agape in Jesus' love for his Father. We see agape in the Father's love for his Son (see John 10:36–38; 14:10–14). Jesus reveals agape in practical ways (John 13:31–34), and even to his enemies (Luke 6:27, 35). Further, Jesus taught us to follow him in his agape. "Love your enemies and pray for those who persecute you" (Matthew 5:44). Even from the cross he prayed, "Father, forgive them; for they do not know what they are doing" (Luke 23:34). Such statements may be interpreted in many ways, but they plainly reveal the essence of costly love.

Note that God's love is never passive. It is not (at least primarily) a sentiment or feeling. God's love is *action*. Love contends for the highest possible good. Love does not force itself, yet it always persists in seeking the good of its object. The New Testament uses only *one* Greek word to describe this kind of love: agape. And this same word is used almost exclusively to describe the love we are commanded to show others. A deeper understanding of this word can reorient our entire life.

Agape: Divine Love

In antiquity the meaning of agape is unique. The word rarely appears outside the Bible. Ancient Greek writers and philosophers used three other words—*eros* (desire), *storge* (affection) and *philia* (friendship). Scholars of Christianity agree that agape names "the steadfast love God has for human beings, as well as neighbor-love humans are to have for one another."[14] The most respected modern study of Greek New Testament words, compiled by premier exegete Ceslas Spicq, notes, "The only adequate translation [of agape], is 'love in the sense of charity'; in Latin, *caritas* or *dilectio*."[15] But this definition is itself controversial. Scholars such as the late Anders Nygren argue that *caritas*, especially as formulated by Augustine, was a *combination* of Greek desire with the primitive Christian understanding of self-giving grace. Nygren further argued that any definition of love that included desire inherently confused *eros* with agape. Only agape was the result of pure grace. It is difficult to *separate* desire from self-giving, but I also believe that Nygren is right to remind us that any emphasis on love that departs from the idea of *unmerited favor* loses the biblical meaning. But I also believe Nygren missed the truth Augustine intended when he wrote: "The whole life of the good Christian is a holy longing. ... That is our life, to be trained by longing; and our training through the holy longing advances in the measure that our longings are severed from the love of this world."[16]

Anabaptist scholar William Klassen provides clarity:

> *Agape* describes a life-enhancing action that flows from God to humans (Rom 8:37; 2 Corinthians 9:7) and vice versa (Matthew 22:37). The commandment to love regulates human conduct within the church: "Love one another" (John 13:34; 15:12; 1 Thessalonians 4:9; 1 Pet 1:22; 1 John 3:11; 2 John 5); and husbands are commanded to love their wives (Ephesians 5:25, 28; Col 3:19). But those outside are to be loved: the neighbor (Romans 13:9) and enemies (Matthew 5:44; Luke 6:28, 35).[17]

Thus the uniqueness of agape. It is the single word that the New Testament's Spirit-guided writers used to express what they meant by *God's one-of-a-kind love*. The revelation of God in Jesus of Nazareth brought this distinct love into the world in a way never known or seen in human history. Agape relentlessly contends for the good. It will pay any cost, even the sacrifice of one's life, in order to love. This means agape is unique for at least two reasons:

1. Agape does not desire to possess or control. Feelings come and go, but agape flows out as a Spirit-given choice. Peter Kreeft captures this idea: "We fall in love, but we do not fall in *agape*. We rise in *agape*."[18] The evangelical scholar Leon Morris (1914–2006) notes that agape is *love given quite irrespective of merit*. (This seems to have been Anders Nygren's *primary* concern in his three-volume work, *Agape and Eros* (trans. P. S. Watson, New York: Harper & Row, 1969). Indeed, agape always seeks to give.

2. Agape seeks the highest good of the one loved, even (especially) if the person is undeserving. This second feature of agape appears to be the central reason for the New Testament writers choosing this unusual Greek word to reveal God's love in the incarnation, death, and resurrection of Jesus. This also demonstrates why agape is far more than just kindness and good will. If God were merely kind, he would simply remove our troubles. Peter Kreeft concludes that lack of belief in God's supreme goodness "stems from this confusion between love and kindness."[19]

> Grandfathers are kind. Fathers are loving. Grandfathers say, "Run along and have a good time." Fathers say, "But don't do this, and don't do that." Grandfathers are compassionate, fathers are passionate. God is never once called our Grandfather in Heaven, much as we may prefer that to the inconveniently demanding and intimate *Father*. The most frequently heard saying in our lives today is precisely the philosophy of the grandfather: "Have a nice day."[20]

God-like Love

Agape is *not* generic love; it is God-like love. Jesus said, "I give you a new commandment, that you love [have agape for] one another. Just as I have loved [have had agape for] you,

you also should love [have agape for] one another. By this everyone will know that you are my disciples, if you have love [agape] for one another" (John 13:34–35). As we will see later, this love depends upon Jesus first revealing God's love to his disciples. He is saying that his love—this *unique sacrificial love*—is so radically different from other forms of love that agape will become his singular mark upon his people. This is how others will see and know God's love.

I would even say that agape is God's *ultimate motive* behind everything he is *and* does. God is far *more* than agape, but agape is his intention and eternal design. Everything God thinks, does and requires is rooted in agape because God *is* love. This is why, to demonstrate love, God went so far as to give up his own Son (John 3:16).

When the Apostle John says "God is love" (1 John 4:8, 16), he makes the clearest and most important *identity statement* about God in the Bible. John is saying that "God is love through and through."[21] *This is who God is.* Yet John does not say that love is God (John 15:13). The first of these statements is amazing truth; the second is colossal error. God *is* love, but love itself is *not* God. Thus agape stands in contrast to all pagan (and modern) ideas of love. God-like love is not the love we discover in romance, sentiment or emotion. The world's love is self-interested and self-protective. It generally arises from demands based on emotion or need. Agape is free. It is not a feeling or a sentiment but a costly choice! It does not play psychological games. It proceeds from the heart and is always directed to the highest good of the other (see 1 Corinthians 13:4–7). When we express agape, we reveal the Spirit's transforming work in us. We freely choose to lay down our lives for others. This love alone will lead us to sacrifice our time, our interests, our money—ultimately our very selves.

All of this underscores an important point in Christian theology. The source of agape is God, and the pattern is always Jesus Christ (1 John 4:7–19). Thus, agape values others and never uses them as a means to an end. Finally, the keynote of agape is devotion, shown in a radical personal commitment displayed in practical action and personal sacrifice

(John 14:1, 24; 15:12–14). In agape the world recognizes true Christians (1 Corinthians 13; John 13:34–35). In agape the Savior is exalted. Through agape Christians look more and more like Jesus. Agape is the true mark of the Christian! If agape is missing, the world finds the church unimpressive.

God's nature is agape. In fact, the word "agape" and the name of God can be used interchangeably. I preached Christ and the gospel for nearly thirty years and never realized this point. Love is *not* God, but where God is actively present, we encounter true love! And when love acts in supernatural power and grace, the God who *is* love is present. *The Amplified Bible* translation puts it this way: "He who does not love [does not have agape] has not become acquainted with God [does not and never did know Him], for God is love [agape] (1 John 4:8). There are two clear points here. First, you cannot know God apart from agape; thus, if you know God, you share in his divine nature of love. Second, a comprehensive understanding of agape in the New Testament makes it clear that love is God's greatest gift. Responding to God's love in true faith leads us to share in his love. It is nothing less than our God-given responsibility (John 15:12–17).

Let me offer two final reflections on agape, what I am calling costly love.

First, it is helpful to think of love in terms of "strong" and "weak" agape. A lot of the talk about agape is really about "weak" agape. Weak agape sees love as charity, a virtue among virtues, but not *most* important. "Strong" agape, by contrast, insists that love is sovereign! In this view, agape possesses *unique authority*. Weak agape sees love as a great good, *similar* to virtues like courage and temperance. Strong agape sees love as *the* singular source of all faith and hope. Strong agape is the basis of everything good in creation, because it is at the center of God's nature. Timothy P. Jackson offers three ways in which Christians are called to understand and demonstrate strong agape:

1. Nothing finite would exist without God's gracious will to create and sustain it, because "God is love."

2. Human sins would not be forgiven without the atoning sacrifice of Jesus in his death on the cross. Jesus lays down his life for us because he is agape. This is the ultimate *cost* of true love.

3. Human persons, made in God's image and redeemed by God's Son, would not develop spiritually and emotionally without an unmerited care that is extended to them by others, a care that comes from God's agape even if the giver is not deeply aware of God's love.[22]

As important as all other Christian virtues are, including erotic love within marriage and deep relationships with our closest friends, these all ultimately depend on strong agape. But this does not lead to love "monism," or the idea that love is the *only* virtue. It means there is no real competition between agape and other virtues. Other virtues are vital, but they all flow from agape.

Second, several years ago I discovered a wonderful way to express agape in plain English: God-Love. I first encountered this hyphenated word in the Catholic writer Chiara Lubich. She said, "God-Love [reveals to us] not a God who is distant, immovable and inaccessible to people. God-Love … meet[s] every person in thousands of ways. … [God is] love in himself, love for all his creation."[23] She liked to say, "God loves you immensely." When a priest told Chiara, in her early twenties, that God loved her immensely she experienced her first *deep moment of transformation*. Her gift of insight into love would ultimately lead her to express *agape* as "God-Love." Her humble way of serving and caring for others touched my life several years ago though the Focolare Movement, a movement birthed through her life and calling. She rightly concludes, "We would not have had any meaning in the world if we were not a little flame of this infinite fire: love that responds to Love."[24]

Agape must be "strong" and "immense" if the church is to recover what it means to follow Jesus. *Costly love is an every-moment, Spirit-given sacrifice that allows us to die to ourselves and then freely give up our desires and comforts for the sake of others.* This love must order all other Christian virtues. And it must reign over all doctrinal formulations because God-Love alone will last forever. "Love never ends. But as for prophecies, they will come to an end; as for tongues they will cease, as for knowledge, it will come to an end... And now faith, hope and love abide, these three; and the greatest of these is love" (1 Corinthians 13:8, 13).

Conclusion

No matter how we feel, or what we think, we are called to love *because* "God is love." We cannot even begin to fathom the mystery of this costly love without putting aside our preconceptions and cultural biases. If we are to become open to the love of Christ in us then we must replace the sentimental greeting-card kinds of love we've embraced in modern culture. We must put on a faith-based, Jesus-centered, love. This love is at the center of the gospel. In the words of Bishop Robert Barron, cited in the Introduction, this love is nothing less than "the radicality of the gospel." God-Love requires us to live "outside the box" of our *human ways of thinking and living.* If we live in a radical gospel way people will likely say of us what they said of Jesus: "He is gone out of his mind" (Mark 3:21). The Apostle Paul is clear about us having this kind of thinking: "Let the same mind be in you that was in Christ Jesus" (Philippians 2:5).

But here is our problem. We have stored our minds with "the 'wheat' of rational and functional ways of thinking, [plus] we also [retain] the 'weeds' of irrational and dysfunctional ways of thinking, cultural biases, personal prejudices, and programming that we have learned."[25] A daily spiritual diet of such "weeds" leads us away from God-Love and imprisons us. This happens so subtly that we may be hardly aware that our daily diet is filled with "weeds." The solution is to consciously receive God-Love moment-by-moment so that we can live love.

My late friend, Robert Webber, helped me understand that the greatest advances we make together as Christians often occur when we recover our ancient ways. In this instance we cannot do better than to end with words from the opening paragraph of Augustine's *Confessions*: "You have made us for yourself, and our heart is restless until it rests in you."[26]

Augustine opens his classic story of conversion with "a design claim." What were we made for and why? We were created by and for God, who is revealed in Jesus Christ. James K. A. Smith says, "We are like existential sharks, we have to move to live. We are not just static containers for ideas; we are dynamic creatures directed toward some *end*."[27] Notice that Augustine places the quest for meaning not in our brain, but in our heart. This richly biblical understanding of our human center says we will only find "rest" when our ultimate end is love, love for God and love for others. Augustine says our hearts are shaped by love; thus only when all our desires and actions are centered in love will we find true rest.

CHAPTER THREE

TWO FACES OF GOD'S LOVE

Love God and do whatever you please; for the soul trained in love to God will do nothing to offend the One who is Beloved.

Augustine, modern paraphrase
from a sermon on 1 John

IN HIS *JOURNAL*, SØREN Kierkegaard writes of the only thing he really knew with deep certainty: that God is love. "Even if I have been mistaken on this or that point: God is nevertheless love." But Kierkegaard also believed it will never be easy for us to grasp this amazing truth since "God is God, and we are men, sinful men."[1]

True God-seekers eventually discover that God loves them with an eternal and transcendent love. They also discover that because God is love he never forces us to love him. If it were coercive, love would not be love. Yet the more God-seekers know him, especially through the knowledge of Christ crucified and forsaken, the more they desire to love him. An old Serbian proverb says this well: "If you love God, you cannot fear him; if you fear God, you cannot love him." Followers of Christ stand in awe before God's holiness and majesty. (Think of Aslan, the majestic and powerful lion in C. S. Lewis's mythical land of Narnia.) Only when people truly know that God is good and that he lives within the mystery of relational love, will they begin to experience divine love. God inscribes on human hearts the capacity and responsibility of love and communion. Such wondrous relational love transcends craven, destructive fear.

In *The City of God*, Augustine writes, "Because a city is held together by some law, their very law is love. And that very love is God. For openly it is written 'God is love' (1 John 4:8). He, therefore, who is full of love is full of God."[2]

As a college student in the sixties I shared my faith via a popular booklet that began with the well-known sentence, "God loves you and has a wonderful plan for your life." Though such a simple statement can be easily misunderstood, I now see the powerful truth of this "first spiritual law." Augustine envisioned this very truth in his prayer about how a community is held together by love. William Penn said that when we fully embrace God's love and purpose "we shall all be lovely, and in love with God and one another."

The Anglican priest William Law (1686–1761) wrote a great deal about holy living. Several of his books profoundly shaped the evangelical revival in Great Britain through men like John and Charles Wesley and George Whitefield. Law says that the greatest idea we can ever frame about God is to conceive of him as infinite love and perfect goodness. This understanding of God's love and of loving God, not fear and self-loathing, fueled the great evangelical revival in both Britain and America. Law reasoned that the happiness of all persons depends on their understanding and receiving divine love.

So if God loves us with "infinite … perfect goodness," how should we respond? William Penn provides the answer: "Religion is nothing else but love of God and man."

Jesus on Loving God

Any attempt to understand loving God must begin with the Great Commandment, a summary of the entire Law given to Israel. It occurs three times in the synoptic Gospels. Matthew 22:15–40 records three conflict stories. In the first episode the Pharisees "plotted to entrap [Jesus] in what he said" (Matthew 22:15–22). They posed a question about paying taxes to Caesar and honoring God. Jesus' response, which avoided a simple "either/or" answer (17:24–27), "amazed" them. Thus, his disciples could be loyal to God *and* pay tax to Caesar (22:37–39). So these religious leaders, "amazed" at his answer, went away for a time. Then, the Sadducees, members of a Jewish sect active during the period of the Second Temple, came with another "trap" question (Matthew 22:23–33).[3] They wanted to draw out Jesus' view of the Resurrection and its relationship to the Law of Moses. As with the response to the Pharisees' question about taxes, Jesus gets the better of the exchange and again the scene ends in amazement.

In a third conflict scene, after the Pharisees heard of Jesus' exchange with the Sadducees, they sent a lawyer to ask him about the "greatest commandment" in the Law. (Remember, there were hundreds of different laws within the whole Torah.)

Here is the story in Matthew 22:34–40:

> When the Pharisees heard that [Jesus] had silenced the Sadducees, they gathered together, and one of them, a lawyer, asked him a question to test him. "Teacher, which commandment in the law is the greatest?" He said to him, "'You shall love the Lord your God with all your heart, and with all your soul, and with all your mind.' This is the greatest and first commandment. And a second is like it: 'You shall love your neighbor as yourself.' On these two commandments hang all the law and the prophets." (Matthew 22:34–40)

A similar story, which might well be the same incident reported from a different perspective, is recorded in Mark 12. A "scribe" questions Jesus, not so much to trip him up as to enable him to demonstrate, as a rabbi, that he could rightly answer the question (12:28, 32–33; Jesus' reply is in verse 34). Along with Luke 10:25–28, which is an entirely different story, these three Gospel accounts provide the clearest insight we have into Jesus' thinking about what it means to "love God." Here we see the essence of true religion.

True Religion Flows from the Inside Out

At its center, *true religion consists in loving God*. God desires and deserves our complete love because he *is* love. He created us because he *is* love. He redeemed us because he *is* love. Therefore, we should seek to love God with "all [our] heart, all [our] soul and all [our] mind." These three elements constitute the *whole person*. Consider Jesus' three specific directives about loving God.

1. *We must love God with all our heart.* In Scripture the heart is the source of passions and feelings. It is the center of willing, choosing, and doing. The heart is the place where all distinctly human activity converges, "the anchor that keeps our soul and mind rooted in the world of the physical and the social. No act is fully human without the participation of the heart."[4] Jesus says we should love God so much that we learn to diligently search, with our whole heart, for what he desires.

2. *We must love God with all our soul.* In Hebrew, the *soul* refers to "the breath of God." This dimension makes us pilgrims who will never be satisfied with this world as it is. "The soul's homing instinct keeps us perpetually moving toward union with God as its first origin and final end."[5] At the center of loving God with all our soul is prayer. If we regard prayer as a duty through which we bring our "lists" to God, we miss this vital connection between loving God and prayer. In true prayer we are directed to look inside ourselves, to do careful introspection. In this way the Spirit enables us to interpret ourselves and gain a deep and growing sense of God's love and forgiveness. The issue here is not the structure of prayer, but deep and loving communion, because prayer is fundamentally our search for God. It centers us in God through a divine encounter in which we experience God's transforming presence and come to know how profoundly he loves us. We pray not only to strengthen *our* love for God but also to tap into *his* love and power despite the noise and clutter inside us. When I am centered on God's unconditional love, I regain divine peace and joy. From deep within my soul I cry out to God, who is always present in me as

relational love. This helps me to remember that when I talk to God, I may envision him as my Father and forget that I am using metaphorical language about a profound mystery. This is why I also remember to speak to the Spirit, because "God's spirit blows wherever it wishes" (John 3:8, Common English Bible). This pattern includes imaginative reflection upon scenes from the four Gospels and the realization that the world has depths I cannot understand. Yet behind this world, at the center of the deepest truths, there are invisible beings. Such recollection and reflection helps me to release any idea that God is sometimes present and sometimes too busy to pay attention to me. And it reminds me that the Spirit's love for me is immanent, caring, and omnipresent.

3. *We must love God with all our mind.* The mind is the faculty that "floods us with the light of truth and enables us to make wise choices in harmony with the truth of [all] things."[6] These three—soul, heart, mind—define what it means to *experience* true freedom. True freedom is responsible, creative, and discerning. It always seeks deeper communion with God-Love. These three "commands" (which comprise *one* command) convey as clearly as any words in Holy Scripture what it means to give and receive true love. Erasmo Leiva-Merikakis, a Trappist monk, concludes:

> Jesus intends this rich answer to make us see the great intensity of the genuine religious life, the fact that the life of faith and devotion by nature engages and exhausts every single aspect of man, whether physical, spiritual, mental or psychological. God claims our whole being for himself, not in the manner of a tyrant who wishes to exploit and annihilate us, but as a lover who deems us so precious that he will not tolerate the slightest capacity of our person going to waste. God delights in the utmost energizing of our being, precisely as a father delights in the fruition of his child's talents.[7]

Because it is centered in God-Love, true religion demands our total commitment. Jesus says, "The *entire law and all the demands of the prophets* are based on these two command-ments" (Matthew 22:40, New Living Translation).

Mark and Luke add a fourth word to these three direc-tives, saying we should love God "with all [our] strength" (Mark 12:30; Luke 10:27). Jesus' command is clear. True re-ligion always leads us to love God and others. Although the Pharisees knew these texts well, they could not "hear" them with open minds and hearts (see Micah 6:8; Isaiah 33:15–16; 56:1; Amos 5:14–15). So we must open our own minds and hearts, in the proper order. We call this teaching of Jesus the Great Commandment, but there are really two inseparable commandments. We must *first* love God; *then* we can truly love others. Costly love does not separate these two com-mands, We love others with God-Love because we first love *God*. Humans are more than just chemical elements. We are all marked by divinity. If we disregard any person's worth, we cannot claim to have God-Love. All of us find excuses for not loving some persons who are hard to love, but true reli-gion always calls us to rise above our self-centeredness and love all others with the love God has shown to us.

This question and response occur in a context "domi-nated by the imperative to perform endless exterior works of piety, charity, and ritual observance."[8] Love indeed may be a work, at least in a certain (narrow) sense, but Jesus clearly says love is *primarily an interior activity* that at first may be difficult to discern. "We love [God], *because* he first loved us" (1 John 4:19). Jesus' words lay the foundations for Christian-ity as a religion of the interior person. True and lasting love flows out of our inner beings because we have *experienced* the love of God.

When Paul affirms the truths that should motivate and inform how Christ's faithful followers act, he appeals to love as our deepest affection *and* motive (1 Corinthians 13:1, 3). God-Love is the only interior work that will completely transform us. Through this gift we are united with the good-ness of the reigning King of Glory. God-Love is thus the *un-common* gift Christians bring to life in this world.

Understanding the Torah

Jesus answers the lawyer's question by appealing to "the greatest and first commandment" (22:34–38). He uses two texts to form his response: Deuteronomy 6:4–5 and Leviticus 19:18. The first is the *Shema*, which comes from the Hebrew word translated "Hear!" or "Listen!" According to Jewish New Testament scholar Amy-Jill Levine, this was "a major part of the synagogue liturgy."[9] Deuteronomy 6:6–9 actually commanded the people to follow these words to the letter. What Jesus understood in his day is consistent with Jewish understanding down to the present time. *The faithful are to love God and their neighbors.* To quote the great second-century Rabbi Akiva, "Love your neighbor as yourself—this is the major principle of the Torah." (Jerusalem Talmud *Nedarim* 9:4). This combination of love for God and neighbor appears in other books from early Judaism, such as the *Testament of Dan* and the *Testament of Issachar*. Levine concludes, "Jesus does not have to be unique in all cases in order to be profound."[10] I agree, but there is indeed something additional here.

The *way* Jesus orders his response and *how* he specifically draws these two primary texts together is unique (Deuteronomy 6:5; Leviticus 19:18). In Mark, Jesus actually weaves together *three essential parts* of Judaism. The first is the creed: "Hear, O Israel! The Lord our God is Lord alone" (12:29). This is the central "creed" of Judaism—there is only one God. Note, the creed and love are *not* separated. Second, Jesus says we should love God above all. Third, we should love our neighbor. As we will see later, Luke expands the meaning of "neighbor" beyond what was ordinarily understood in Jewish culture of the time. So these three stories show us *how* Jesus uniquely weaves three elements together and then *demonstrates* what love for our neighbor means in actual practice.[11]

A proselyte once asked Hillel (the great Jewish scholar who lived a century before Christ) to instruct him in the whole law. He replied, "What you hate for yourself, do not do to your neighbor. This is the whole law, the rest is commentary. Go and learn." Simon the Righteous said, "On three things stands the world—on the law, on the worship, and on the works of love." These answers clearly resemble one another, but put into their first-century context, the uniqueness of Jesus' teaching becomes evident.

Jews and Christians have often debated which language best expresses what love for God means and how love for God is to be understood in actual practice. But one thing is clear: *Jesus did not introduce something completely new.* Levine notes that while philosophers and theologians can debate the difference in these statements within their two traditions, they should never pit Jesus against his own Jewish tradition:

> Such an approach hardly demonstrates love of God and neighbor. Perhaps if church and synagogue stopped debating who had the better formulation of the Golden Rule—which is by no means restricted to Jesus and Hillel—and started living by it, we'd all be better off.[12]

Keeping in mind that the Golden Rule was well-understood in Jesus' time, it should be noted that Jews had several different schools of thought about the law. Some believed that there were lighter and weightier matters in the law. Others were stricter and argued even the smallest detail was important precisely because God had revealed it. This is what makes the lawyer's question (Matthew 22: 34–36) so subtle. If he could "trap" Jesus, he could find a way to undermine his claims. While Jesus' answer may not have been *entirely* original, the way that he framed it is *unique*.

So How Can We Obey the Great Commandment?

Can anyone keep God's commandments? Before answering no, recall that this text was *not* given during a sixteenth-century Reformation debate about the role of human works in salvation. In Matthew 15, Jesus had said the heart must be *renewed* if we are to produce the fruit of true religion. (Remember, *true* religion is *not optional*; see James 1:27.) In the

Sermon on the Mount (Matthew 5–7) Jesus issues a challenge to live in a manner that reveals this renewed heart.

There are many ways to order Jesus' kingdom teaching in the Sermon on the Mount. The one I prefer says that after the Beatitudes, his teaching can be divided into two parts, which correspond to the two parts of the Great Commandment. First, Jesus teaches that in his kingdom, agape is specifically focused on our neighbor. This is why a "sharp" tongue can "murder" our neighbor and lust can easily lead to trouble in personal relationships. Godly love in marriage should be valued because this discourages divorce, which negatively impacts the lives of so many others. Our oaths should be kept by letting our "yes" be "yes" and our "no" be "no." We should turn the other cheek to those who attack us, thus showing love even for our enemies. Each of these statements comes from the Old Testament. But Jesus also builds on this foundation by expanding the depth and breadth of agape. Thus in Matthew 6–7 we see several more specific ways in which we should love God. For example, we can give to those in need quietly. We can pattern our prayer after a *model* "kingdom" prayer. We can fast in private without looking somber so as to draw attention to ourselves. We can intentionally store up treasures in heaven rather than on earth, thereby trusting God so fully that we stop worrying about tomorrow. And by not judging others we actually learn to leave judgment to God alone. In our prayer we make our deepest needs known to God in private. The most important directive is, perhaps, that we be sure we've entered the narrow gate that leads to kingdom life. When this happens we will bear fruit *like* good trees and build our lives on the love of God, the love that is like a solid rock!

Do you see the central point here? *A renewed heart of love precedes all our actions.* How then do we live the Christian faith if true religion must be rooted in love? Or, to put the question another way, "What does a relationship with God solidly built on agape look like?"

What Jesus says about true religion and the law makes sense within the larger context of the good news of the kingdom. The apostles would come to understand that Jeremiah had prophesied about a time when God would "put [his] law within them, and ... write it on their hearts" (Jeremiah 31:31). This time came about when Jesus died for the sins of the world and rose to give new life. Then Messiah would "pour out" the Holy Spirit on those who were joined to him (see Ezekiel 39:29; Joel 2:28–29; Zechariah 12:10; Acts 2:17–18). N. T. Wright explains this point:

> What Jesus says here about loving God, and loving one another, only makes sense when we set it within Matthew's larger gospel picture, of Jesus dying for the sins of the world, and rising again with the message of new life. That's when these commandments begin to come into their own: when they are seen not as orders to be obeyed in our own strength, but as invitations and promises to a new way of life in which, bit by bit, hatred and pride can be left behind and love can become a reality.[13]

A popular view in Second Temple Judaism predicted that the Davidic Messiah would be a warlike person who would trample Israel's enemies "under his feet." But this view missed the true purpose of Psalm 110. The "enemies" that this coming Messiah would defeat were *not* the enemies of ethnic Israel. They were "the ultimate enemies of the whole human race, and indeed of the whole world; in other words, sin itself, and death, which it brings."[14] In these narratives Jesus directly opposes *the pride of special status* that promotes nationalistic standing and religious separatism. Unless the Messiah defeated sin and death, *true religion* (James 1:27) could never be possible. Wright concludes, "Jesus knows that sin and death can only be defeated by David's master going to meet them in single, unarmed combat that continues his work ... all the way to the cross itself."[15]

You've Got to Love

Out of love, God created humankind in his own image. Out of love, God told Adam and Eve to love him and obey him. As we saw in Augustine's *Confessions*, God has inscribed on the human heart a capacity and desire for love. Sin did not destroy this desire. We are made for relational oneness, and only through relational love can we experience it.

The second commandment, or the second part of the Great Commandment, is "like" the first. (That means there is a distinction here *without* a separation.) By calling our love for God "the first and greatest commandment" and by saying the "second [is] like it" Jesus is saying the first can never stand alone without the second.

Through the second commandment, God makes a *complete* claim on our self-giving, relational love. And through the second commandment we can know that we *truly* love God. We can easily be deceived, so it provides a way for us to test our love for God.

God's Love Has Two Faces

Scottish writer George MacDonald said God is "easy to please but hard to satisfy." That is, God's love is not sentimental conviviality. At the beginning of this chapter I said the servile fear of God hinders our love. So what is the solution to this apparent predicament?

God's love has two faces. God is both good *and* holy. He is forgiving *and* demanding. God is both good *and* hard! (Not "hard" as a ruthless taskmaster but "hard" as a good Father!) This is what George MacDonald means.

True love is always hard if you are to reach your human potential. True love costs deeply. It has two faces.

One of the greatest problems the church faces today is realizing that the absolute, unchanging, eternal God will not compromise. This is why we misperceive his love. The very fact that God is absolute and unchanging is the only solid reason for trusting in his perfect goodness and love. He is tender, compassionate, and truly kind. Kierkegaard was right in concluding that the command to love God can redeem love from the fear of failure, because God's will cannot fail.

Catholic philosopher Peter Kreeft says, "God shows us these two faces of his love in the opposite way and at the opposite time from the way the devil shows them. Before we sin God warns us about the great harm sin will cause." He then adds, "If we are sane ... we ought to fear sin more than sickness, suffering, or death itself."[16] When we are tempted to disobey God, Satan assures us our sinful choice will be just fine. God warns us of the dangers ahead. When we have sinned, the opposite occurs. Satan attacks us to make us believe there is no hope for us. But God shows us his mercy and reveals his loving desire for us to come home. This is why MacDonald says God is "easy to please and hard to satisfy."

Conclusion

Although Thomas Aquinas (1225–1274) is considered one of the greatest theological minds, his fellow students called him "the dumb ox" because initially he had so little to say. Over his lifetime this extremely quiet man built an entire system of theology—expressed in nearly sixty published volumes. Yet near the end of his days, he called his entire life's work, a huge store of intellectual and spiritual food, "straw." No one ever accused Thomas of arrogance! He desired to bring everything he thought into Christ's love and service. And with that motivation he pursued his goal—true purity of heart in God's love. Like true theologians before him Aquinas was not a pure academic, but a pastoral practitioner. He wrote theology as a "doctor of souls." But somewhere around AD 1300 Christian theology became a university (academic) discipline. This caused unexpected harm. *Deep spirituality was cut off from the enterprise of trained thought.* Bishop Robert Barron concludes, "[T]his disjunction proved disastrous for both sides, giving rise to a theology void of life and a spirituality too often void of substance."[17] Theologians who debate thinkers like Aquinas can be filled with pride in their erudition, yet miss the experiential aspect of his way of life and thought. When this happens, they miss his most important contribution: Life is about seeking God alone for the purity of heart that is true love.

The Greek New Testament often uses an important word here: *nous*. This important word has been translated in a variety of ways, and in the process has lost its richness. In English, *nous* has been taken to mean "intelligence," even "common sense." In the New Testament it should be understood more like *noetic* prayer, a prayer of the mind and heart that is at the center of true life. *Nous* refers to the means by which we apprehend God's presence and will. The inner springs of our human person are all *noetic*. Orthodox Bishop Kallistos Ware refers to *nous* as "the intellective aptitude of the heart."[18] Here, in the innermost being of the human person, mind and matter meet. Scott Cairns thus concludes, "[This is] where the human person is mystically united to others and to God."[19] In the image of God, personhood is relational. *Nous* is the faculty by which the relationship we have with God and one another comes alive.

During a debate some time ago a professor of biochemistry and molecular biology was asked, "What are the three most-important words in the English language?" He answered, "I love you." Then he was asked, "What are the second three most-important words?" He replied, "I don't know." When we grasp these two answers in the right order we discover our true meaning in life. Thomas Aquinas understood these two answers with everything in him. So did the ancient fathers and mystics of the church. We can do so as well if we make love our aim.

PART TWO

WHY SHOULD WE LOVE?

We love because he first loved us.

(1 John 4:19)

CHAPTER FOUR

FALLING IN LOVE WITH GOD

> Being a Christian means learning to love with God's love. But God's love is not a warm feeling in the pit of the stomach.
>
> Roberta C. Bondi

THE BIBLE STATES CLEARLY the origin of love: Love comes from God *because* God *is* love. His holy love emerges out of his creative and reconciling purpose. God's love makes human love possible, and because he first loved us, he commands us to love. We will never reach our God-designed joy until we love as God loves. And to obey this command we must keep before us that our love is always a *response* to the gift of God's love. This is why the essence of Christianity comes down to this: In *Jesus Christ, God's love is made visible.*

God powerfully manifests his love in his sovereign acts of creation and in his covenant. This is why Jesus, as a faithful rabbi, taught love for God is *the greatest commandment.* The *Shema Israel* (Deuteronomy 6:4–6) indicates the centrality of this relationship to Israel's life. But Israel did not generally understand love for God as intimate affection, though this idea begins to appear later in the Old Testament. Rather, love was first understood as wholehearted "obedience to God's commandments, serving God, showing reverence for God, and being loyal to God alone."[1] As stated in chapter 2, no single Hebrew word translates as "love" in the same way agape means God-Love in the New Testament. Yet the

Hebrew words I mentioned (*hesed, rahamim*) indicate covenantal faithfulness. This faithfulness refers to "experiences of close relationship, although not all of them denote (sexual) intimacy."[2] When the Old Testament was translated into Greek (*Septuagint,* or *LXX*), "agape" was chosen for a wide range of Hebrew words that carry this idea of covenantal love. For this and other linguistic reasons, early Christians used "agape" in order to avoid profane or philosophical concepts of love. For them, love was rooted in the Scriptures and in the worship of Israel's God, the almighty, faithful Creator.

Under the old covenant, loving God meant accepting and respecting his faithfulness and powerful presence. But it also meant "loving the other human being and one's own emerging self."[3] That is, we love God and others, and in turn, we grow in our awareness of doing so. These core ideas are summed up in the Mosaic Law (Deuteronomy 10:12–20).

The three Gospel stories considered in the previous chapter (Matthew 22:34–40; Mark 12:28–34; Luke 10:25–37), show Jesus' teaching about love for God is anchored in this rich covenantal understanding. The Mosaic covenant provides the framework for a proper human-divine relationship. Many biblical scholars note the authority with which Jesus interprets the Law. In these narratives, the commandment to love God rests not on one rabbinic interpretation but the absolute authority of Rabbi Jesus. The new covenant, established though his death and resurrection, becomes the central event in history and defines God's love. Jesus is clearly calling us to *concrete action, not empty religious performance.* In an "ever-widening horizon" his command redefines Israel's core identity beyond biological family and national loyalties. Jesus is calling his followers to enter into a radically new community that will be defined by his love:

> [Jesus'] mother and his brothers came to him, but they could not reach him because of the crowd. And he was told, "Your mother and your brothers are standing outside, wanting to see you." But he said to them, "My mother and my brothers are those who hear the word of God and do it." (Luke 8:19–21)

In this passage, Jesus is not rejecting the traditional pillars of Jewish religious life and identity (family, temple, Torah, and land); he is showing that in a proper messianic context, their significance is relative to God's love. He wants his disciples to understand God is subordinating all of these markers of Jewish life to one purpose: his singular love. Werner Jeanrond concludes, "The coming of God's reign will be promoted through love, not through the preservation of established religious tradition."[4] This makes the command to love God and neighbor central to everything we are to become as baptized followers of Jesus. Thus, the reign of God's kingdom will be explained in this fundamentally "new" way. We see this with particular clarity in John's Gospel and first epistle.

Can We Grow in Our Love for God?

To gain true knowledge of God we must center ourselves *in* his love. The three Gospel narratives about loving God and our neighbor show clearly that we cannot truly love God until we first love him with all our being. The English translation of Matthew 22 does not make this point as sharply as the original Greek conveys. The future indicative tense actually says, "You *will* love!" This underscores the *imperative force of the command while reminding us that God must work in us to prompt this response.* Jesus says we must love God with all our mind *and* all our soul (Matthew 22: 37; Mark 12:30; Luke 10:27). Loving God includes our rational thoughts as well as the *mysterious fire of love* within us. Thus, loving God first is an interior activity produced by God's Spirit, but then it becomes an activit*y in which we must become fully engaged.* He wants us to consider this carefully. Our love for God must be rooted in *both* our mind (truth) and our will (heart). We don't program love once and for all through a single act. We can't Google-search "how to love God" and then "Just Do It!"

True knowledge of God comes in a dynamic way, just as a spouse learns to love in a fruitful marriage:

> The knowledge husband and wife have of each other includes a profound respect for the otherness of the other; based in love, each seeks to preserve the integrity of the other, allowing the other to be [who he or she is] without simply becoming an extension of the spouse. It is a knowledge that comes out of living together, responding to each other's daily interests and needs, being shaped by deep caring for the other. It is a transforming knowledge.[5]

Over decades, I've learned that to love God we must cultivate definite life-patterns (habits) that fuel the fire of our growing love for God. But we won't care deeply about these patterns unless we first *intend* to love God with all our being. So before we look at the second part of the Great Commandment—"you shall love your neighbor as yourself"—let's pause to ask, *how can we learn to love God?*

A Dedicated Activist

In my earliest memories, I recall learning I should love God by faithfully engaging in four activities: reading the Bible daily, daily prayer time, going to church, and witnessing for Christ. These activities, while good, never *directly* helped me to grow in my love for God. Several decades into my adult life, and after more than a decade in pastoral ministry, I ran out of gas. Many times I "felt" great love for God, but I was not transformed by it. The result was internal spiritual mediocrity, even spiritual and emotional burnout. Of course, I couldn't help but go to church. I even went to seminars to learn "new" ways to do these four activities better. I continued them as faithfully as I could, but the more I did them, the more I sensed something was lacking. I hungered for an intense experience of God-Love. But I had hit a wall and had no sense of how to go further.

Then, in my forties, I was exposed more and more to Christian tradition that reached back over two thousand years. My understanding deepened as I read writers from *before* and *after* the Protestant Reformation. I began to move "outside the box" I referred to in chapter 2. Eventually, in the great love stories of Jesus, which are found in his parables and profound metaphors, I discovered that "I am the true vine" (John 15) defines the depth of the love bond between him and us. I further realized that whether actively loving him or not, I was still connected to the vine (Jesus), the *source* of my life and his love. Jesus maintains this intimate relationship so that we will know him better and then pass on his costly love to those who need the "fruit" of his love. I finally understood why John Paul II described this love as "a dynamic relationship of faithful self-giving with others. It is in faithful self-giving that a person finds a fullness of certainty and security."[6] The gift of love I now receive moment-by-moment will empower me to love others with God's love whether others have a close relationship with me or not.

Finally, I began to enter into Jesus' love stories. These stories are not about my own happiness but about living intimately in God-Love. When this happened my own private practices of faith began to change. Being in love is not about seeking for my personal happiness, but about serving others. "The love in which we spend our lives in serving others will not give us the temporary happiness of romantic love stories but, rather, the lasting, everyday, all-one's-life-and-then-some happiness Jesus refers to as *joy*."[7] I discovered a profound truth: "The joy of the Lord is your strength" (Nehemiah 8:10). Jesus commands us to give ourselves away in costly love *so that* his eternal joy might become strong in us. When his love abides in us then our joy is made complete in him (John 15:9–17).

Learning to See Jesus in Scripture

When I began to listen to many Christian voices from the past, and how they understood Jesus, I engaged Scripture and prayer quite differently. For example, I discovered *Lectio Divina* (Latin for "divine reading"), a third-century Benedictine practice of reading, meditation, and prayer that promotes deeper communion with God. Instead of seeing God's Word as a text to be mastered, I began to engage it as a means to entering into God's heart. Traditionally, *lectio* involves reading a passage of Scripture in order to reflect on it slowly and carefully, then praying over the words (or even a *single* word) and contemplating what God is saying to you. This cannot be hurried. *Lectio* enhanced the spiritual transformation of Augustine, who wrote more about loving God and neighbor than any other Christian writer after the apostles.

Here's an example of how *lectio* works in modern practice. Popular author James Martin, S.J., says when he reads the four Gospels, he asks, "How was Jesus able to make such bold statements?" Martin says he gradually "realized that not only did everyone in the synagogue know Jesus, but Jesus probably knew them. [Thus Jesus could clearly anticipate their response.] So Jesus most likely anticipated their rejection." How could Jesus be so bold? "One reason he was able to speak out was because he was free, unfettered by worries of acceptance or rejection, perfectly embodying what Ignatius called 'detachment.'"[8] Martin describes what I began to learn and experience: to rest in God and to be bold, because God has taught me I am totally free!

The Spiritual Disciplines

Perhaps no modern Protestant writers have had a greater impact on my private life than Dallas Willard (1935–2013) and Richard Foster. Willard's book *The Spirit of the Disciplines: Understanding How God Changes Lives* (1999) opened my eyes to transforming love. If you want to make daily progress in loving God, there is no book I would recommend more highly. Willard, a Baptist, taught philosophy at the University of Southern California but moved beyond his own evangelical background by embracing the catholic spiritual tradition of the wider church.

Richard Foster, a Quaker professor, authored the pioneering book *Celebration of Discipline* (1978) and founded Renovaré, one of the best ministries I know concerning the spiritual disciplines. In the opening line of this book Foster writes, "Superficiality is the curse of our age. ... The desperate need today is not for a greater number of intelligent people, or gifted people, but for deep people."[9]

These authors believe the spiritual disciplines give us solid patterns for growing in love. They have created two categories of Christian disciplines: abstinence ("letting go") and activity ("engagement"). The disciplines of abstinence include solitude, silence, fasting, frugality, chastity, secrecy (see Matthew 5:15; 6:1), and sacrifice. The disciplines of activity include study, worship, prayer, fellowship, and submission.

These disciplines are not meant to provide a rigid program that guarantees specific outcomes. They are best understood as tried-and-true courses upon which we can run a long-distance race to love God more deeply (1 Corinthians 9:24; Hebrews 12:1). These practices allow us to relinquish things that we are free to do but can hinder us from growing in transformative love. We practice the disciplines to gain something we deeply desire. For example, we abstain from something not because it is law but because abstaining helps us experience God's love more fully (1 Peter 2:11). The point is not practicing sin-management but rather entering into the experience of divine love.

We can liken these disciplines to the personalized regimen athletes use to prepare for competition (1 Corinthians 9:24). Willard and Foster are helpful places to begin basic training. Another helpful place to start is Fr. James Martin's *The Jesuit Guide to (Almost) Everything: A Spirituality for Real Life*. The Christian tradition has more to offer than many of us realize. Begin to explore, and you won't regret it!

Virtue and Vice

James K. A. Smith notes that the ancient way to make love our fundamental orientation is to develop love as a habit. When this happens love becomes the supreme virtue, not something that comes and goes. Paul exhorts the first Christians in Colossae to adopt love as a *pattern of life*:

> As God's chosen ones, holy and beloved, clothe yourselves with compassion, kindness, humility, meekness, and patience. Bear with one another and, if anyone has a complaint against another, forgive each other; just as the

Lord has forgiven you, so you also must forgive. Above all, clothe yourselves with love, which binds everything together in perfect harmony. (Colossians 3:12–14)

Paul uses *clothing* as a metaphor here. Just as we clothe our bodies with outward garments so "clothe yourselves with love" in your personal relationships. We are "to put on the Lord Jesus Christ" (Romans 13:14). And then over all these items of clothing (virtues) we are instructed "to put on love" (1 Thessalonians 5:8). Love is something like a belt that holds all our clothing (the virtues) together.

These character qualities Paul enumerates in his epistles as *virtues*. A virtue is a good moral habit. Virtue means more than good ethics. (Obviously, vice is a bad moral habit.) Such good habits should become *internal dispositions* to do the good, not just occasional choices. They can become patterns, patterns formed by practice. Just as we breathe without thinking, we practice these virtues as a kind of second nature when we've developed them over time. When we possess these virtues we do not have to *think* about being considerate, compassionate or forgiving, at least most of the time. We *are* considerate, compassionate and forgiving as a way of life.

So the $64,000 question is: "How do I *acquire* these virtues as a follower of Jesus?" It's obvious you can't work your way into virtue through study and better thinking. We can learn laws and obey them, but virtue is different. Acquiring virtue is more like practicing my skills through writing this book. I may read books on how to write better, but writing only becomes second nature by writing. (Reading books on writing has helped me!)

Let me illustrate this more specifically. A young son will often mimic his dad. In the same way we can learn to mimic people who live the virtue of love. We need role models if we are to learn *how* to love. (Great souls, sometimes called the saints, help us to cultivate the virtue of love through real life stories of virtue!) This is exactly what Paul means when he says, "Brothers and sisters, join in imitating me, and observe those who live according to the example you have in us" (Philippians 3:17). *We learn the supreme virtue of love by modeling those we live with who love just like Jesus!* This takes lifelong practice, and it requires us to learn love in relationship *with others* since all of these virtues must involve others. These are not private thoughts; they are public virtues. This is also why unity can became a reality only through the virtue of costly love.[10]

Longing for What I Knew All Along

Christians long to be devoted followers of Christ, but the pressures of life and unseen spiritual powers hinder us (Ephesians 6:10–20). Like Paul, we desire our "hearts [to be turned] to the love of God and to the steadfastness of Christ" (2 Thessalonians 3:5). Our common problem is we cannot see *how* to do this. We try simplistic methods and fail. Our love grows cold. Our lives feel empty. Much of what we do inside the church doesn't help. Sermons may be only pious talks or classroom lectures. In time, these practices become mere rituals that no longer touch our hearts. It's easy to see how we lose love for God at the center of our being.

In addition to all these, we misunderstand prayer. It is not primarily about asking and receiving. Authentic prayer is about opening ourselves to a mutual interchange with our loving Creator. It is about *being*, not doing. Real prayer gives us self-awareness and thus directly affects how we walk in love.

Our culture tells us that self-improvement and positive affirmation are the keys to life. Modern psychology has helped us in many ways, but it can never teach us how to draw our hearts and minds into the love of God.[11] We need fresh ways to receive God's love so that we can genuinely love him.

The spiritual disciplines will indirectly help us to love God. But becoming fully alive to God's love is something only he can accomplish in us. Our ingrained habits and longstanding patterns of sin predispose us to miss God's love. What we deeply desire—"righteousness, peace and joy in the Holy Spirit" (Romans 14:17)—*is* the kingdom of God at work within us. God graciously invites us to "seek" first his kingdom of love (Matthew 6:33). This takes us back to the Sermon on the Mount, as we saw in chapter 3.

In the preface to her book *To Love as God Loves: Conversations with the Early Church*, Roberta C. Bondi says we need a "real fleshing out of what Christian love is: God's love for all of us, ours for each other, God's world, and God."[12] We need to know what being a *real* Christian actually means. Bondi creates a lovely conversation with Christians from the late third century—a time when, after the legalization of Christianity in AD 313, the church was becoming more and more like the surrounding culture. God raised up a small group of believers to challenge the status quo. They gave up everything and moved to the desert. They attracted small communities who followed them because people wanted to be holy in practical ways. We know of these Christians because of the writings they left about how they *learned* to love God. While I don't agree with all of what these monks wrote, I believe they offer something we truly need. They desired above all else to *perfect* their love for God (Matthew 5:48; 6:33).

Humility Is First

One Desert Father, Anthony (251–356), came to realize humility preceded loving God, because humility was centered in valuing others above self. In the wilderness he sought perfection in God's love, something most of us can't grasp because we do not understand perfection. (We think it means *complete sinlessness*—an idea closer to Greek thinking than Christian!) Anthony believed humility alone made love possible. It also made it possible to forgive and love others. Our problem, he reminds us, is *not* that we live with messed-up people. (We are prone to think that holiness requires us to get far away from "messy people" because they'll tear us away from God's love.) Genuine humility allows us to see that love for God and neighbor go hand-in-hand. True humility is the only solution to the bipolar way we profess to love God yet fail to show costly love to real people.

I suggested earlier we cannot really know how much God loves us until we humbly enter the relational life of the Trinity. There we begin to grasp that we are "rooted and grounded in love" (Ephesians 3:17); thus we can "know the love of Christ that surpasses knowledge, [and] be filled with all the fullness of God" (Ephesians 3:19). Here we discover God's love is not a flimsy or powerless emotion but a costly and powerful reality that changes us completely. But we will not experience the magnitude of this divine love until we know true humility. God's love will then create a unifying process through which all our relationships become central to our costly love for God. These relationships will bring us into a realized oneness with the divine mystery whereby God becomes "all in all" in our actual experience. This is how we enter into the reality that nothing in all of creation can "separate us from the love of God in Christ Jesus our Lord" (Romans 8:37–39).

"Blessed are the poor in spirit" is the first beatitude of our Lord (Matthew 5:3). I preached from these words decades ago, yet they remained a mystery for me until I learned the practice of *lectio* and contemplation. James Martin says if practicing Christians are asked if they should be charitable and loving, they will answer yes, but if asked if they should be poor in spirit, they'll reply, "Huh?" As a young Jesuit, Martin discovered poverty of spirit when, assigned to serve two years in Nairobi, he was sent to an office where he was bored and alone. He was sent a modern classic titled *Poverty of Spirit*, by German theologian Johannes Baptist Metz (b. 1928). Metz says only through poverty of spirit can we realize our highest good lies beyond self-reliance. Through spiritual poverty we can *see* God, and we see this by experiencing our great need to love him above everything else.

Poverty of spirit describes a stance of utter dependence upon God. It is not demeaning but rather refers to making God our true foundation in life. It is a way of saying we depend on God entirely for our happiness and fulfillment. It also means joyfully accepting that we face disappointment, pain, suffering, and death so that we will let go of everything that keeps us from costly love. But here we face a great danger. Our culture has encouraged us to ignore this reality. Metz says, "We are all members of a species that is not sufficient unto itself" and "we are all creatures plagued by unending doubts and restless, unsatisfied hearts."[13] The sooner we embrace our poverty of spirit, the sooner we will love God and others more profoundly.

But another danger lurks on the other side of understanding humility. We can *overemphasize* our sin and sinfulness. Don't misunderstand: Personal, social, and systemic sin is truly devastating. But we need to remember that "where sin increased, grace abounded all the more" (Romans 5:20). When we overemphasize sin, we can lose sight of our God-given goodness and forget that we are called to be co-creators of divine love in a world being filled with the love of Christ![14]

Ignatius of Loyola (1491–1556) created a series of spiritual exercises, called the *examen*, to help Jesuits pursue love for God. Loyola's aim was to lead Christians to choose one course of action over another. But he was a realist. He knew real depression and spiritual struggle. One of the keys in his *Spiritual Exercises* is to discover humility through poverty of spirit. He says the central way of doing this is to strive to be free of the desire for wealth, honor or even long life. Ignatius called this "indifference" or "detachment." We must not only do the right thing but also become *free enough to accept what God allows* us to undergo. But in Loyola's path there is an even higher way toward humility. Besides doing God's revealed will and striving for detachment, we can actually choose the way of humility. We can choose to be poor and rejected just as Jesus was. A modern Jesuit writer explains, "Here ... your desire is to share the whole being and condition of the Beloved."[15]

To gain humility, we must overcome a variety of false views. The word *humility* does not resonate with modern people, and has lost its distinctly Christian sense. It has become shorthand for accepting an inferior position in the world because you can do nothing else. Women and minorities were once expected to be particularly humble because of their lot in life. Even the oft-used Christian phrase *selfless love* is problematic. For some, it has come to mean we must deny all our likes and desires. If we do this, we will likely lose our *distinct* personalities. But Jesus makes it clear we should be aggressive and intentional in seeking true greatness by choosing to serve in humble love (Matthew 16:24–28; 20:20–28; Mark 9:33–37; 10:35–45; Luke 22:24–27).

Love Is the Goal

The previous chapter said loving God is the *goal* of the Christian life. In this chapter we've seen how we must "learn to love God" above all else. Here's the critical point: There is a huge difference between love as a *spontaneous emotion* and love as a *cultivated and settled disposition*. Not understanding that difference will defeat our attempts to love God with all our being. Indeed, here lies the true distinction between costly love and every other kind of love. Let me explain.

Austrian-British philosopher Ludwig Wittgenstein (1889–1951) argued that an emotion cannot be commanded. He was right. Jesus is not commanding an *emotion*; he is commanding us to *make a choice, one that will cost us everything*. We can make *this* choice because "God's love has been poured into our hearts" (Romans 5:5). We can count the cost, understand Christian discipleship, and choose to be a generous, self-sacrificing person. German Mennonite scholar Ethelbert Stauffer (1902–1979), says Christian love "is a matter of will and action." Roberta Bondi adds, "We must not for one minute think that Christian love is something that arises in our heart as a gift of God's grace from the moment we become Christian, or we set ourselves up for despair or hypocrisy."[16] Love, she concludes, is the *goal* in the same way that becoming a good minister is a goal. If you are a minister, this calling did not come to you all at once. Yes, you must learn skills, but having done so does not make you a *fully* competent minister. No true minister ever concluded, "I am now a minister. I have arrived at my goal." Ministry remains a *goal* in the sense that it continues to shape your decisions, actions and attitudes. In much the same way, love is the *goal* of the every Christian's life. You must continue to "strive" for the kingdom (Matthew 6:33).

Remember, purity of heart *is* love for God. Love for God is our true goal in life, but the blight of sin blocks our pathway to the experience of divine love. Only the grace of God can forgive our sinful self-centeredness, purify our hearts, and turn them back to God and true goodness.

Philip Melanchthon (1497–1560), often just a footnote in the story of the Protestant Reformation, was Luther's most trusted partner and good friend. He was also a genius in his own right. In 1521 he wrote the first systematic presentation of Lutheran doctrine, *Loci Communes*, a work Luther considered a masterpiece. Elizabeth I is said to have memorized it so she could better discuss theology. Of all the doctrines Melanchthon presented in his large body of work, none was more important than his consideration of the human self, or the heart. He said, "The chief affection of human nature is self-love, by which it [the heart] is drawn away to wish for and desire only what seems to its nature good, sweet, pleasant, and glorious."[17] Trained as a humanist scholar, Melanchthon did not deny the role of human reason but argued rather that reason could only nudge the heart toward God's love. Love alone can rule the heart and bring about communion with God. But he also understood this love could be received only as a gift of inward purity through grace. Reliance on grace alone brings this genuine purity of heart and this God-given purity leads us into the experience of God-Love.

Melanchthon considered the heart central to Christian experience, and love alone could transform the heart. He leaves no doubt about where his own redeemed heart was in this regard. We hear his witness in a written prayer: "O God of Wisdom and Goodness, Truth, Mercy, and Loving-kindness; with all my heart full of thanks I remember thy favors and blessings which are so many and so great that I cannot count them or reflect upon them."[18] God's love revealed by grace produces gratitude, and gratitude leads us to deeper love for God.

Conclusion

We've come full-circle. Love is a costly choice, *not* an emotion. Yet the more we make this choice to love God, the more we will actually fall in love with him. But can we actually *fall in love with God*?

A journalist once asked former head of the Jesuit order Pedro Arrupe, S.J. (1907–1991), "Who is Jesus Christ for you?" Many would answer rightly, "He is my Savior," or "Jesus is my Lord, the Son of God." But Fr. Arrupe answered, "For me Jesus is everything!" He then wrote about *falling in love with God*. His explanation captures everything I've written:

> Nothing is more practical than finding God, that is, than falling in love in a quite absolute, final way. What you are in love with, what seizes your imagination, will affect everything. It will decide what will get you out of bed in the morning, what you will do with your evenings, how you will spend your weekends, what you read, and who you know, what breaks your heart, and what amazes you with joy and gratitude. Fall in love, stay in love and it will decide everything.[19]

CHAPTER FIVE

TO WHOM SHALL I BE A NEIGHBOR?

> From faith flows forth love and joy in the
> Lord, and from love a cheerful, willing, free
> spirit, disposed to serve our neighbor volun-
> tarily, without taking any account of ingrati-
> tude, praise or blame, gain or loss.
>
> Martin Luther,
> *Concerning Christian Liberty*

ANTHONY DE MELLO, S.J. (1931–1987), a Jesuit priest, well-trained in psychotherapy, gave us some simple but powerful insights into love for God and neighbor. One of them helps me conceive of God's love through *identification*. De Mello employed several metaphors to explain "identity." For example, he said a holy and loving person is *like* a rose: "Have you ever heard a rose say, 'I am going to give my fragrance only to good people who smell me, and I am going to deny my perfume to evil people'? No, it is of the very nature of the rose to spread fragrance." This is what de Mello means by *identification*.[1] It allows us to see how our experience of being loved by God will give off the fragrance of true love. This idea of *identification* between our human nature and God's divine nature brings us to the second part of the Great Commandment.

Jesus employs identification when he tells us to be "like" our heavenly Father. God's mercy "makes his sun rise" on the good and the evil and "sends his rain on the righteous and the unrighteous" (Matthew 5:45). We've seen that

73

dedication to God's love will lead us deeper and deeper into the mysteries of eternal love. But if we understand love in terms of *identification*, we must actually *love people*, not just abstract ideas. De Mello conveys this in a question: "Have you ever experienced that millions of us make up a single Christ?" Paul says we are all one, a single body of Christ. Thus, as individuals, the people of God are different, yet they become one in Christ. Through such identification we "sit down and get in contact with [ourselves and other members of Christ's body] ... and achieve silence. All we do is prepare the soil. In a world where minds are corrupted and suspicious, can you think of a better route to God?"[2]

So at this point I wish to help prepare the soil of your mind and heart by identification with costly love. We will do this by gaining a clearer understanding of what it means to love our neighbor.

Our Culture and Love

Jesus says, "You shall love your neighbor as yourself" (Matthew 22:39). We know the commandment, but what lies at its heart? Erasmo Leiva-Merikakis, a translator, commentator, and an expert in Ignatius, says,

> No one can love himself or another fruitfully unless he first loves God absolutely. Human love must continually nourish itself from the wellspring of uncreated, eternal love flowing from the Heart of God. Created love can never be autonomous. Not for a single moment can it exist outside the increased Being of the God who *is* Love.[3]

Our culture leaves little place for costly love. We constantly compete, even against ourselves. We feel a deep need to use others and consume products and entertainment. Yet God still calls us to love our neighbors.

Romantic love stories and music have conditioned us to expect that everyone will "live happily ever after." So when younger persons die we say, "They died before their time." We even attempt to "keep them alive" (if only inside our minds and words) so we can feel something for them we call love. This thinking has become ingrained in our culture.

> Such love stories are not about being in love but about being happy.... We attach our happiness to having a relationship, to marrying whomever we desire, to acquiring whatever we want, to behaving however we feel. If we should ever be unhappy, it is never our fault. It is always someone else or society that is the cause of our unhappiness and bears the responsibility for making us happy. In this kind of love story, we are the center of the universe and the story is all about us and our happiness.[4]

But as we saw in John 15, Jesus' love stories are *not* about our happiness; they are about his joy being completed in us. Unless we are prepared to get "outside the box" of our common ways of thinking we will settle for conventional wisdom. *But to experience costly love we must die. There is no other way to be raised to new life.* The old ways of the world will never fulfill the desire for love God has planted in us. But dying is profoundly disturbing. We rightly fear it even though we know it must happen. "Our fear is not so much a fear of the new and unknown in Jesus' way of love; it is the fear of leaving behind the place we have and familiar ways of feeling and thinking."[5]

Only by dying can we enter into divine love, a love not based on feelings and common sense. We must make a profound choice. It is inescapably true that this choice will be costly. I only entered into the love I write about after thirteen years in my "ministry desert." In calling me to a unique life-changing experience God took away almost everything I treasured about my public ministry. He placed me in a quiet place where I learned just how much he loved me. In the light of this revelation nothing else mattered. No one could explain this to me by arguments, though some tried. I learned that in the school of holy love, the cost of following Jesus would become evident. Over these years God taught me in a deeply personal manner that: "One does not live by bread alone, but by every word that comes from the mouth of God" (Matthew 4:4).

As we saw in chapter 4, the earliest monastics believed they could not live "in the world"—within a family and a vocation—and still be empowered by God's love. They chose a radically different way of life—giving away their personal property, giving up marriage and denying themselves of other vocations. They renounced other ways of life not because they believed such choices were inherently evil, but because they saw these activities as a potential source of self-deception. Physically fleeing from people and stuff was a singular, prayerful choice rooted in a deep desire to seek humility. When we read their writings carefully, we see they did not believe everyone had to move to the desert to be filled with love, but these desert writers remind us that stuff (money, homes, vacations and retirement) will never satisfy us. Only love for God and our neighbor will allow us to thrive spiritually.

So we begin our deep striving to love our neighbors by remembering that true spirituality is rooted in one great, common fact: "While we still were sinners Christ died for us" (Romans 5:8). The sick need a physician even if they don't know how ill they are. Our neighbors have the same need of divine grace that we do. What we do have, even if we differ in the realm of grace, came to each of us as pure gift. "Every generous act of giving, with every perfect gift, is from above, coming down from the Father of lights, with whom there is no variation or shadow due to change" (James 1:17). When we judge our neighbors we act like Satan, the accuser (1 Corinthians 6:2). We are not to judge but to love, our neighbors. The Father of heavenly lights shows mercy to our neighbors because he is perfect love!

Who Is My Neighbor?

In Matthew 22, Jesus' two great commandments are *inseparable*. We cannot conceive of loving God or our neighbor *without loving both* God and our neighbor. This is why it's called the "Great Commandment."

Our growing love for God naturally overflows into our growing love for our neighbor. The rose gives off its fragrance so others receive its sweet smell.

But who is this "neighbor" Jesus refers to? (Leviticus 19 defines neighbors as only one's "fellow countrymen.") So the question remains: "Who is my neighbor?" The answer is so *critical* to Christian faith and practice, we need to consider it more deeply. The parable of the Good Samaritan (Luke 10:25–37), should be our starting point in hearing and following the teaching of Jesus. Yet before we can grasp what Jesus says in the story of the Good Samaritan, we must again confront the basic question of God's nature. Is God love?

God-Love

When the God of Abraham revealed himself to Moses, he said he was the sovereign God. He called himself "I Am Who I Am" (Exodus 3:14). In Hebrew this oft-discussed revelation is quite dynamic. It literally means "the one who is always there." God is contained in himself and always projected toward the good. Implicit in this ancient revelation is the truth that God is always love. As we've seen this implicit truth unfolded over time and in Christ, the God who was revealed to Moses as "always there" is the perfect and eternal love. Thus, John can twice write, "God *is* love" (1 John 4:8, 16).

John Paul II, in explaining the unity of all that has been revealed, says: "God is love. This is the name of the one who is."[6] Catholic theologian Walter Kasper concludes that this means *the very essence of God is life and love.* If this were not so, then God could not be the God of human persons but rather a detached and impersonal Creator. *In a profound and mysterious sense, love and God are an eternal unity!*

My own life was radically altered when I realized God is everything that is eternal and thus, everything that eternally matters is love! In chapter 2, I spoke of Chiara Lubich (1920–2008), who taught me this truth *inside* of human relationships. She used the term "God-Love" to express what she understood as costly love. God, she explained, "is not a God who is distant, immovable and inaccessible to people. God-Love…comes to meet every person in thousands of ways [and is] in himself, love for all of his creation."[7]

For Lubich this "immense discovery" of God-Love created in her and her companions an "entirely new faith in him as love." This new faith caused her young companions to discover Christ in others relationally, because they believed their entire being could be "perennially [moved to respond] with God's infinite love." Chiara deduced that we would "not have any meaning in the world if we were not a little flame of this infinite love; love that responds to Love."[8]

Thus the starting point of a true and abiding Christian spirituality is God-Love. We must understand this truth with every fiber of our being. Love is not something God *does*; it is who he *is*. Love fully discloses the nature and heart of God. God-Love is what it actually means to say the word God in a fully biblical sense. Richard Rohr, citing a saying from within his own Franciscan tradition, expresses the same idea: "Jesus did not come to change the mind of God about humanity; Jesus came to change the mind of humanity about God." This is why costly love, the love we've so easily missed but that has so powerfully re-emerged in various ages of Christian practice, is nothing less than God's nature in us; thus it is God-Love.

The Good Samaritan

Perhaps the toughest task we face in interpreting this parable is readjusting how we've heard it. It has passed into our Christian vocabulary as a metaphor for "doing good to strangers." It's become a story about moral "do-goodism" and so has lost its connection with costly love. People often say that what really matters is Jesus' teaching about love. In other words, Christianity is not about worshiping the person who told us to love our neighbor, but about showing the love he taught. Throughout church history people have separated the ethical teaching of Jesus from the doctrine of the gospel (*kerygma*). Once we grasp what is going on in Luke 10, we'll see the problem with this view.

The mutual animosity between Jews and Samaritans was well-known. It parallels the modern enmity between Jews and Palestinians. When Temple officials passed a beaten, bloody Samaritan, especially on a dangerous road, they re-fused to get involved lest they pollute themselves. What the lawyer asks in Luke 10 is quite shocking: How can someone "inherit eternal life" (verse 25)? Jesus' answer is even more shocking: "What is written in the law?" (verse 26). The lawyer replies by citing the Great Commandment (verse 27). Jesus' response is intended to shock us. Why? In context it shock-ingly cut away ancient religious trappings with a simple and clear answer. In our modern context it should also shock us. Why? When Christians hear a question about how to receive (or inherit) eternal life they generally read "belief" (or faith) into the text. Few popular preachers would answer a ques-tion like this with a direct answer. The lawyer answers and then Jesus adds, "You have given the right answer; do this, and you will live" (verse 28). At first glance Jesus might seem to be operating on the same legalistic basis as the lawyer. Is eternal life the *byproduct* of a loving and ethical life? Is Jesus saying that if we love God enough we will "inherit" eternal life? The answer is critical to understanding costly love.

In *The Essential Commandment*, Greg Ogden suggests Jesus is saying, "OK, let's take your position and see where it leads. You want to do something to inherit eternal life. Very well. Just continuously love God and your neighbor with the totality of who you are."[9] But complete obedience to the law is impossible. We can learn to walk in obedience through faith and love, but can never attain an "inheritance" by *keep-ing the whole law*. Besides, an "inheritance" is never earned.

Notice the motive Luke ascribes to the lawyer: He "want-ed to justify himself" (verse 29). This is why he asks, "Who is my neighbor?" He could be saying, "I don't want to rush into this. I need to really be sure who my neighbor is. Perhaps we could have an extensive conversation about this." Or he could be saying, "I need to justify myself and my actions in my own mind," something all of us are prone to do. We are thus rightly shocked to learn that *truly loving God and our neighbor means to love all persons with costly love*. But note further that Jesus does not rebuke this man for asking his question. Surely Jesus knew he had come to trap him. But he

79

does not condemn the man for his misguided ideas. Rather, Jesus rebukes certain prejudices and then draws him into the meaning of true compassion, or costly love. This is why Paul concludes Jesus' love transcends human barriers like Jew/Gentile, slave/free, male/female (see Galatians 3:28).

In Jesus' era Jews often engaged in this type of debate. One of the great rabbis said that all Jews should love their fellow Jews, as well as those who were proselytes. Gentiles were *not* included. Another prominent rabbi said it was wrong to conspire in the death of a Gentile, but if a Gentile was in danger of dying because of an accident, Jews were not obliged to help because a Gentile "is not your neighbor." Thus it appears this lawyer is looking for an answer within the context of this first-century debate. I think he is saying something like this: "Give me a definitive answer so I know who I am *not* obliged to love."

At the end of the parable Jesus expands his response by asking another question. Here we discover several important truths about love for our neighbor.

First, Jesus indicates our neighbor is *any person* in need. "As in the case of God himself, I am henceforth to love, impelled not by subjective inclination and whim, but by another's need for my love."[10] Our neighbor may live in our immediate community or on the other side of the world. Our neighbor may be a person we bump into during the ordinary events of life. Ultimately our neighbor, because he or she is made in God's image, is the next person we meet. And our neighbor is precious because that person has God's life within, even if he or she denies God or hates us. (I'll return to this point later.)

Second, the lawyer's question and Jesus' answer don't quite line up. To this lawyer, neighbor meant his *Jewish* neighbor. But Jesus is saying Israel's God is a God of grace for *the whole world, because he is love.* By the end of the story Jesus asks the lawyer which person in the story (the priest, the Levite or the Samaritan) showed true mercy. The lawyer rightly answers it was the Samaritan because he alone got involved and showed God's love. New Testament scholar T.

W. Manson suggests Jesus doesn't really answer the original question, but instead asks a new, more searching question: "To whom am I willing to *become* a neighbor?" Manson adds, "The lawyer's question is unanswerable and ought not to be asked. For love does not begin by defining its objects, it discovers them."[11] While Manson provides an interesting reading of this dialogue I think he profoundly misses the central point of the story. The point is *not* nearly so complicated. In fact, so far as I can tell, Jesus was asked many *direct questions* in the Gospels but he rarely answered them explicitly. Here, and in at least two other places, he answered a *direct question* with a *direct answer*. He does the same in answering a question about *how to pray* when he answers by giving what we refer to as "The Lord's Prayer." And when he was asked about *how often his disciples should forgive* those who sinned against them he also gave a direct response by saying "seventy-seven times." (This is a hyperbolic way of saying we do not stop forgiving!) In most instances Jesus replied to questions with indirect responses. On other occasions he asked a question that revealed just how much the questioner had missed a greater truth.

Jesus also says that those who love a neighbor use their physical and emotional resources to meet the needs of the person in trouble (verse 37). N. T. Wright captures the sense of the story: "Underneath the apparently moral lesson ('go and do the same'), we find a much sterner challenge, exactly fitting with the emphasis of Luke's story."[12] The challenge is clear: Will you *recognize* everyone is your neighbor and then *respond* with true, unconditional and costly love? Jesus exposes the lawyer's agenda by showing just how far-reaching the grace of God is for all people. He loves the whole world![13]

This story presents a crucial question: Will we love only as a way of supporting our isolation (independence) and religion (security)? Or will we love as an expression of our divine calling to share God-Love with the whole world? Christians and churches that allow an easy definition of God, or soothe their consciences by focusing only on themselves, will generally miss the Great Commandment. People are living and dying all around us, and we can make a real difference by our actions, so is not our love anemic if we remain comfortably uninvolved? Our love is not costly when we refuse to reject racism as well as ethnic and cultural stereotypes. Why? Costly love will lead us to embrace the dignity of all people because all people are precious to God (Acts 10:35; 14:17; 17:27). Evangelical pastor Bill Hybels established an entire church—and ultimately a wide-ranging global ministry—on a simple expression of this belief: *People matter to God.* All people, in all circumstances, matter to God. God expressly desires we treat our neighbors "without a trace of partiality or hypocrisy" (James 3:17). Nothing more clearly defines the Christian faith for the world than God-Love; i.e., love without partiality. Pope Francis expressed this well in a Tweet (July 16, 2013): "Prayer, humility and charity toward all are essential in the Christian life: they are the way to holiness." I believe the world listens to Pope Francis because love is his obvious priority. As a Christian reformer he is not seeking to tear down other people or institutions, but to build up the kingdom of God. He understands that true power is found in costly service of others, a costly service rooted in God's love.

The Priorities of Love

The text Jesus cites commanded the Israelites to love their neighbors because God said, "I am the Lord." But Jesus doesn't quote this part of the Old Testament. Why? Because "Jesus *is* Lord!" (Acts 2:36; 10:36; Romans 10:9). And as the Lord he becomes *our* love. Jesus, through the Holy Spirit, has been poured *into* our hearts. Thus in a mystically real way Jesus *becomes* our love for *our* neighbors. He is the *living* text in us. He *shows* us the *way* of love, and then he *empowers* us to follow in his relationally transforming love. This is not self-help religion. On this specific occasion, in first-century Palestine, Jesus commanded us to love God *and* our neighbors *absolutely.* He alone has the power and authority to speak this way, because he is Lord, perfectly one with his Father in eternal love (see John 1:18; 6:46; 8:38; 14:9). Thus this relationship of eternal love between the Father and Son is the very *basis* for our love.

Let's go back to the story of the Good Samaritan. People need to grasp the truth of the antipathy between Jews and Samaritans (which I mentioned earlier). Greg Ogden says, "If Jesus were to tell this story in the United States today he might have chosen a 'good Muslim' or maybe, God forbid, a 'good homosexual.' Jesus' hearers cut their teeth on hatred toward the Samaritans, and now Jesus is using one as an example of the embodiment of righteousness."[14] Jesus says this Samaritan was "moved with pity" (Luke 10:33). He actually "felt" compassion, which is perhaps the truest emotion we can ever have because it reflects God's heart. When we *act with compassion*, we actually get involved (Luke 10:34) even at great cost. So love always acts, because we know God's love is moving us toward deep compassion within.

An Important Distinction between the Two Great Commandments

There is a clear distinction between the first and second commandments. First, we love God. Second, we love our neighbors.

We love God *alone* with wholehearted adoration. Our total self-surrender in love is to God who is love. Further, "We love [God and each other] *because* he first loved us" (1 John 4:19). This means our love for God *began* in divine love. Yet the words *God loves me* can sound so trite. Only a robust understanding of the greatness of God's love will prompt us to see that he alone is eternal love. We don't love God because he is nice. We will never truly love God because we believe he is nice. Nor will becoming outwardly religious prompt God-Love to grow within us.

We surely don't love God just because we rightly understand the creeds. (Sadly, they're silent about love and this commandment. This point should give us pause, which we will explore again later.) We love God *because* we personally know love with our *entire being*: "with all your heart, and with all your soul, and with all your mind" (Matthew 22:37).

I can know more and more *about* what Scripture says about love, but one burning question remains: Do I *experience* this love deep within me? Jesus has made it clear that if I do, the evidence of this God-given experience will be seen in how I treat others. I must *become* active love. To follow Jesus is to love as Jesus loved. Mother Teresa was right. "What is important is not how many actions we perform, but the intensity of the love that we put into each action." I've slowly learned that it is better to love a few neighbors truly and make a real difference in their lives, than to love the whole world and miss the person right in front of me.

Jesus *is* the Good Samaritan

A few years ago at a theology conference I struck up a friendly conversation with Kenneth Bailey (1930–2016), a teacher and writer I had long admired. His books have all proven a great help, especially *Jesus through Middle Eastern Eyes*.[15] In that book Bailey suggests *Jesus is* the Good Samaritan!

If this insight is true, then Jesus' story is a self-portrait. He was hated and despised by the religious leaders. John's Gospel says, "Are we not right in saying that you are a Samaritan and have a demon?" (8:48). The Samaritan is willing to become the object of a blood feud in order to become intensely involved with an unnamed stranger. The Samaritan paid all the man's expenses to meet his needs. This story should not be turned into a morality play titled "Be Good to Those in Need." And it cannot be separated from Jesus. Jesus came to reveal God's love.[16] His sacrificial life and death demonstrate the fullest meaning of costly love for us and our neighbors. At the cross we discover the fullest meaning of his love in the holy mystery of his sufferings for the salvation of the world (John 3:17; Colossians 1:15–20). He died to defeat the dark powers arrayed against God and us (1 Peter 3:22) and rose to justify us from sin and death (Romans 4:25).

The real question is not "Who is my neighbor?" but "To whom shall I be a neighbor?" We can answer this only as we live day by day in the presence and power of God's love. *The condition of our heart is the real issue.* The question we must ask each day, if we follow Jesus as *the* Good Samaritan, is this: "When we meet a neighbor, what will we do?"[17]

A Loving God with a Big Heart

We must come to understand that any attempt to love others not rooted in God-Love can destroy us. We cannot love another well except *in* God and *for* God. All our own attempts to love, particularly if our love is passionate and heroic, will end up consuming both us and the beloved.[18]

I first was able to visualize this truth through an idea called *triangulation.* Triangulation frees me to *be* love. Erasmo Leiva-Merikakis says, "Truly life-giving love can never be a dyad; it is always a triad."[19]

I can live costly love *only* by loving God and my neighbor. I certainly cannot experience God-Love by centering my actions and thoughts on myself. It flows *into* us from the triune God and then elicits a *flowing out from us* into our neighbors. *God-Love bears fruit because it is active, costly love.*

So how does understanding love as a triad help?

> The only medicine for this affliction is an ascesis of heart and mind that breaks the attachment to the reductive only-God-and-me dyad and introduces me into the wide, liberating spaces of a triangle defined by God-neighbor-self. Love must flow through all three if it is to flow at all.[20] [The word *ascesis* here refers to the kind of self-denial we saw in the last chapter, self-denial rooted in love and discipline.]

The great change for me came through deep anguish, followed by a series of unfolding moments that blinded me to myself and then led me to bask in God who is love. Chiara Lubich, attesting to something similar, called it "a flash of lightning." She spoke of such love as "the fiery brilliance of an Ideal."[21]

Similarly, in 1946 a young teacher in India named Sister Teresa was traveling by train to her yearly retreat in the Himalayan hills. Sister Teresa had an extraordinary experience of this same mystery of costly love when she became aware of the meaning of Jesus' cry from the cross, "I thirst!" This teacher, who we now know as Mother Teresa of Calcutta, later said all three persons in the one God "thirst" for us with eternal love. She referred to this experience as her "call within a call." Within two years it led her to leave teaching so she could care for the abject poor of Calcutta.[22]

I discovered all my efforts to love others were rooted in an external religion of outward forms that defined God and relationships in terms of theological concepts and personal efforts at sanctity—a sanctity I often measured by the distance I kept from the irreligious. In my church circles, "how well we explained and followed *our* doctrine" was often the standard for holiness. If you follow this path for long, you'll eventually become so sure of your beliefs that you will never open up your inward being to others in relational love. Your faith will become argumentative, lacking in tenderness.

Over the years one story haunted me. In both Matthew 11:7–19 and Luke 7:18–35 Jesus was asked about the contrast between himself and John the Baptist. Both accounts have similar conclusions. In Matthew we read, "For John came neither eating nor drinking, and they say, 'He has a demon'; the Son of Man came eating and drinking, and they say, 'Look, a glutton and a drunkard, a friend of tax collectors and sinners!' Yet wisdom is vindicated by her deeds" (Matthew 11:18–19). What haunted me were these words: Jesus was "a friend of tax-collectors [perhaps the most despised people of the time] and sinners!" I often asked myself, *Are you a friend of despised and hated people? Would sinners come to my funeral and say, "John Armstrong was a man who really loved me!"*?

According to Jesus the kingdom of God is present wherever people act with mercy in love. If God's presence is to become visible, we must re-introduce compassion into life. Mercy must take root in us and develop. If we are to have anything to offer our world, the whole church must be baptized in this compassion. We must seek God's pity when we look at lost and confused souls. We must become truly concerned for those who do not have food and clothing. Because of justice and mercy, wonderfully joined in the love of Christ, we must resist injustice and racism. When Jesus arrived, he offered God's forgiveness and mercy to all, acting with compassion even toward those he rebuked.

Because of our misunderstanding of sin and human depravity, in both ourselves and others, we easily adopt a wrong emphasis on being separate from the world. This leads to judgmentalism. We do this when we fall into attitudes and verbal responses that condemn the world as inherently evil. Yet Scripture says that creation, and all living creatures, are "good" (Genesis 1:31). This kind of separation from the world can be seen in the Pharisees, a devout and conservative sect of the Jews. Sad to say, this separatism is still present within some forms of Catholic, Orthodox, and Protestant Christianity. We'd rather set aside the messiness of our neighbors and embrace our private understanding. For many successful Americans, charity is about making lots of money and giving some away. While being a steward of wealth can be a blessing, those who are wealthy need to be reminded of the grave danger of their position (Ecclesiastes 5:19; Matthew 6:24; 23:25; 25:45; Mark 10:23; Luke 12:15; 16:13; Colossians 3:5).

James says the "royal law" is to "love your neighbor as yourself" (James 2:8). Before he drew this conclusion, he warned the church against showing partiality to the wealthy (2:1–7). His teaching is consistent with what Jesus said about the kingdom (Matthew 25:31–46; Mark 10:23–25; Luke 6:20).

One thing is clear. My true capacity for loving my neighbor reveals the genuineness of my love for God. Only in loving my neighbor will I know I *truly* love God. Not living within this life-giving triad has dire consequences. When we stand before Jesus on the Last Day, the measure of our lives will be true love: "'Truly I tell you, just as you did not do it to one of the least of these, you did not do it to me.' And these will go away into eternal punishment, but the righteous into eternal life" (Matthew 25:45–46).

Conclusion

This order of the imperatives in the Great Commandment is important. We learn to love others by first loving God. This means that we must *experience* God-Love daily or we cannot love God or our neighbors.

Satan offers us inverted love—what I call the love of the dyad. When he tempted Jesus "to fall down and worship him" (Matthew 4:8–9), his strategy was to destroy the *love triangle* between Jesus, his Father and the world. His attack was centered on love as *relational oneness* with God and others, or triadic love. He sought to turn the love of Jesus into self-centeredness. Self-centeredness lies at the very heart of sin! We are created as loving, desiring, affectional beings but our selflessness (sin) profoundly twists in upon ourselves. The answer to this inversion is God-Love, the kind of love that is always trinitarian *and* deeply relational. We will discover this answer when we recover a core truth of our faith: God is one but he is not solitary. God is a "we," a communion of persons.

Because we human beings tend to pervert the reality of true love in one way or another, God gave us twin commands regarding love. God knows that through these two commandments we can fulfill our deepest desires. He has not made love into an arbitrary commandment to test the limits of our perseverance. God knows us and loves us unconditionally. For this reason he seeks that we pursue love as a triad between us, the Holy Trinity *and* our neighbor.

I began this chapter with an idea called identification. When we live in identification, we give off the sweet fragrance of God's love. I then asked, "Who is my neighbor?" If Jesus *is* the Good Samaritan, then loving and following him will always lead us into the triad of eternal God-Love. Only within this triad will our love become costly, a divine love filled with the sacrifice that makes it life-changing.

PART THREE

HOW CAN LOVE BECOME

OUR GOAL?

For the love of Christ urges us on, because we
are convinced that one has died for all; therefore all have died.

(2 Corinthians 5:14)

CHAPTER SIX

CAN THE CHURCH REGAIN LOVE AS ITS GOAL?

Love is not something you choose to do, but what you choose to be.

Dallas Willard

OVE IS WHAT WE become within the triad of God, ourselves and others. Love therefore is the true basis for living a Christian life. But Christ's love is not easily understood. In *The Problem of Pain*, C. S. Lewis called what sometimes passes for love "senile benevolence." But living Christ's love is not something we choose to add to our faith or religion. We *enter* his life and death in our innermost being (*nous*) and then are continually raised with him into newness of life in the Spirit (Luke 9:23; Ephesians 2:19–20). This is why God-Love is always free, yet totally costly.

Without doubt, we need a Christian renewal of God-Love. Real renewal must lead us to see that above all else divine love is something *we are freed to become*. Each day we experience God-Love and thus become love by living in a relationship within God's triune love. Love becomes not an occasional heroic action, but our pattern of life. Yet how many Christians miss this central point of the New Testament? I did, for a significant part of my Christian life. Paul's words are clear: "If I gave everything I have to the poor and even sacrificed my body, I could boast about it; but if I didn't love others, I would have gained nothing" (1 Corinthians 13:3,

NLT). Without love, no action of ours gains a single thing that will last. There is a radical difference between choosing to *do* something and choosing to *be* someone. One is an action step; the other is a character trait. Can we, as the visible community of the church, recover this distinction? We must!

Jesus said his disciples would be recognized by their fruit (Matthew 12:33). Peter underscored this (1 Peter 2:12), and Paul said love was *the* fruit of the Spirit (Galatians 5:22–23). The principle is simple: *A good tree bears good fruit.* Little by little the Holy Spirit produces the fruit of love in the followers of Jesus who "abide" in him (John 15). Love is the result of relationship established by grace. "We know how dearly God loves us, because he has given us the Holy Spirit to fill our hearts with his love" (Romans 5:5, NLT). The love of Christ cost God everything so that our hearts can be filled with divine love.

When I began to understand the spirituality of love, I came to see the Jesus of history, who interacted with people by revealing love through his words and actions, cannot be separated from the crucified and risen Jesus who is Lord. There is *one* Jesus. Slowly I began to understand that his abandonment in the final hours of his sufferings reveals the depths of *who he is* in the mystery of his immense love. Many Christians, including myself, were taught to follow the Jesus of doctrine and biblical stories in terms of our intellect and activity. But too easily we missed *who he is* through his suffering and victory over the grave for our salvation. As a result we often miss what Jesus' abandonment on the cross means for showing us what costly love really involves (see Matthew 27:46; Mark 15:34).

Only by passing through abandonment did Jesus enter into the triumph of his resurrection. This abandonment profoundly shapes how I understand what I mean by costly love. A theologian familiar with Chiara Lubich's experience of love expresses this insight succinctly.

> The fact is that if "Jesus is Jesus Forsaken," that is, the Son who entrusts himself to the Father, without residuals and

> conditions, in the act in which the Father seems to hide the name of Abba in the most cruel and darkest trial—*if Jesus is this, then our faith in him is a partaking, through grace, intimately, in the very event of his abandonment. Our faith is carrying within us the faith of the abandoned One in the occupations of our day.*[1]

In declaring that God is his Father, Jesus made it clear that when reborn by the Spirit, his disciples would assume a new attitude toward God and others. God would place on them a distinctive, *special mark of the Spirit,* one that would be clear to all who read the Gospels: "Love one another" (John 13:34–35). This mark of divine love would flow out of their entering into the life of Jesus forsaken and abandoned because of his great love.

Chiara Lubich concluded that Jesus' cry of forsakenness from the cross was the "climax of his pain [and] the climax of his love." She concludes, "Whoever finds this man has found the solution to every problem human and divine. He will reveal the solution. We only need to love him."[2] Here is the true heart of costly love—complete abandonment to "Jesus forsaken" *in* love and *for* love. This is both the cost and the gift bound intimately together in a revealed mystery!

This is why Mother Teresa of Calcutta spoke eloquently of love when she said that Jesus forsaken "is thirsting for our love when [he] was dying on the cross." What is this thirst she speaks of here? She says it is *Jesus on the cross forsaken* and "[yet he is] thirsting for souls, for love, for kindness, for compassion, for delicate love." She concludes:

> By each action done to the sick and dying, I quench the thirst of Jesus for love of that person—by my giving God's love in me to that particular person, by caring for the unwanted, the unloved, [the] lonely, and . . . all the poor people. This is how I quench the thirst of Jesus for others by giving his love in action to them.[3]

The church Jesus built cannot be reduced to rituals, commandments, theories or organization. These things have their proper place, but *the church of Jesus Christ is fundamentally a society of love who share their life in the "crucified Christ"* (Galatians 2:19–20). The Bible calls the church a "family" (Matthew 25:40; Galatians 1:2; 6:10; 1 Peter 2:17) distinguished by "love for one another." Jesus said this new "family" would have priority even over our biological one (Matthew 12:50; 19:29; Mark 10:29; Luke 14:26). It draws its power from the life of Jesus, crucified and forsaken.

Should Love Be Our Explicit Goal?

Christian history includes many attempts to understand agape. In too many instances it is apparent that the church failed to show the love of Christ to the world. Our struggle with one another inside the church generates massive disunity and relational chaos. It can't be denied: Love is a considerable challenge, both conceptually and practically. But if we do not grasp the basic concept of agape, how can we understand the many New Testament commands about love?

Several years ago Dallas Willard (1935–2013) presented a paper, "Getting Love Right," to the American Association of Christian Counselors. His insights provide amazing clarity. Willard said we easily praise love, but because grasping it proves so difficult we actually back away from it, preferring "practical alternatives."[4]

> It is hard to find a church or para-church staff that is practically oriented around Jesus' instruction: "Love one another, even as I have loved you" (John 13:34). You might think this would be their primary explicit goal, but it usually turns out otherwise.[5]

What Willard decries here has been my experience. I've heard many messages about love, read countless books on Christian love, yet rarely experienced a church or group where it was *the* "primary, explicit goal." That is why in earlier chapters I discussed Chiara Lubich and the Focolare. When I was first introduced to this ecclesial movement, I began to experience friendships with people who *explicitly* centered their shared life in God-Love. They carefully teach love, but more often than not I've seen my Focolare friends live love in simple and practical ways. Their literature, stories, gatherings and conversations are all *explicitly* centered in love. They make love their aim (see 1 Corinthians 14:1)!

Lamentably, though modern preaching and teaching acknowledge love's importance, very little has been done *practically* to form and sustain loving churches. Clearly, we hold some mistaken notions, such as the idea that love is merely a noble ideal or wonderful religious sentiment. Best-selling author M. Scott Peck says liking, or affection, is primarily a *feeling* but love (agape) is a decision. Christian love is a *costly decision* to become an entirely new person who lives in the relational life of the Trinity. Love is *an action verb*!

Paul presents a clear objective for the church: "Let love be your highest goal" (1 Corinthians 14:1, NLT). Perhaps it would help if we inscribed the words *"Our highest goal is love"* throughout our church buildings. It surely couldn't hurt.

When Paul wrote to his young apprentice Timothy, he said, "The purpose of my instruction is that *all believers would be filled with love* that comes from a pure heart, a clear conscience, and genuine faith" (1 Timothy 1:5, NLT). Not one believer should be left out! Every minister should ask, "In serving this congregation, is my aim to love?"

Dallas Willard is right to say that love was Paul's "primary explicit goal." Isaac of Syria said God brought the world into existence in love, and in love God will bring the world back into a wondrous transformed state. A Latin proverb says it well: "A man is not where he lives but where he loves."

The Central Problem in the Local Church

Over the course of twenty-one years I pastored three churches. In 1992 I left the pastorate of my last local church to embark on a ministry to the church at large. My first pastorate, with a very small congregation, lasted only one year while I did graduate studies. The second was a church-plant that grew out of a vision in the early 1970s for establishing new local churches. My ministry in this new church lasted four years. My third congregation was an established church that went into a period of deep crisis following my first year. I served this congregation for sixteen years.

In the last two churches I believe we genuinely liked one another. We had powerful times of congregational prayer. We joyfully preached the gospel. But relationships were often difficult. My first church, formed from a schism before I became their pastor, had a short history. My second church grew in numbers rather quickly, but our love lacked depth. Finally, I returned to the town where I'd finished college. Before I arrived as pastor of this existing church it had suffered two painful divisions. I was chosen as pastor because I was young and the people believed I was driven by a strong vision. My preaching quickly led to an increase in our numbers. Initially, the future seemed bright, but things did not go so well when I began to preach doctrinal sermons. Before we could resolve our differences (more than a few of which I caused) we descended into rivalries and power struggles. This led to grievous schism and the exodus of members. I was left with a long-term *rebuilding* project. What strikes me after all these years is that none of the three congregations I served could honestly say that "love was [our] highest goal."

In truth, I've seen Christians tolerate, ignore, even openly despise one another. When people in the American church disagree strongly enough, they'll "church-hop." In my second and third pastorates, the churches had several great leaders, but when our team broke down, it was *always* because love was not our real aim. I now believe almost every battle I've experienced *inside* the church, especially since I left the pastorate in 1992, began because "love was not the highest goal." Can this disturbing trend be reversed?

Over the last twenty-five years I cannot recall experiencing a single church where it was *obvious* that love was their *clear and specific aim*. In many churches doctrine is extremely important. In others, the highest priorities are outreach, worship, youth ministry, leadership development, denominational concerns, or discipleship. In others the priesthood and the sacraments are most important. (I'll return to the matter of discipleship in the next chapter.) But in none have

I seen a congregation for whom love was clearly the highest goal.

Role Models of Love

One of my high school teachers taught me the importance of history for understanding the present. When I began to question *why* the church did not make love its highest goal, I looked more closely at various eras of church history to discover how we went wrong. What I found stunned me. From the apostolic era to the present, it seems to me, love has *always* been the greatest struggle *inside* the church. The real struggle has not been about evangelism, heresy, money, or programs—not even discipleship, at least as it is commonly understood. *Love* has been our constant problem. Yet almost everyone I know thinks our greatest struggles as Christians concern sound doctrine, especially that of Christ and salvation. Although doctrine is immensely important, it is often an excuse for a lack of love. Even Paul, the greatest doctrinal teacher in the early church, made love his highest aim.

John said, "The Word became flesh and lived among us, and we have seen his glory, the glory as of a father's only son, *full of grace and truth*" (John 1:14, emphasis added). Jesus is the absolute truth. But he is also absolute grace! We see love clearly by focusing our attention not on concepts but on Jesus. Sadly, however, love has become just another concept among many. Down through the entire history of the church, I am sure that the *guiding goal* has not been love.

The more I study church history, the more I see a recurring motif. At critical times for the church, the Spirit would anoint a person or raise up a movement to face a crisis—and often, to witness to the centrality of love. Francis of Assisi (1181–1226), as mentioned in the Introduction, demonstrates this very pattern. Francis, the son of a wealthy Italian family, had everything. Then in 1204, a serious illness caused him to reflect on his life. In 1205, after a profound vision of Jesus, he lost his desire for money and power. (His actions at this point were both strange and wonderfully radical.) He took a vow of poverty and gave everything away. His father tried every means imaginable, even physical beatings, to prevent it, but Francis could not be stopped. He *made love his goal.* He loved God *and* the poor. He loved animals and all of God's wondrous creation. One thing stands out in the life of this layman: Francis loved God and his neighbors in a totally *intentional* way.

Time and space preclude a survey of the whole story of the church concerning this recovery of love. Before the Protestant Reformation, Antony of Egypt, Pope Gregory the Great, Thomas à Kempis, Catherine of Siena and John of the Cross were all lights pointing people back to love. After the Reformation, Protestants such as Johann Arndt, Philipp Jakob Spener, Count Nikolaus von Zinzendorf, William Law, John and Charles Wesley, and William Penn did the same. So did scores of Catholics and countless Orthodox men and women *after* the Reformation. I could name hundreds of such great souls. My point is this: When the church reaches a low point, God raises up men and women who are captured by God-Love. They understand anew that love is *the true goal* of the church. They learn again how to truly love the poor, the oppressed and the weak. Some of these great souls have touched my life through their writing and stories. I've also been privileged to know friends who have shown me *how* to love God and my neighbors. More than impressive and gifted leaders, what we need now is great lovers. *We need great role models.* Let's look at one.

Paul: An Apostle of Love

John highlighted Jesus' love and his teaching on it, but Paul is the great theologian of Christ's love. While shaping the development of the young church in a way not clearly seen in the Gospel narratives, Paul consistently underscored that the love seen in Jesus' life and teaching was central to Christian practice.

Consider the following examples:

> Owe no one anything, except to love one another; for the one who loves another has fulfilled the law. The

commandments, "You shall not commit adultery; You shall not murder; You shall not steal; You shall not covet"; and any other commandment, are summed up in this word, "Love your neighbor as yourself." Love does no wrong to a neighbor; therefore, love is the fulfilling of the law (Romans 13:8–10).

You were called to freedom, brothers and sisters; only do not use your freedom as an opportunity for self-indulgence, but through love become slaves to one another. For the whole law is summed up in a single commandment, "You shall love your neighbor as yourself" (Galatians 5:13–14).

Paul says something staggering: "Through love [we should] become slaves to one another" for "the whole law is summed up in a single commandment."

The verse just before Paul's famous "love" chapter, 1 Corinthians 13, says the church "should strive for the greater gifts," adding that love is "the more excellent way" (12:31). A few verses later Paul reveals the core of his counsel.

Love is patient; love is kind; love is not envious or boastful or arrogant or rude. It does not insist on its own way; it is not irritable or resentful; it does not rejoice in wrongdoing, but rejoices in the truth. It bears all things, believes all things, hopes all things, endures all things. (1 Corinthians 13:4–7)

Paul states plainly the God-given "mark" of a genuinely Christian congregation is *not* great knowledge, incredible insight or power encounters. It is certainly not money. *The singular mark of the church is love.* In Romans, Paul addresses the church's internal and external life. How should Christians treat those who believe? How should Christians treat those who are weak? How should they treat those still outside the church? Paul works out the doctrine of love in the most practical way:

Let love be genuine; hate what is evil, hold fast to what is good; love one another with mutual affection; outdo one another in showing honor. Do not lag in zeal, be ardent in spirit, serve the Lord. Rejoice in hope, be patient in suffering, persevere in prayer. Contribute to the needs of the saints; extend hospitality to strangers.

Bless those who persecute you; bless and do not curse them. Rejoice with those who rejoice, weep with those who weep. Live in harmony with one another; do not be haughty, but associate with the lowly; do not claim to be wiser than you are. Do not repay anyone evil for evil, but take thought for what is noble in the sight of all. If it is possible, so far as it depends on you, live peaceably with all. Beloved, never avenge yourselves, but leave room for the wrath of God; for it is written, "Vengeance is mine, I will repay, says the Lord." No, "if your enemies are hungry, feed them; if they are thirsty, give them something to drink; for by doing this you will heap burning coals on their heads." Do not be overcome by evil, but overcome evil with good. (Romans 12:9–21)

Love: The Heart of the Gospel

Many Bible readers do not realize the first New Testament scriptures read in the earliest churches were Paul's letters. Several of these letters had been written only twenty to twenty-five years after the death of Jesus. Read carefully, they reveal that Paul's greatest concern was the gospel. Bible scholar Daniel J. Harrington writes,

> At the "heart" of Paul's theology was the "Gospel," or "good news," about Jesus as the revelation of God's love and the source of all benefits that accrue to us from it (liberation, reconciliation, redemption, justification, access to God, sanctification, and so on). The proclamation of this mystery is what Paul called the "good news," and his primary concern was that those whom he brought to Christian faith might fully participate in the Paschal mystery and its benefits.[6]

Harrington describes Paul's experience of Jesus as a "Christ-centered mysticism." Some may find the word *mysticism* unusual but by it he seeks to name the deep internal apprehension of knowledge not directly accessible to the intellect. Such knowledge, or truth, is often granted through contemplation and self-surrender. It may come in moments that seem more like divine intuition than conscious reasoning. Mysticism is clearly present in New Testament narrative and teaching, and has always been a vital part of Christian practice and tradition.

Harrington says Paul's hope was rooted in Christ's sufferings *and* the power of his resurrection (Phil. 3:10–11). Indeed, Paul's gospel was grounded in the saving power of costly love (1 Corinthians 13:1; Romans 8:38–39). He was convinced that in the gospel God's love is made clear: Christ's death and resurrection is "the ultimate revelation of God's love [and this] changed everything in his life and became the basis for his total identification with Christ (Galatians 2:20). ... [Paul] regards love as the 'super' virtue that joins together all the other virtues in perfect harmony."[7]

Thus in the earliest New Testament churches Paul established love as "the super virtue." Several decades later John expanded this by giving the church a theology of love centered in costly grace. Everything the church needed can be found in the Trinity, because at the heart of the relational union of the Father, Son, and Holy Spirit is love itself.

Harrington's idea of love being a "super virtue" is made clear in the evangelical *Cape Town Commitment* (2011): "The mission of God flows from the love of God. The mission of God's people flows out of our love for God and for all that God loves."[8] Love is primary!

This Pauline truth was powerfully expressed by the Bohemian-Austrian poet and novelist Rainer Maria Rilke (1875-1926), himself a mystic.

> We know little, but that we must trust in what is difficult is a certainty that will never abandon us; it is good to be solitary, for solitude is difficult; that something is difficult must be one more reason for us to do it. It is also good to love—love being difficult. Love is perhaps the most difficult task given us, the most extreme, the final proof and text, for which all other work is only preparation.[9]

The Only Thing That Counts

If Rilke is right, that "love is perhaps the most difficult task given us, the most extreme," then we should not be surprised at how, in Galatians 5, love becomes one of Paul's most-staggering ideas about doctrine and life. The apostle was battling a heresy that threatened the gospel. Nowhere else in his letters does he defend it with such direct, aggressive, and passionate language. After explaining the freedom that Christ has given us, he concludes, "The only thing that counts is faith expressing itself through love" (Galatians 5:6, New International Version).

> Twentieth-century martyr Dietrich Bonhoeffer (1906–1945) understood. The first demand which is made of those who belong to God's Church is not that they should be something in themselves, nor that they should, for example, set up some religious organization or that they should lead lives of piety, but that they should be witnesses to Jesus Christ before the world.[10]

Bonhoeffer grasped the danger of witness without love, of discipleship based on cheap grace. It's why he wrote his classic book *The Cost of Discipleship*. He believed the German church in the 1930s was abandoning Christ in two specific ways: (1) It had reduced the gospel to rules, which easily became the antithesis of the "easy yoke" Jesus taught about. We've so burdened the church with extra-biblical practices and concepts it's hard for people to find the real Jesus in the gospel. Without this real Jesus, people find it difficult to encounter the love of Christ. (2) The church had also created a doctrine of "easy" grace, an idea that has become a collective excuse for shallow discipleship and pervasive acceptance of sin in the body of Christ. In its most basic sense Christians in the West today have been taught a not-so-costly discipleship. Compounding our own shallow understanding, we've exported our various versions of cheap grace and prosperity to other continents. For multitudes, grace means you can live as you please and accept God's love without any significant cost. For Bonhoeffer, cheap grace described the very problem in the German church under Nazism. Today I believe this same "cheap grace" has led us to embrace what I'd call "cheap love." This explains why, despite Bible study, prayer, and Sunday worship, so many churches do not see radical outcomes. Bonhoeffer actually believed that religion was the problem. He wrote, "Jesus calls men not to a new religion, but to life."[11] The only solution rests in an intimate relationship with Christ that grows and matures in costly God-Love.

The Christian church carries one divine mandate. It is not to shame people or to slam the world in its pain and misery. It is not to elect candidates or to advance religion or Christendom. It is not to win "culture wars." The Christian church is commanded to bear witness to God's love for the world. But we have so misunderstood God's love and so poorly embraced it, our witness has not had an effect. I could write an entire chapter about how the modern church has substituted agendas and human ideologies for the good news. Because our love is anemic, the church in the West is in decline. Our ministries are mocked, and most people reject our witness.[12]

How can the world "see" Jesus? The New Testament provides a clear answer: Jesus said when we love God, our neighbors, and one another, the world will see why the gospel is gloriously good news: "On these two commandments hang all the law and the prophets" (Matthew 22:40, emphasis added). Everything we do "hangs" on these two commandments.

Everything "Hangs" on Love

The image is vivid. Jesus is not saying there are no other laws or commandments, a conclusion of extreme reductionism. None of us can live as Christians in the nitty-gritty of life's routines without some concrete guidance about purity and godliness. I believe we also need the wisdom of the past to express our love wisely. But when we read the Great Commandment, we should note that everything "hangs" on love!

There are two ways to read the Bible. One is to read with no preconceived Christian notions or insights. This reading asks, "What did this text mean in its own day, and what bearing does this have on our present moral life?" Many opt for this approach. *The second way is to read the entire Bible as a story centered in Jesus.* If Jesus is the goal or aim (*telos* in Greek) of the story, then I ask, "What does this particular passage mean for living in the way of Christ?" At this point Matthew 5:17–20 becomes an indispensable text for understanding why everything "hangs" on loving God and our neighbor.

The key word here is "fulfilled" (verse 17). Scot McKnight places the Great Commandment at the center of the Jesus story. His best-selling book, *The Jesus Creed: Loving God and Loving Others*, explains what he means.[13] McKnight says it is a misinterpretation that some first-century religious leaders considered Jesus' teaching about the law to be "soft." In reality Jesus expanded the teaching of the commandments in Matthew 5–7:

> It was not that Jesus had an Ethic from Above, Below, or Beyond, but that he had the audacity to think he was the Messiah and taught a Messianic Ethic, reorienting the whole Torah and Prophets. This is what disturbed some of his contemporaries.[14]

Jesus did not come to "abolish" the Torah or the prophets but to "fulfill" them. Correct interpretation requires we understand the word "fulfill" properly. Jesus is saying something akin to this: "All the patterns, morals, and predictions of the Old Testament come to their complete realization in me." No wonder the religious leaders conspired to kill him. The entire Torah takes on a human face and finds its authority in Rabbi Jesus! His claim is completely Jewish (Isaiah 2:1–5; Jeremiah 31:31–34) yet deeply troubling to his enemies. McKnight concludes, "The first lesson we get in reading the Bible is this one: Look to Jesus as its central story."[15]

So when we read the Great Commandment, we are not left to "create" everything anew, as if the Holy Spirit did nothing before Jesus. From tradition we receive secondary forms of faith and practice. But what remains primary is the commandment Jesus gave us regarding love for God and for neighbors. All our religious practice and piety "hangs" on these commandments.

Love Is a Disposition

It is dangerous, however, to think agape is an easy choice. We've seen love is not an emotion or good intentions. And it's not a simple, one-time choice. We must understand that love gives rise to intention, and intention leads to action. And as we saw earlier, actions become habits and good habits lead to the internal formation of true virtue. Agape does involve feelings and emotions. (As an example, agape will lead to compassion, and compassion is the most Christlike of all our human emotions!) We are not Stoics, but love is not primarily a feeling.

Here's the point: Agape is holistic. We can't turn it off and on at will. Love dwells in what is good and always acts in support of what is good wherever it is found. God-Love is fed by what is good, right, and beautiful (Philippians 4:8). Our love is our whole soul responding with joy to God's love. We can see why Thérèse of Lisieux concludes, "God does not demand great acts from us, but only surrender and gratitude."

Conclusion

Dallas Willard is right: "We do not achieve the disposition of *agape* love by *direct effort*, but by attending to and *putting into practice* the conditions out of which it arises" (italics added).[16] Paul says, "Love does no wrong to a neighbor; therefore, love is the fulfilling of the law" (Romans 13:10). The biblical story is the greatest love story ever told.

The nature of our feelings differs from agape. They are the result of human impulses empowered by God's grace, not human choice. Love is always a choice to be, to become. This choice leads to an orientation that consistently seeks the good of the other person. (This is why the public face of love will lead us to seek for justice since love inherently leads us to seek impartiality and fairness in all our dealings with others.) Yes, love allows us to refrain from hating our enemies, but it does much more. It actually empowers us to bless those who hate us. This is how God in Jesus Christ treated us. To love others is to be like Jesus.

The church that learns to love genuinely will become a church that continually makes loves its aim without placing a list of demands on people. We may do many impressive activities within the church, but none of them matters if we do not love. The most powerful principle for our life together is right here: "Make love your aim."

CHAPTER SEVEN

HOW DISCIPLESHIP IS
ROOTED IN LOVE

It is not by ideas and programs or by conscience, duty, responsibility and virtue that
reality can be confronted and overcome, but
simply and solely by the perfect love of God.

Dietrich Bonhoeffer

LOVE HAS INFINITE VALUE. "The entire finite universe
disappears like a speck when placed on the scales of
value next to the love of God."[1] Augustine said, "God
gave love. God bestowed love. There brothers you have the
scriptures of God."[2]

Love alone has *infinite, eternal value*. When everything
else passes away, love alone remains. Why? If God is love,
then love remains because the triune God remains. Jesus
came to bring the reign of God into the world. When we
pray "Your kingdom come," we are praying that Christ's love
will reign in all that we do and say.

Through Christ's life, death, resurrection, and exaltation,
love wins. Jesus' kingdom is here, and like yeast in dough it
is quietly spreading throughout the world. In the final act of
this age, Christ will finish what he began. Jesus will return
and give his kingdom to the Father, who will reign over all
that he created in eternal love (see 1 Corinthians 15:12–34).
Revelation 21:4 indicates that this finite, temporal universe
will "pass away" and only one thing will remain—*God's perfect love*.

The Basis of Discipleship: God's Radical Love in Christ

Ultimately our lives consist of a series of thoughts and experiences. We experience love and acceptance, fear and rejection. We embrace ideas about God, truth, and ourselves, often unknowingly at first. All of us have known both love and fear, to a greater or lesser degree. It has become increasingly evident to science how powerfully the earliest stages of life shape who we are and what we believe. This also seems true with regard to our earliest views of God, whether we were directly taught specific religious views or not. These early influences, or the lack thereof when faith has been absent, shape all of us in some way. Though the outcome of this early development is never entirely certain in any individual, the power of early formation is undeniable. But can the results of these early influences be altered? Can we change?

Reading the Gospels introduces us to a truth about this idea of change. Trusting Jesus can slowly and powerfully change our entire life scenario through what he called *discipleship*. At its core Christianity teaches that following Jesus in true faith and obedience really can radically change our lives. Most followers of Jesus do not change overnight but change marks their life as they develop and mature.

Christian discipleship is rooted in what the Bible calls repentance. The Greek work for repentance means *to experience a complete change of mind and life.* Our human story can be radically reshaped by the expulsive power of a new affection working from inside out. Christians have always believed that Jesus is that someone and the Holy Spirit is the power of Jesus working in us in his physical absence. Clement of Alexandria expressed this well: "Therefore let us repent and pass from ignorance to knowledge, from foolishness to wisdom, from licentiousness to self-control, from injustice to righteousness, from godlessness to God."[3]

I was once asked to describe the Bible in one sentence. I answered: "*The Holy Scripture is God's open love letter to humankind and thus it should only be read with a deep hunger for the experience of eternal love.*"

To understand the Bible in this way is life-changing, yet many Christians miss this message. In the process they have also missed the fact that God's love is central to Jesus' mandate to "make disciples" (Matthew 28:18–20). To make disciples, we must become *intentional transmitters of love*. When I know love through God-given *experience*, I can then love *as* he loves. I believe it is this experience of love that leads to *true* discipleship.

Should We Love Ourselves?

Popular modern theories of the self shape the thinking of many Western Christians. Christians often cite Matthew 22:39, "You shall love your neighbor *as yourself*" to bolster ideas they've received from pop-psychology. It is argued, almost *ad infinitum*, that we *cannot* love our neighbor *unless* we *first* love ourselves. But such reasoning does not exactly fit with what Jesus says. He knows we have *an inherent desire* to serve and protect ourselves; thus, he calls us to turn this inherent self-love *outward* toward our neighbor. To read modern psychology into this text is a mistake. But how *should* we respond to what is popularly called the "self"? By "self" I mean the combination of emotions, feelings, and thoughts that make up our human essence. I have in mind what psychology refers to when it speaks of our inward identity as related to our experience(s). In this latter idea, psychology refers to me as a *"subjective knower of Me,"* the object that is known.

Nicaraguan Catholic leader Ernesto Cardenal argues that "we should not therefore fall into self-love, because self-love cuts us off."[4] What does he mean, especially in the light of Jesus' statement that we should love our neighbors *as we love ourselves* (see Leviticus 19:18; Matthew 22:39; Mark 12:31; Luke 10:27)?

Mother Teresa sums up my understanding: "Love, to be real, must cost—it must hurt—it must empty us of self."[5] But if this is true, as I have argued throughout this book, then how should we love ourselves?

When God touched my soul with divine love, I entered a place I'd never known. I had thought I knew what love was, but I discovered I'd known a *concept*, not a lover. *To know love relationally is entirely different.* The waves of God's love poured over my heart and penetrated deep down into the roots of my being. My love has slowly become a *grounded* reality that defines who I really am. If I am a "high tension wire" (Ernesto Cardenal) carrying divine love as electricity, then the power station is God, the holy Trinity. The ground wire must be the Scripture expressed through the living tradition of the church. I can be a decent and kind person *without* God's love. But I cannot enter into the story of eternal, reconciling, divine love *without* entering into Jesus as the vine (John 15:1–11).

God's love can change us in many ways, seen and unseen. At times we do not even know this is happening until we look back upon years of growth. When the power of love began to transform my mid-life relationship with God, I *began* a process of slowly ceasing to judge people. I also stopped trying to *convert* people to my religion or doctrine. *I entered into what I call the "dialogue of love."* When disagreement comes, I now seek to remain inside a relational circle of love. My desire is not to change others, but to love them. This is liberating. Inside of love there are no winners and losers, just people who love and need to be loved. Christian therapist Adolfo Quezada expresses what this means: "It was as though I had ceased to exist as a separate entity, yet I was fully aware of my individuality. It was a paradox filled with splendor."[6] Indeed, a paradox filled with splendor!

Quezada says the human soul moves toward the reconciliation of opposites. I once "hated" myself, which was really an inverted form of pride. But now I understand that dying to self is a daily commitment to follow the crucified and risen Christ in the love that cost him his life. I have learned to die to myself by becoming "lost in wonder, love, and praise," to quote the hymn "Love Divine, All Loves Excelling." I refuse to hate or despise myself. Why? Because I am moving toward the reconciliation of all things, thus deeper and deeper into the gospel. What I had seen previously as complete opposites, I now understand as a duality that confirms living faith. I embrace this diversity and continue to work at repairing brokenness. God is empowering us in relationships *together* to become our authentic selves in love. This is what he created us to be; thus in our redemption he is restoring us to who we are in him.

So, back to the question I posed earlier: "What about self-love?" Should we reject this idea entirely? I think not.

Is Love Selfless?

Before I explain "self-love" in an ancient Christian way, let me correct another common error. Two concepts that Paul uses ("flesh" and "Spirit") are vital to biblical understanding. He contrasts them with each other. I used to regard these two words as standing for two *aspects* within my human nature. I no longer understand anthropology (human nature) in this dualistic way.

These two Pauline words describe what some scholars call "two power-spheres." These two spheres are associated with *two ages*, ages distinguished by the coming of Jesus Christ. Apart from Christ, humans are captives to "flesh." Here, "flesh" does *not* mean sex or the body; it is what we were when we lived under the "power of sin." To be "in the Spirit" means we have been liberated (Romans 8:4; Galatians 5:16, 25). Christians are "led by the Spirit" (Romans 8:14), "sealed with the Spirit" (Ephesians 1:13), and should be "filled with the Spirit" (Ephesians 5:18). Each of these Pauline descriptions—led, sealed, and filled with the Spirit—implies a *positive self-image.* I am no longer a slave to my flesh, the person I was without Christ. I am free. There is indeed a struggle between my old and new self. But I am not garbage, a lowly worm, or a rotten sinner. *I am beloved by God.* The gospel affirms our humanity and then offers us a powerful cure in the holy medicine of love. Because we matter to God, we have profound personal dignity. Don't misunderstand. I still sin but I am not a sinner in the old way. I am a Christian who is living in God's love. Sometimes I do not live in that love as I should, thus I still sin. I confess my sin because I am loved, not because I am filled with terror (see 1 John 1:9).

Loving God and my neighbor are thus interconnected with who I am, the "self." Fourth-century monk Anthony (Antony) of Egypt argued that people who sin against their neighbor actually do real harm to themselves. Those who do good to their neighbor will do good to themselves. Likewise, he says (paraphrasing 1 John 4), whatever good we do for our neighbor, or for our brother or sister in Christ, we do for ourselves.[7] This is not to say we should nurture a self-directed inner desire for attention. It means that in loving God and others, we find a genuinely healthy self-life. This is ancient faith Christian teaching, not modern pop-psychology. Let me explain this important idea further.

After wrestling for years with this idea of the self, I am quite sure that no human act can ever be *entirely selfless*. (Excepting the human person of our Savior, Jesus!) We all get satisfaction from our acts of love. This is why some philosophers believe that Christian love is ultimately impossible. (I would agree except Jesus *gives* us the power to truly love with his love!) Let's explore this question of selflessness and personal satisfaction further.

Søren Kierkegaard took self-love as the actual measure of our loving others. "To love yourself in the right way and to love the neighbor correspond perfectly to one another; fundamentally they are one and the same thing."[8] Aristotle reasoned that if we love the other we must first love ourselves and then regard the other as we do ourselves. Here it seems we are not denying self so much as we are affirming the goodness of ourselves and others. No less a Christian theologian than Thomas Aquinas said that God alone is a maximal giver since he gains nothing by his loving and giving. (Aquinas says our giving reminds us that we are still on the way but we've not yet arrived.) But this does not mean everything we do in love has an *ulterior motive*. We must realize our acts of love benefit us and the other. The point of being selfless is to be reminded that love involves sacrifice, thus God-Love will always be costly. Let me illustrate with a personal example.

Last year my daughter gave birth to twin sons. For many years she had longed to have children. To say these little boys have changed her life is an understatement. Her love for them is so deep and real (It is also fun to witness!). This love involves costly sacrifice. Why? She loves her boys deeply. She will discover, as did my wife and I, that one of life's greatest joys is having children. Then she will begin to see how her sacrifice for them will result in greater blessings as well. Here is my point: the sacrifices of love, which most often involve profound self-denial, are as much for the joy of the beloved as for the lover. When you give the needy a meal you have helped them by your act of love but you have also gained even more by your gift. Mother Teresa said true love causes us pain and hurt "yet [it] brings joy. That is why we must pray and ask for courage to love."[9]

So love brings us personal joy. We seek the courage to love knowing that in the end love benefits us. Yet loving does not mean we make the benefits of love our motive for loving. *The very thought of loving for my benefit is a direct denial of costly love.* Philosopher Chad Engelland concludes, "In love, our self and another become entwined, so that sorting our benefits becomes absurd. Do good for loved ones and gratefully receive the good that comes from doing so."[10] I have discovered this: Such love increases our love and then enlarges us so that in the end our love cannot be entirely selfless, at least not in an absolute sense.

Here's another way to understand this question about our self-life: "In what sense is costly love selfless?" Greedy, self-centered people are devoid of true virtue. They can't love, at least not in a God-Love way. They seek good for themselves through their love because of what love does for them. (I do *not* deny that non-Christians can love in costly ways. Because of the innate desire for love in all of us we can love through other means of grace. I only deny that this other kind of love is transforming *in the same way* that it is in the one who knows the love of Jesus!) But self-love *requires* Jesus-directed desire. Love is recognizing the community of the self and the other by letting go of our egoism so we can love. By such love we become our true selves as God created us. *Remember—the virtue of love requires us to humble ourselves. The antidote to selfishness is not absolute selflessness but* costly love!

One last illustration may help convey what I am saying. I am a mentor and writer. Why do I mentor and write when it is such hard and demanding work? At times this commitment costs me sleep, even health. I do it because I love God *and* love this calling to serve others. This is my high calling because these are my God-given gifts. *But love motivates me to persevere in my teaching and writing.* Students and friends gain from my sacrifice. I've seen that over the course of many years. But I also gain an incredibly deep satisfaction from seeing my friends grow in his love. Nothing summarizes what I am saying better than this: "Give and don't count the costs, but don't give because it costs. Give because there is a love for the recipient and glory in giving."[11]

Roberta Bondi explains further:

> A real love for God arises out of the knowledge of what God is like. But at the same time that we begin to have this knowledge, we also come to know what being in the image of God means. We long to have that image, covered over with the muck of everyday life, restored to what it was meant to be. Then we are able to seek our own salvation not out of self-hatred, but rather out of a love of our own life. We begin to see that if God loved human beings so much that we were given the gift of the incarnation, the terrible crucifixion, and the resurrection, then no one can offer any Christian justification for despising or hating any human being, ourselves included.[12]

For ancient spiritual writers, love was a way of being that included a right way of feeling, seeing, and understanding. God's grace makes us aware of divine love, prompting us to make good (free) choices. Love functions as the goal, yet love is also the *means* to the goal. For these ancient writers, love was of two kinds—emotion and long-term attitude of heart. Love requires a choice, but grace enables us to make

this choice. I see an important difference between temperament (seen in qualities like introversion and extroversion)
and disposition (seen in our nature as rooted in our deepest
loves and fears). We are all born with a temperament, but it is
our disposition toward specific behavioral response that will
form us as we follow our choice to pursue a long-term heart
adjustment. This alteration of our inner disposition should
be linked with discipleship and this inner disposition will
result in virtue becoming second nature within us.

Love and Discipleship

When I began my journey into divine love, I wondered
how all these ideas fit with the biblical teaching of discipleship. Matthew 28:18–20 has been rooted in me from childhood. I've always believed God's changing me into a more
Christ-like person (sanctification/maturity) was at the center
of discipleship. I also understood the true purpose of good
theology was personal transformation, to love God and my
neighbor. But I lost this healthy emphasis by thinking my
disposition was shaped entirely by a mental grasp of doctrinal concepts. I now know that experiencing God-Love is the
only solid foundation for true discipleship. Love is the language of the covenant, and the basis for discipleship.

From childhood I believed every Christian should share
the Good News so the church could make true disciples.
Over time I found the idea of people making decisions for
Christ and calling it discipleship was problematic. I came to
question this practice. If evangelism is proclaiming the good
news of Jesus, then those who love others will desire that
people know the love of God revealed in Christ. The Good
News invites—indeed, I would say commands—all people
everywhere to repent and believe in Christ (Acts 16:30–31).
But when we truly believe, we must understand discipleship
is much more than believing the Good News once and for all.
It does not stop at *initial* belief. Jesus invites us to take up a
yoke and follow him. Bonhoeffer expressed this well when he
said that Jesus calls us "to come and die." This call is to enter
into divine rest:

> Come to me, all you that are weary and are carrying heavy burdens, and I will give you rest. Take my yoke upon you, and learn from me; for I am gentle and humble in heart, and you will find rest for your souls. For my yoke is easy, and my burden is light. (Matthew 11:28–30)

Teachers in Jesus' day were demanding and strict. The Pharisees and scribes tended toward perfectionism. No one could measure up. New Testament scholar Dale Bruner says, "Jesus presents himself as gentle and simple, as almost the exact opposite of [these] contemporary teachers." He elaborates:

> As we all know from experience, a teacher's manner is nine-tenths of the teacher's impact. Jesus apparently believes that his manner is one reason why studying with him will bring students refreshment. His gentleman-liness means that he will be patient with slow students and thoughtful in correction. Jesus will later rebuke Bible teachers of his time because "they tie up heavy burdens; but they themselves are unwilling to lift a finger to move them."[13]

Knowing and living the Christian faith is a dynamic, lifelong process. God unites us with himself in relational love and then forms and shapes us through a Spirit-directed process. *Jesus is the true disciple-maker.* We have substituted "data processing" (an entirely mental process) for heart transformation (a deeply spiritual process). Many churches have equated this data processing of Christian information with lifelong discipleship. When this happens, spirituality and life drain out of Christian education.

Some disciples experience God's love suddenly. Others—most, I think—find this experience of divine love rather gradual. Either way, God-Love must become transformational. "The love of God is always with us, but it is not until we stop what we are doing and open up our hearts and minds that we can consciously receive the gift and become vessels of divine love."[14] That's it. God's boundless love toward us in Jesus Christ reveals his overflowing love. His love empowers us to become growing disciples.

I finally understood the love of God is the *only* basis for understanding Christian discipleship. Indeed, *the life of Jesus* is the basis for understanding and entering into divine love.

Be Perfect as Your Heavenly Father Is Perfect

I now believe *every* article of Christian faith comes down to this: God *is* love! We can never exhaust his love; it is infinite, and infinitely more than we can understand. The Father loves us. He sent his Son into the world to reveal this love to save us. The Spirit loves us and draws us into the redeeming, relational love of the triune God. We see this in Paul's prayer for the church in Corinth: "The *grace* of the Lord Jesus Christ, the love of God [the Father], and the *communion* (*koinonia*) of the Holy Spirit be with all of you" (2 Corinthians 13:13, emphasis added). God's love is rooted in the Trinity.

The next chapter will consider our Lord's words in Matthew 5:43–48 about loving our enemies. Here my focus is on verse 48: "Be perfect, therefore, as your heavenly Father is perfect." The word *perfect* sounds like a state of being that needs no improvement. When we think of *perfect* in this way, we have adopted a Greek idea. We reason we can never be "perfect" because only *God* is perfect. He is static, unchanging. This is divine perfection. Humans are subject to change; thus, we will always be *defective*. Turning this pagan notion upside down, Gregory of Nyssa says *to be a human being, one has to change*. Roberta Bondi says, "It is the way God made us when God set us in creation, for creation itself is changing. The real issue is not physical change at all, but moral or spiritual change, over which we [do] have control."[15]

This understanding of *perfect* sounds so strange. The Greek word for it is *telos*. This word is used here, as well as in Matthew 19:21; James 1:4; 3:2. It means "complete maturity." But there is a danger in the word *maturity*. We can miss what for centuries the church understood about "becoming perfect as God is perfect."

We speak of having a perfect day or of seeing a perfect ball game. We even say a piece of music was perfectly performed, or a meal we enjoyed was perfect. What we really mean is we saw, or experienced, *completeness.* Limiting *perfect* to mean "never changing" is to use this dynamic word as pagan philosophers did. The heirs of Aristotle and Plato believed human beings cannot be perfect as God is perfect, whose perfection must be unchanging and complete. Herodotus captures the idea: "Call no one blessed until that one is dead."[16]

Most Christians I know never talk about being *perfect* in the love of God because they believe it is impossible. They read Jesus' words and say, "This is the law; thus it condemns us!" So, they conclude, we should never *seek* for perfect love. We should merely acknowledge we have sinned. Yet this is *not* how the church understood this word *perfect* in Matthew 5:48.

Gregory of Nyssa (335–395) says in order to be truly human we *must* change. Creation is always changing. What if the real issue in Matthew 5 is not physical but *spiritual change*? We have little control over our physical change, generally speaking, but moral and spiritual change is something we have considerable control over. We must cease from our not-so-clever excuses for spiritual failure—"I'm only human!" or "I can't help myself unless God changes me." These are forms of fatalism. We must take full responsibility for ourselves. Roberta Bondi captures my point: "Change has to do with the balance we strike between these two spheres. We become more [fully] human by gaining freedom from the enslaving quality of appetites and emotions, more able to love as we move toward God. Understood this way, perfection cannot be unchanging."[17]

Why then does Jesus tell us to be perfect when he knows we can never be perfect in moral righteousness? Ancient Christian writers answered that at the center of this commandment is love, and love is a *growing, dynamic response to God.* God's love has no limit, so we can never reach the full limit of love. We may love fully at one moment and fail to love at another. Gregory of Nyssa says, "This is truly perfection: never to stop growing towards what is better and never placing any limit on perfection."[18]

We all sin, and Christians confess their sin (see 1 John 1:9–10). Yet we were made for authenticity and wholeness. This means we can *grow up (mature) into the perfect love of Christ, even for our enemies.* We cannot arrive at moral perfection, but this should actually be "a cause for celebration,"[19] because this means that we can grow into the likeness of God in divine love!

True Faith Gives Birth to Love

In many Protestant and evangelical contexts, the answer to the question "What must I do to inherit eternal life?" is stated in words like these: "Believe in Jesus as your Lord and Savior, and you will be saved" (see Acts 16:31). Another common response is, "Pray this sinners' prayer (already written out), and Christ will save you." These answers are not *wrong*, but they are seriously deficient. They lend themselves to several common errors, one of which is leading people to believe something like this: "If you believe the right things, or make the right decision in this moment of time, you will be saved no matter what follows." This distorts and reduces Jesus' actual teaching. Perhaps this is why we have failed to present the cost of discipleship rooted in costly love.

Besides the fact that this formulaic approach is not what Jesus actually says, these types of answers fail to grasp that salvation is about more than believing something, or saying something, once for all time. Salvation is God's costly gift that comes to those who repent and believe.[20] When the Spirit stirs us inwardly we seek Christ. But the Spirit *also* leads us to seek Christ for his transforming, *active* love. Without faith we cannot be saved, but if we have faith, we will also have love (James 2:24). We cannot obey God unless and until we actually love him. Anything else leads to moralism, not the Spirit-filled life of Christ. We cannot love God unless we know him, and we cannot know him unless we truly believe; thus, there is a vital link between faith and love, one that must never be broken.

During the eighteenth-century Evangelical Awakening, John Wesley held these same ancient Christian views of love and discipleship and helped many Christians grasp this proper sense of discipleship. (His views are widely associated with his *particular* teaching about Christian perfection.) I believe Wesley's actual views are easily misunderstood. In his treatise *A Plain Account of Christian Perfection*, he wrote, "Sinless perfection is a phrase I never use, in order to avoid the appearance of contradicting myself."[21] Wesley made a critical distinction between *actual* sins and *human faults*. He believed that sins are voluntary transgressions of God's commandments, while faults are unknowing violations of God's commands. By virtue of our humanity all of us are subject to faults, but we can live in God's love and rise above sin.[22] He is saying that we cannot have perfect knowledge, ability, or strength, nor can we cease entirely from error or avoid all temptation, but *we can attain God's love in real discipleship*.

Though I do not feel all of Wesley's distinctions can be completely sustained, I do believe his understanding corresponds more closely with the ancient Christian idea of discipleship than do our popular modern views. Wesley was often asked what constituted Christian perfection. His answer: "Christian perfection is loving God with all our heart, mind, soul and strength. This implies that no passions contrary to love remain in the soul. It means that all thoughts, words, and actions are governed by pure love."[23]

John Wesley's doctrine of love and discipleship is profoundly *relational*. God is renewing us in our inward being by conquering and ruling our hearts through God-Love. He is restoring his divine image by grace alone. Christians should delight in God through experiencing his love. Wesley called love God's "reigning attribute, the attribute that sheds amiable glory on all His other perfections."[24] For Wesley, all God is and does was motivated and governed by divine love. This is the very thesis of this book, even though I am not related to the Wesleyan tradition.

Finally, John Wesley believed God's love was most fully revealed in the life and (especially) death of Jesus Christ. *It is the man Christ Jesus who defined the meaning of love.* The goal of salvation is not to lead us to embrace right ideas but to *restore the image of God in us by renewing us in divine love.* Wesley went so far as to say the incarnate Christ enables us to become more fully shaped into the image of God than was possible *before* the Fall. Why? Before the fall we could not know the depth of God's love as we can now through the death of Jesus on the cross. Because we know *this* suffering, dying love of Jesus, we can love one another just as he loved us. On his deathbed, Wesley asked that his sermon on the love of God be read to him. Biographers say his dying wish was the passion of his entire life, namely, that everyone might come to know personally God's love in Jesus Christ!

Conclusion

One of the greatest Christian thinkers of all time is Blaise Pascal (1623–1662), a scientific genius and the father of integral calculus. He invented the hydraulic press and did pioneering work in atmospheric pressure. Some even believe his principles led to the invention of the computer. But more important, at least for Christian faith, are his two works that defended and explained the Christian faith: *Lettres Provinciales* ("Letters to a Provincial") and *Pensées* ("Thoughts").

Pascal, a Catholic, possessed a profoundly biblical understanding of the human heart and divine love. He said his mind and emotions were unified in his response to God's love. But what truly transformed him was the evening of November 23, 1654, a "night of fire." This baptism in God's grace and love lasted for about two hours, giving him a purity of heart and mind and making him fall in love with God as a disciple of Jesus. He describes this baptism as "fire burning away doubt and distress," a fire in the mind and the heart, a forgiving fire that brought "renunciation, total and sweet."[25]

Thus we see again how the Spirit immersed a person, Blaise Pascal, into the experience of God-Love. This immersion comes by grace and it works as "fire in the heart," cleansing and renewing everything it touches.

The conclusion should be clear. Christian behavior, asceticism, or learning can never replace love. To misconstrue the Gospel texts about following Jesus as a disciple will dull the radical impact of what Jesus actually teaches us about Christian discipleship. It will lead to apathy and indifference, which kills love faster than anything else I know. St. John of the Cross was surely right when he concluded, "In the twilight of our lives, we will be judged on how we loved."

But here is the radical good news of gospel discipleship: We are God's "new creation" (2 Corinthians 5:17), and by God's grace we *can* change. By being filled with God's love, in ever-increasing ways, we become true disciples of Christ.

CHAPTER EIGHT

THE MOST ASTOUNDING COMMAND EVER UTTERED

> It took me a long time to understand that
> God is not the enemy of my enemies. God is
> not even the enemy of God's enemies.
>
> Martin Niemöller

IN MY OPINION, NOTHING should astound a reader of the Gospels more than Jesus' clear command to "love your enemies" (Matthew 5:43–44; Luke 6:27, 35). Every Christian I know has at least heard this command. Many non-Christians know it as well. But it seems the church has so reduced the impact of this command that it rarely astounds us. Have we become so comfortable with our own characterizations of love that we have found many ways to avoid this incredible command?

The Command Itself

Our Lord's commandment to love our enemies first occurs in the Sermon on the Mount (Matthew 5–7). This account contains a series of sayings in which Jesus challenges several moralisms common in first-century Judaism that led to a popular misreading of Scripture. Six times Jesus says, "You have heard that it was said. . . . But I say to you." He addresses weighty issues such as anger, adultery, divorce, oaths, retaliation and one's enemies. The last such statement comes at the end of Matthew 5:

> You have heard that it was said, "You shall love your neighbor and hate your enemy." But I say to you, Love your enemies and pray for those who persecute you, so that you may be children of your Father in heaven; for he makes his sun rise on the evil and on the good, and sends rain on the righteous and on the unrighteous. For if you love those who love you, what reward do you have? Do not even the tax collectors do the same? And if you greet only your brothers and sisters, what more are you doing than others? Do not even the Gentiles do the same? Be perfect, therefore, as your heavenly Father is perfect. (Matthew 5:43–48)[1]

When "love your enemies" is understood in terms of costly love, the command *exceeds all natural human capacity*. Christ's proposal is not simple, realistic, or manageable. It can only work if "God is love" in us. God is the ultimate realist. He takes into account the violence, hate, and evil in the world, and still loves *all* sinners. Clearly this love, which alone can overcome huge obstacles, does so either by winning over the enemy or by bearing faithful witness to God's love in the face of deeply evil opposition. In Matthew 5 all six of these commands stress the immense power of love, since all are in the future indicative tense. This means that each of them speaks of Jesus' desire *and* of his promise. This command had to sound like "sheer madness or subversive politics to the ears of [Jesus'] contemporaries."[2] I have come to wonder why people understand this essential commandment in such widely divergent ways. What has caused so much confusion in interpretation? Has human logic so trumped our relationship with the truth that we have reduced this command to a doctrine that costs nothing?

A Radical Hermeneutic

Scot McKnight says the law was not limited to 600-plus commandments. (Biblical scholars differ concerning the precise number of commands in the Old Testament.) Alongside these recognized commandments there were various *halakhic* rulings. One example concerns these commands.

It appears that in Jesus' time approximately forty activities were constituted "work" that could not be performed on the Sabbath. The discussion in Matthew 15:1–20 concerned similar laws about ceremonial purity, such as the proper cleansing of one's hands. Jesus specifically calls such *halakhic* rules "heavy burdens" (Matthew 23:4). Peter concludes that the weight of Torah has become a "yoke" that neither Jews nor Christians could truly observe (Acts 15:10). He is not saying the law is bad, but rather that people create burdens from their particular readings of the law.

Given these and similar passages, McKnight concludes, Jesus stepped into a first-century context where the rules had become burdensome and complex. Jesus' response that was "nothing short of a radical hermeneutical guide for proper observance of the Torah: love God and love others."[3] *He cut through all the inconsequential statements that surrounded the law and made the radical center profoundly clear.*

Thus, the command to "love your enemies" became one of the most important moral imperatives ever uttered. Few who heard Jesus speak these words would have added an easygoing *"Amen!"* Some would have grumbled, "Love a Roman soldier? Are you kidding?" Zealots in the crowd would even have said this command was traitorous. *Let's not miss the simple fact that Jesus' words were controversial.* No respectable member of Jewish society would have quickly embraced these words, words which turned their world upsidedown. Jesus' radical hermeneutic brings into sharp focus the essential feature of his kingdom teaching: *radical God-Love.*

Did the Law Teach Israel to "Hate" Their Enemies?

We've observed that Jesus prefaced this commandment with "You have heard that it was said" (Matthew 5:43). Nothing in the Old Covenant suggests God's law blesses "hatred" for one's enemies; this was *implied* by zealous nationalists who had lost the spirit of the covenant, a covenant that included the blessing of "all the families of the earth" (Genesis 12:3).

Law and love are not in conflict. Love is part of the law, and the law commands love. It seems the particular law was intended to restrain hatred, not to justify it against non-Jewish neighbors. But endless debates revolved around this law and how Jews should apply it. Some teachers reasoned that if God loved Israel and commanded love for their neighbors, then the opposite must follow—Jews should hate their enemies! This was a popular distortion in Jesus' time. Ultimately this came down to one specific question, as we saw in chapter 5: "Who is my neighbor?"

Hating your enemy was not the majority teaching of Judaism even in Jesus' day.[4] Moreover, this interpretation is not found in the Old Testament, though one might attempt to prove it by citing Psalm 139:21–22. There was fertile ground for an idea like "hating" if the Old Testament is read in a way that favored one's instinctive bias. (This is true of many of our favorite interpretations of Scripture.)

McKnight summarizes the central truth behind Jesus' command: "Loving those we like and hating those we don't like is as common as sin."[5] Lest we blame Israel for "hating [their] enemy," we must understand this particular interpretation flourished among the Pharisees, Zealots, and Essenes, causing many Jews to debate what the word *neighbor* signified.

The word *hate* (*miseō*) denotes both active hostility and "loving less" (see Matthew 6:24). For Rabbi Jesus, all this tradition was a false interpretation of the law. But in the Sermon on the Mount he takes the law to a level of understanding and application no Jew had ever heard, at least not in such a clear manner.

We saw in chapter 5 that when a lawyer asked Jesus about the greatest commandment (Luke 10:29), the Lord didn't offer an off-the-cuff response. Sinclair Ferguson says, "His reply was one of the great theological talking points of the day. Jesus' answer then, as his teaching here, was revolutionary in the moral challenge it presented to the disciples."[6]

The real contrast, which careful readers can see through-out the entire biblical narrative, is between reliance on the power of the state (however it was understood) and trust in God. To trust God is to pursue obedience in the way of peace and love. While the Old Testament can't be interpreted as teaching pacifism, some texts such as Proverbs 25:21–22 seem to foreshadow Jesus' teaching about radical love for one's enemies. What might have been only imagined in the Old Testament, we could say, came to fruition in Jesus. No other text says this more clearly than these words that call us to love our enemies in a radical and remarkable way. But how should we understand Jesus' teaching in the face of state power (see Romans 13)? For twenty centuries Christians have wrestled with this tension. It's not easy to confront this question, but there is one response we cannot allow: ignor-ing the implications of the commandment by toning it down with civility or sentimentality. Martin Luther King, Jr. was surely right in saying "Love is the only force capable of trans-forming an enemy into a friend." But for this to happen, love for my enemy must be robustly centered in Jesus' life and kingdom message.

Who Then Is My Enemy?

This command to love our enemies comes as the culmi-nation of six antitheses. Jesus plainly says we are never justi-fied in hating our enemies. Then he says, "Love your enemies." He gives two concrete ways we can do this: "pray for those who persecute you" (Matthew 5:44) and welcome outsiders (Matthew 5:47). The word *persecute* likely refers to the oppo-sition some Christian missionaries would face (see Matthew. 10:23; 23:34). The word *greet* (*aspazomai*), in verse 47, means to welcome and wish for the well-being of the enemy.

So what does Jesus actually command? In first-century Judaism your "neighbor" was Jewish. Your common "en-emy" was Rome, and your personal "enemy" was whoever persecuted or opposed you and your family. *Jesus says the ethic of his kingdom teaches us to love all our enemies.* The English word "enemy" comes from the Latin word *inimicus*, from the prefix *in* ("not") and *amicus* ("friend"). *Defined broadly, an enemy is the opposite of a friend.* In *Loving Our Enemies: Reflections on the Hardest Commandment,* Jim Forest offers a striking anecdote about what it means to be a non-friend. At age seven his son Daniel told another boy to "go away and drop dead." Daniel's plain language illustrates the meaning of "non-friend."[7] The *Oxford English Dictionary* elaborates the meaning of "enemy" as "an unfriendly or hostile person, one that cherishes hatred, and works to do ill to another." This underscores an element of the truth we must grasp. We are prone to think an enemy is *another* person, nation or group of people. But if I am unfriendly or hostile toward *anyone* I have treated that person as my enemy. If I cherish hatred, which creates an angry emotional reaction that wishes someone ill, I have become that person's enemy. Jim Forest says, "If I wish to break the cycle of enmity, I had better keep in mind that the only enemy over whom I have much influence is myself."[8]

Aleksandr Solzhenitsyn, held captive for eight years in the labor camps of the Soviet Union's Gulag, tells us that in those terrible conditions he learned something about enmity and enemies:

> If only it were all so simple! If only there were evil people somewhere insidiously committing evil deeds and it were necessary only to separate them from the rest of us and destroy them. But the dividing line between good and evil cuts through the heart of every human being, and who is willing to destroy a piece of his own heart?[9]

Gandhi once said he had three enemies. The first was the British nation. The second was the Indian people who opposed him. Finally, "My most formidable enemy opponent is a man named Mohandas K. Gandhi. With him I seem to have very little influence."[10] I'm reminded of Walt Kelly's cartoon figure Pogo, who said "We have met the enemy and he is us." Anyone I feel threatened by, or whom I believe I must defend myself against, is my enemy. My enemy is often a former friend, or a group of people I once belonged to, or even a member of my own family. In most instances my enemy is a very specific person.

This idea of the enemy is underscored through abuse or violence. Police officers will tell you that most violence occurs between people who know each other. A husband, wife, coworker, boss, neighbor, family member, or former friend becomes the target of violence. You can add to this list all kinds of categories or stereotypes: blacks, whites, Hispanics, Muslims, Arabs, Jews, Democrats, Republicans, gays, punks, pro-abortionists, pro-lifers. You can also add other nations, illegal immigrants, dictators, jihadists, and those who carried out the 9/11 attacks.

It may be helpful to reflect on the great challenge of being called to love our enemies. We're bombarded on television and social media with news about terrorism and evil. All this tends to inflame our passions. Our passions become especially dark when we connect our fear to others who differ from us. Movies, television shows, the 24/7 news cycle all prompt a growing hostility toward our enemies. We then create categories and labels that become a subtle form of *marking out* our enemies. We view images of people walking into public places and blowing themselves up, intending to kill others. Tragically, religion gets connected to the story. Our government sanctions drone-strikes upon nameless, faceless persons we will never meet, killing them as if they were nothing more than images in a computer game. Some of these people have actively sought to do harm, killing and enslaving others. I believe governments are right to protect their citizens against such violence, but even when this requires deadly force we have no right to adopt a response of violence linked with hatred. All too easily we become inured to real people who have become our personal enemies in one form or another. This toxic cultural setting, which marks so much of modern society, undermines love. But the command still stands: "Love your enemies."

In all circumstances Christians should promote peace, not war. We should especially be careful of glorifying war out of fear and anger. This is particularly important today, when armed conflicts threaten our way of life through the strategy of terrorism. Building a culture of life, rooted in God's love, means that war is never a reflection of what ought to be. It reflects a failure of human dignity at multiple levels. If Jesus' words are taken at face value and we affirm a proper use of armed force (through what is called "a just war" theory), then we should especially pray for the victims of war, not just for our own soldiers. To not hate our enemies must mean we always seek first to resolve conflicts through peaceable means, even at the highest levels of our society. A culture of violence can be built by our response to violence. Christians all too easily embrace this culture and then adopt the language of hatred for others. This commandment must be allowed to address these very human, yet sinful, responses.

The Command Expanded

Luke underscores additional aspects of the commandment in Matthew to love our enemies. For example, "But I say to you . . . love your enemies, do good to those who hate you, bless those who curse you, pray for those who abuse you" (Luke 6:27–28). Here the enemy is a persecutor, someone who intends injury because of our beliefs. Loving means praying for our persecutors and welcoming them with genuine concern. It means to labor for reconciliation. *This ethical idea suffuses the New Testament.*

We should not forget that the word for love here is still agape. William Barclay defines "agape" as "unconquerable benevolence, invincible goodwill."[11] However others treat us, whether insult or ridicule or even bodily harm, we are to regard them with agape.

The central reason Jesus gives for loving our enemies should shock us (Matthew 5:45–48). God loves his own enemies in this way! The example is straightforward: Every single day God treats both the just and the unjust, the good and the bad, with the same gracious and loving provision (verse 45). So what is Jesus saying?

First, he commands us to be *with* our enemies. This includes both physical proximity and gracious *attentiveness*. We are to be like our heavenly Father, who longs *for* and works *for* the good of his enemies! Love cannot be rendered mere "tolerance." Loving our enemies means "striving for them to become the sort of person God wants them to be."[12]

Second, Jesus commands us to *will* this agape. We almost never *feel* this love, at least not initially. In this way agape allows us to overcome our natural response. This is how we adopt a supernatural response to those who oppose, hurt or offend us. This love, a gift from God, will never alter us unless we seek for it. My own *initial response* is *never* to love my enemies. Then God reminds me I must make a conscious, intentional choice. It matters not if I *like* someone or if that person likes me. It matters not how awful or terrible that person has been. Agape, in this active and radical sense, is how Jesus helps us overcome anger, bitterness and strife with complete goodwill. *We bless our enemy.*

Agape will shape me into the person God wants me to be. It's not a formula that "works" by turning our enemies into friends through psychological self-talk. That may help, but it is *not* radical love for my enemy.

The frequency of this command and the many allusions the first Christians make to it in their writings is remarkable. We remember Jesus on the cross, asking the Father to forgive his persecutors (Luke 23:34). Stephen adopted the same language and action at his death (Acts 7:60). Paul's counsel is the same (Romans 12:14; 1 Corinthians 4:12–13; 1 Thessalonians 5:15). And Peter's teaching about being in the fiery furnace of suffering for the gospel encouraged his readers to follow Jesus in loving their enemies (1 Peter 3:9).

This commandment shows up in the New Testament, as well as throughout the literature of the early church. It seems to have become a primary way Christians *overcame* their opponents. History suggests the church actually changed the ancient world through the practice of love for one's enemies. We see this idea in *Polycarp's Letter to the Philippians* 12:3:

"Pray for all the saints. Pray also for kings and powers and rulers, and for those who persecute and hate you, and for all the enemies of the cross, in order that your fruit may be evident among all people, that you may be perfect in him."

Clement of Alexandria (150–215) writes, "The spiritual man never cherishes resentment or harbors a grudge against anyone—even though deserving or hated for his conduct.

Cyprian (200–258) says, "Even our enemies are to be loved." Late in his life Lactantius (250–325), a prominent Roman teacher of rhetoric, converted to Christianity. He had much to say about the way Christians loved their enemies.

> What if a man gives way to grief and anger and indulges these emotions (which he should struggle against)? What if he rushes wherever injustice will call him? Such a man does not fulfill the duty of virtue. For he who tries to return an injury desires to imitate that very person by whom he has been injured. In short, he who imitates a bad man cannot be good.[13]

Golden-Rule Christianity?

"Love your enemies" is often connected with Christian pacifism. It's also used to explain how governments should pursue peace. Christian history reveals that both ideas commend themselves to us for prayerful and deep consideration. In the first instance this commandment of Jesus offers a strong case for *personal* pacifism. We see evidence of this in early church history. (I cannot *explicitly* speak about this here. If you accept the reasoning of the "just war" tradition, you ought also examine the logic of *Christian* pacifism.) I acknowledge it is hard to use this specific text about our enemies as the basis for relationships among nations. Furthermore, I do not think we should turn this command into a broad Golden Rule anyone can undertake with or without the experience of Christ's love. By truly loving our enemies, we partake in something more—the power of costly obedience.

It is easier to lobby for peace than to love our enemy. The political and social left and right can both profit from the no-nonsense response of the late William Barclay: "First and foremost, this commandment of Jesus deals with personal relationship. This is a commandment of which we should say first and foremost: 'This means me.'"[14]

The Golden Rule says, "In everything do to others as you would have them do to you; for this is the law and the prophets" (Matthew 7:12). One religious tolerance website suggests something akin to this teaching can be found in twenty-one major world religions.[15] But this specific commandment to "love our enemies" goes far beyond religious tolerance and kindness. Yes, we should do to others as we want them to do to us. But this is not what Jesus is specifically teaching here. At best, the Golden Rule is a step toward loving your enemy. The second step will take you far beyond. This is precisely why, if we properly hear it, this teaching remains shocking.

One other point should be made before we apply this ethic. As noted above, we are exhorted to do two things. Verse 44 tells us to "pray." I've discovered we cannot pray for others for long and still hate them! When we pray for another, something happens within us. It may take time, but we will change. A simple practice I adopted some years ago with regard to my enemies has transformed my life. I keep a private prayer list with a section called "My Enemies." I'm always the first person changed by this practice!

Sadly, many of my harshest enemies have been other Christians. In some cases these were once my friends, or at least I thought they were. The people I have in mind have caused me deep harm emotionally and spiritually. They've even impacted my financial well-being. They've attacked my character and motives in public and private because they disagree with me about some issue(s). They seem to think they must warn others of the harm I might do. I have approached some of these people to seek peace, but my attempts have not always resulted in a restored relationship. In many instances these persons will still not talk to me. So I am forced to make a choice. I choose to embrace agape. But what can I do if I cannot have peace with them? I must pray!

If this sounds pious and simple, I assure you it is not. Jesus has united us with himself and made us "ambassadors of Christ"; thus we can undertake "the ministry of reconciliation" (2 Corinthians 5:17–20). Reconciliation means the restoration of relationship. Much as electricity turns on a light, the current that turns on the possibility of reconciliation is God-Love. When the electricity of divine love flows through me, I cannot hate others. In fact, the more I pray, the more I appreciate the great good I see in them; my heart is filled with joy at their success and pained by their burdens. I cannot explain this naturally. William Barclay is right: "The surest way of killing bitterness is to pray for the man we are tempted to hate."[16]

The Consequence of Enemy Love

One of the most troubling parts of Jesus' teaching is why we should love our enemies. In Matthew 5:45 he tells us to love "so that you may be children of your Father in heaven." The words "so that" should be read in the context of Matthew 5:9: "Blessed are the peacemakers, for they will be *called* children of God" (emphasis added); as well as in Luke 6:35: "Love your enemies, do good, and lend, expecting nothing in return. Your reward will be great, and you *will be* children of the Most High" (emphasis added). The word "that" in Matthew 5:45 indicates the greatest consequence of enemy love will be the revelation that we are indeed the children of our heavenly Father.

Jesus is clearly speaking of reward, prompting Scot McKnight to call this the "Ethic from Above." He writes, "By using reward language Jesus is telling us what God ultimately thinks."[17] Reward theology often appears in Matthew's Gospel (see 5:12, 46; 6:1–2, 5, 16; 10:41–42; 20:8), but this language makes some Christians uncomfortable because it can sound as if Jesus is saying we are redeemed by works. So how do we understand Matthew's intention?

In a Jewish context, "reward" and "merit" are words that express the way people thought and spoke. They thought of sin in terms of a debt; thus, salvation was a (gracious) "reward." Based on this Jewish rhetorical use, "reward [is] expressed as a promise."[18] Said in a slightly different way, we can see this as a rhetoric of motivation, not a theology of personal merit. Jesus is not saying we earn eternal life by balancing the scale by good works. *He is saying we are to live the gospel of the kingdom in a way that reflects who God is, proving that we truly belong to him because of our continual experience of divine love.*

Conclusion

So Jesus is telling us who God is and what kingdom life looks like. God's love is demonstrated in this: "[H]e makes his sun rise on the evil and on the good, and sends rain on the righteous and on the unrighteous" (Matthew 5:45). This is how Jesus says that God loves both observant and non-observant Jews. He loves the people of the Abrahamic covenant, and he loves Gentiles who sin without the law. This is consistent with the declaration in John 3:16–17 of God's love for the whole world.

Jesus is teaching what really matters—"your righteousness exceeds that of the scribes and Pharisees" (Matthew 5:20). Jesus is using conventional first-century stereotypes his audience would have considered religiously and politically correct. After all, he was a friend of tax collectors (Matthew 11:19) and had deep concern for Gentiles (Matthew 21:43; 28:19). His rhetoric indicates his love is accepting and embracing. His love is radical. He loves those who hate him. McKnight concludes, "To love humans is to love all humans."[19]

Jesus shows us how to deal with our enemies by making them into our neighbors. This humanizes them. We see God's great love for them and act toward them as God acted toward us in Christ.

Jim Forest tells the story of meeting Father Mikhail, a Russian Orthodox priest. Mikhail Gorbachev, in his second year as Russia's new head of state, had ended religious persecution. Forest asked the priest if he was surprised. "Not at all," he said. "All believers have been praying for this every day of our lives. We knew God would answer our prayer, only we did not know when. I am only surprised that our prayer has been answered while I am still alive." Forest responded, "Still, surely you must hate those who caused so much suffering and who killed so many." Father Mikhail answered, "Christ does not hate them. Why should I? How will they find the way to belief unless we love them? And if I refuse to love them, I too am not a believer."[20]

In 2016 my good friend Frank Lesko, director of Catholic-Evangelical Relations for the Glenmary (Catholic) Home Missioners, wrote a blog titled "What Makes a Christian?"[21] Frank says he sometimes thinks of the collective witness of Christianity as "the elephant in the living room." If you close your eyes you can begin to imagine millions, even billions, of Christians in this big room. They're all talking and milling about and being energetic about their faith. But there is one big problem. They all are ignoring the giant elephant right in the middle of them all. They even have to bend and contort to see around this huge animal, but they just keep ignoring it. What is the elephant in the room? The Greatest Commandment. Yet if we hear Jesus saying anything clearly it's this: "Of all the things you do, do this! If you are going to invest time and attention in my kingdom, do it right here. Love God and your neighbor more abundantly. Practice my love, because it is of singular importance!"

PART FOUR

HOW CAN WE RECOVER

THE COMMANDMENT

JESUS GAVE?

When he had gone out, Jesus said, "Now the Son of Man has been glorified, and God has been glorified in him. If God has been glorified in him, God will also glorify him in himself and will glorify him at once. Little children, I am with you only a little longer. You will look for me; and as I said to the Jews so now I say to you, 'Where I am going, you cannot come.' I give you a new commandment, that you love one another. Just as I have loved you, you also should love one another. By this everyone will know that you are my disciples, if you have love for one another."

(John 13:31–35)

CHAPTER NINE

THE NEW COMMANDMENT

Why does Jesus describe as "new" the commandment that must characterize the life of
his disciples? ... Essentially because the love
itself is new in nature: It is the filial love of
Jesus, which is the origin and foundation of
a new dispensation of relations that establish
an entirely new human family.... The relationship which [Jesus] has had with his disciples during his earthly life and which was
a reflection of his oneness with the Father,
must now be changed after his departure into
a fraternal love in the new community.[1]

Gerard Rossé,
Community of Believers

THE PORTRAYAL OF CHRISTIANITY in popular media—
radio, television, social, and print—can be painful. But
sometimes it's even more painful to listen to how we
speak of ourselves. Multitudes in the West have written off
Christianity, opting instead for no religion, new religions, or
(most often) private spirituality. Christianity is seen as profoundly negative.

In the United States, some "progressive" denomina-
tions and religious groups have been called "the Democratic
Party at prayer." Others, from a more "conservative" political stance, are seen as the Republican Party seeking to enforce Christian morality. Such associations between partisan

politics and Jesus' teaching have become common. Some say we should confine Jesus to our private worship because the church has no place in a secular society. But the gospel itself repudiates such a separation. Why? *Discipleship is never a private matter*:

> You are the light of the world. A city built on a hill cannot be hid. No one after lighting a lamp puts it under the bushel basket, but on the lampstand, and it gives light to all in the house. In the same way, let your light shine before others, so that they may see your good works and give glory to your Father in heaven (Matthew 5:14–16).

Jesus says we cannot live our faith in private because we, the church, are "the light of the world." In fact, the church exists to *be* Christ's mission, not just to do mission activities. The essence of being Jesus' disciple is being on mission with him. When we turn inward, and occupy ourselves with our own existence and place in the kingdom, we lose our purpose. Our entire mission is to give ourselves away for others, through costly love. As we saw in chapter 7, discipleship leads us to express God's costly love in and for the world. *Being* and *doing* God-Love touches all of life. This is the most fundamental reason why we must demonstrate love *publicly* through deep and thoughtful concern for human justice. Jesus said to a group of pious religious leaders that "the weightier matters of the law [are] justice and mercy and faith" (Matthew 23:23). Growing up in the Deep South, in the pre-Civil Rights Era, I never knew a Christian man who lived justice and mercy more than my own dad. Thomas Armstrong, a dentist, loved all people, black and white. He quietly lived a way of racial inclusion that showed respect for every person he met. When I preached at his funeral, I summarized his life with a biblical text that to this day has powerfully framed how I understand costly love in public:

> He has told you, O mortal, what is good;
> and what does the Lord require of you
> but to do justice, and to love kindness,
> and to walk humbly with your God? (Micah 6:8)

This profound concern for justice and mercy *is* nothing less than costly love for our neighbors and neighborhoods. Thus, avoiding controversial public and social issues is not an option if we truly embrace the discipleship of costly love. (We can and must debate *how* we should do this in effective and faithful ways.) I think this is close to what Paul had in mind when he wrote, "Every time we get the chance, *let us work for the benefit of all*, starting with the people closest to us in the community of faith" (Galatians 6:10, *The Message*, emphasis mine).

The Key to Costly Love

Earlier I mentioned Matthew 28:18–20, one the most familiar texts in the New Testament. We call this the Great Commission. In this passage we often miss that Jesus commanded not just individuals but the *entire* church to make disciples. This is not merely a private task, but a corporate mission. The Scriptures establish two parts in making disciples: baptizing, and then, corporately, "teaching them to obey everything that I have commanded you" (Matthew 28:20). The word *commanded* is significant. The New Testament uses it several different ways. For our purposes, I want to show how in its various forms (*entellomai/entole*) this word is connected with the word *love*, a connection that underscores the costly nature of true love. Here are several examples:

> I give you a new *commandment*, that you love one another. Just as I have loved you, you also should love one another. By this everyone will know that you are my disciples, if you have love for one another. (John 13:34–35)

> If you love me, you will keep my *commandments*. (John 14:15)

> They who have my *commandments* and keep them are those who love me; and those who love me will be loved by my Father, and I will love them and reveal myself to them. (John 14:21)

> I do as the Father has *commanded* me, so that the world may know that I love the Father. (John 14:31)

> If you keep my *commandments*, you will abide in my love, just as I have kept my Father's *commandments* and abide in his love (John 15:10).[2]

The linkage of the words *command* and *love* occurs more than thirty times in the New Testament, and thus is a significant theme throughout. The above verses clearly show this connection between costly, Christ-like love and Jesus' commandments. This is why our Lord calls this imperative the "new commandment."

The Discourses of Jesus to His Disciples

The four Gospels *comprise* the teaching of Jesus. But, surprisingly, only two commandments are *specifically* attributed to him. The first is in the Great Commission. The second is in John 13–17. Here Jesus tells his disciples specifically how he wants them to relate to one another, and he calls this commandment "new":

> When he had gone out, Jesus said, "Now the Son of Man has been glorified, and God has been glorified in him. If God has been glorified in him, God will also glorify him in himself and will glorify him at once. Little children, I am with you only a little longer. You will look for me; and as I said to the Jews so now I say to you, 'Where I am going, you cannot come.' I give you a new commandment, that you love one another. Just as I have loved you, you also should love one another. By this everyone will know that you are my disciples, if you have love for one another." (John 13:31–35)

The so-called "Upper Room Discourse" of John 13–17 actually includes several discourses Jesus gave on the night before he suffered and died. Biblical scholars agree that all these discourses center around one commandment: "Love one another."[3]

The Gospel of John has been called the "book of signs" (2:11, 23; 3:2; 4:48; 6:2, 26; 7:31; 9:16; 11:47; 12:37; and especially 20:30) for good reason. Yet in spite of these "signs" the apostle shows how the world, even though it was given the testimony of a divine witness, finally rejected the Light. In a parallel theme, John shows how those who received Jesus (1:12) became sons and daughters of God. Most scholars agree that chapters 13–17 are John's version of *the final private teaching* Jesus gave his apostles.

Everything in John 13–17 centers on union with Christ rooted in the eternal relational love between the Father, Son, and Holy Spirit. The life these disciples will enjoy after Jesus is gone will be the direct result of this mutual indwelling of the Father, Son, and Holy Spirit. When the Spirit is given (John 16:4–16) the holy Trinity will live in those who follow Jesus. Our own mystical union with God, if we read John 13–17 in sequence, is rooted in our union with the Trinity and that unity of persons is a unity of eternal love.

After Jesus washes his disciples' feet, demonstrating what self-giving love truly looks like, he dialogues with these men. (Remember, all this occurs on the eve of his greatest display of love—his death.) Jesus quietly identifies his betrayer, and Judas flees. Faith is a progressive experience of trusting God's love for us but Judas follows a different pattern, one that leads him to reject love and friendship. Jesus knows Judas will betray him but he still invites him into the fellowship of his love. After these tragic events John says Jesus' glorification *began* (13:31–32). He will return *to* his Father, yet still be *with* his disciples (13:33). He will hear their prayers and send his Spirit (14:15–17); thus, they will never be orphaned (14:18–21). The costly love Jesus commands of them will soon reside *in* them because of the gift of the Spirit (14:15, 21; 14:22–26). In chapters 15–16 John develops the subjects Jesus introduced in chapters 13–14—the mutual indwelling of Christ and the gift of the Spirit. These chapters are almost entirely a monologue about Christ and his church. The disciples will live in a hostile world (15:18–16:11), but the Spirit's action through them will be enough to empower them to live faithfully until the end (16:12–16). In the metaphor of the vine and branches, Jesus provides one of the New Testament's most powerful images of relational love (15:1–8). He further reminds the disciples that the world will be judged because it rejects the Light. This is why the world will hate them (15:18–16:11).

The New Commandment

On the final evening before his suffering and death, Jesus tells his disciples they will no longer have him in their midst to protect them. The Gospels have several different accounts of the disciples disputing among themselves about which of them was the greatest (Matthew 18:1–4; Mark 9:33–37; Luke 9:46–48; 22:24–27). These episodes are the definitive *backdrop* of John 13:34–35.

Here Jesus shifts their hearts from the ecstasy of the Father glorifying Jesus and Jesus glorifying his Father, and calls these friends "little children" (13:33), underscoring his tender love for them.[4]

In this rich context Jesus commands his disciples to "love one another" (13:34). What should amaze you, especially if you've followed my thought to this point, is Jesus specifically calls this commandment "new." *How can it be new when love is not a "new" commandment at all?*[5]

This commandment is *not* entirely new. The moral counsel to love others is ancient. General parallels occur in the Old Testament and in rabbinic literature. Even ancient classical moralists wrote about love. What is truly original here is the *context of the command*—the new era following the coming of Jesus and the outpouring of the Spirit at Pentecost. There will now be a *new* internal motivation and a *new* personal relationship that did not exist before Jesus came (see Jeremiah 31:33–35 to grasp the way the prophet foresaw this era).

The *newness* of Jesus' command can be seen this way: It rests on the reality of his relationship *with* his disciples. It grows out of *relational* and filial love. The Father loved the Son, and the Son loved the Father. They mutually indwelled each other in eternal God-Love. This is *why* "God is love." What is "new" here is this: The love of God the Father and the Son (and later the Spirit) has *now been revealed for all the*

world to see in Jesus of Nazareth. In other words, the newness of this commandment rests on the *uniqueness* of Jesus'
love for his disciples. This love will be seen more powerfully
after Pentecost. These disciples' lives will be changed when
they learn to live with one another in Jesus' relational love.
This will be *the singular mark* of their *new* relationship with
Jesus. Pope Francis captures this truth well: "Our mission as
Christians is to conform ourselves evermore to Jesus as the
model of our lives."[6]

The translations of this command to "love one another"
are often weak. As a result we can miss the power of what
Jesus actually said. Here are several good renderings of the
new commandment (italics added):

> Love each other. *Just as* I have loved you, *you should* love
> each other (NLT).
>
> *Just as* I have loved you, so *you must* love one another (J.
> B. Phillips).
>
> You *must love* each other, *just as* I have loved you (Con-
> temporary English Version).

What is crucial is very clear when we examine accurate
translations of the commandment. Jesus' disciples are to love
one another with *the same love* Jesus had *for them* during
his sojourn. The *relationship* they enjoyed with him is the
model for how they are to relate to one another. This mutual love, rooted in the narratives of the Gospels, is *tough*
and *tender,* plainspoken yet gentle. It is honest, yet it doesn't
use the truth to hurt another person. This love is rooted in
the Golden Rule but it goes far beyond, moving directly into
the cares and fears of the other person. Jesus designates it
to express *the continuing relationship* between him and all
believers.[7] This love "opens up the possibility of community
with God and Jesus and community with one another, but
it is not an easy word to keep."[8] This is another reason I call
this "costly love"!

This new commandment love *defines* our relationship with other Christians. Anabaptist scholar Willard M.

Swartly says it is "the foundation and impulse of the hospitality and humble service permeating the chapter." The new commandment in John 13, as well as in 1 John, exemplifies the Johannine ethic "internally directed, with positive impact upon the church's mission to the world."[9] This is why I call this *missional love*! It leads to what I called *missional-ecumenism* in my book on unity (John 17:21).[10]

The disciples will no longer have Jesus in their midst to hold them together. There will be pressures upon them to divide or to pull apart. One of them has already been exposed as a traitor. And Peter will shortly deny Jesus and act in ways that could cause division. Whether these first disciples will hold together in Jesus' love will depend on their complete trust in Jesus and his promises. Will they be filled with the love he has given them or not?

Finally, we must not miss the historical redemptive context of the new commandment. The fullest demonstration of Jesus' love will come in his death on the cross. Just as he lays down his life for his disciples, so they must lay down their lives for one another. We've seen that Jesus commands us to love our neighbors as well as our enemies. But this *new* commandment to love is specific in a different way. *It is focused on other Christians.* Perhaps the Johannine community, to whom this Gospel was likely addressed, was faced with the loss of their aged leader, the Apostle John. None of Jesus' original apostles would be left after John passed away, so these Christians needed clarity about their future. The command to costly love would serve to recalibrate their life together. When Jesus' followers love one another his love will directly create a continuing mode of life experience within the Christian community that is "his presence" in the world. His love would remain in believers even when all the original apostles were gone. The Spirit would enable them to live this "love for one another." But John says more.

Our Love Is God's Sign to the World

In this new commandment Jesus conveyed what I believe to be the greatest apologetic ever given for the gospel: "By this everyone will know that you are my disciples, if you have love for one another" (John 13:35). For all the great intellectual work the church has done in defense of the faith, this is *the unique sign* that Jesus gave us to show how much he loved the whole world! *This is the mark of genuine Christianity.* God is real. Jesus is Lord. The Christian faith is true (John 17:21–23). When the *new* commandment is at the center of Christianity, the world can hear the gospel.

John's emphasis on intra-communal love is often seen as a license for sentimental complacency. "Let's all just get along," some say. This severely diminishes our Lord's new commandment, a distinctive call to costly sacrifice. Citing 1 John, biblical scholar Richard B. Hays says, "The Johannine talk of love does have practical implications. Love within the community is not merely a matter of warm feelings; rather it is a matter of action."[11] Yes, *action.* God-Love is never passive. It cost the Father the life of his own Son, and it cost the Son unimaginable torment in both body and soul. Hays adds that words like those in 1 John 3:11, 16–18, and 23 cover a wide range of activities. The point is clear: There is no sectarian retreat in the new commandment. We cannot hide in it and then write off the world. (Soon enough we will see why.)

The Scandal of Origen

Jesus is not commonly apprehended by direct physical sight. If the world believes in him, it will be because God's power and grace is made known to them through love. The world is most likely to believe in him when it *sees* Christians living together in relational love. Jesus continues to deal with the world in love until the end of this age. Perhaps so many in the West do not believe God is love because they have not seen Christians obey the new commandment.

Luke says Jesus came to seek, find, and free those held captive: "The Son of Man came to seek out and to save the lost" (19:10). How does the world know this profound truth? Certainly they know it through the preaching of the good news of the kingdom. But if we don't exemplify the greatest sign Christ gave to us—"love for one another"—then our preaching of the gospel will not work as God intended. The "world may [never] know that [the Father] ... sent [Jesus the Savior of the world]" unless we Christians obey the new commandment. This calls each of us to contribute to the preservation of the unity Jesus gave us (John 17:21–23). Pope Francis perceptively says, "Our mission as Christians is to conform ourselves evermore to Jesus as the model of our lives."[12]

I first became interested in Origen (186–253), one of the more intriguing figures in early Christian thought, because of two controversial issues in his life. First, he possessed a deep desire to know purity of heart in God's love. This is why he mistakenly took Matthew 19:12 literally and castrated himself. Second, he held several doctrines that some early Christian theologians consider heretical (e.g., he appears to have taught universalism, or the ultimate salvation of the entire human race!).[13] Although there are extremes in Origen's doctrine and practice, modern scholarship has taken a new look at his writing and now tends to see him as perhaps the greatest and most comprehensively *biblical Christian thinker* between Paul and Augustine. This fact alone should make us pay attention to Origen's thought. But what difference does this make?

Origen was the church's first writer to attempt a systematic theology of Christian teaching. Clearly a genius, at eighteen he became head of the famous Catechetical School in Alexandria. Demetrius, the bishop of Alexandria, asked Origen, a layman, to be the headmaster because of his brilliance. He studied and traveled widely, teaching in many cities of the ancient world. In AD 215 he went to Palestine, where the bishop asked him to preach. This put him in conflict with Demetrius, who felt laymen should not preach. When Origen returned to Palestine in 230, the bishop there ordained him, further alienating him from Demetrius. (His self-mutilation was condemned in Jewish law and was considered abhorrent in Roman culture; thus, a century later, in 325 the church officially condemned him.) Following the condemnation by Demetrius, Origen remained in Caesarea, opening another school and continuing his travels as a master teacher.

I tell this story because one of Origen's greatest personal trials was maintaining purity of heart in his conflict with the bishop of Alexandria. He was deeply hurt by the anger Demetrius directed toward him. (By this time he had come to realize the error of his self-mutilation.) Origen desired more than anything not to hate Bishop Demetrius. He wanted to love him with purity of heart. "The Logos (reason or the Word)" he wrote, "called him to stand firm for the contest and to preserve the inner self, lest haply evil thoughts should have power to bring the storm against my soul also."[14] History tells us Origen did weather this personal storm and that he did so by the power of Christ's costly love. Maybe his theology contained some error, but no theologian is always right.

In the end, I can only conclude Origen was profoundly flawed, yet a wonderful model of what it means to be forgiven and seek Christ as a disciple with a pure heart of love. He aimed, in his own words, to "see life steadily, and [to] see it whole."[15] We can draw encouragement from his aim.

Conclusion

In the blog article I cited at the end of chapter 8 my friend Frank Lesko referred to the elephant in the room for Christians—the clear commandment to love.[16] Like me, Frank laments that "we fail a most basic mark of the faith" so easily. He says it is "a downright scandal how rarely it is preached." But Jesus could not be clearer about this commandment and its priority. So what happened?

Frank writes, "We don't outright deny the Greatest Commandment. Oh no, we would never be so bold. Rather, we do something far more sinister—we just sort of brush it aside, put it on a pedestal and otherwise ignore it. We box it in, limit it, put the ropes around it because, in truth, it scares the living daylights out of us." My life experience confirms Frank's assessment.

Rarely, if ever, have I heard a Christian repudiate costly love. We know too much to do that. So what do we do with love? We box it in with rules, doctrines, rituals and all kinds of distractions. We replace Jesus' central teaching with something secondary. In doing so, we do not deny costly love outright. Instead, we do something far, far worse. We give it lip service and relegate it to an inconspicuous place. In a word, we become *indifferent*. I have come to realize that the true opposite of love is *not* hate, but *indifference*. Because of our growing indifference we believe that talking and singing about love means we are loving. But Jesus would have no part of this type of Christianity. He solemnly warned the first century church in Ephesus to regain their *first love* or he would remove their witness (Revelation 2:1–7). Could this be what Jesus is saying to today's church in the West?

CHAPTER TEN

HOW THE NEW COMMANDMENT WAS LOST

> By and large, love has remained only a sub-
> set of Christian truth and teaching. It has not
> been given priority as a core commandment
> of authentic Christianity.
>
> Gaylord Enns,
> *Love Revolution*

IN 1943, WORLD WAR II was raging around and over the Italian city of Trent. The German military occupied the city. The Allies dropped bombs almost daily, killing people, destroying property, and shattering youthful dreams. Young women were particularly broken as they saw everything they had hoped for passing away. But a young schoolteacher named Chiara Lubich asked a question God used to begin a new movement of love: "Is there a reason for living, a dream that does not die, an ideal to which we can give ourselves wholeheartedly, that no bomb can destroy?"[1] Chiara and her young friends discovered the answer in God-Love, a truth that dazzled their hearts in the midst of so much death and suffering. Because these humble Christians experienced a God who was very close to them, they could face their extreme circumstances with joy. Chiara later said,

> Our joy and amazement was so great that we did not hesitate an instant in choosing him, God-Love, as the Ideal of our life, just as we did not wait a minute to communicate

to the people around us (relatives, friends) our great discovery: "God is Love, God loves us. God loves you, God loves you all."[2]

These young women had found an ideal, but they realized at once that such great love called them to love God in return. They knew doing his will was the way to God. While the sirens were sounding, as often as eleven times a day, they'd run to the air-raid shelters for cover, taking with them their small copies of the four Gospels. They began to "live the gospel" one sentence at a time. They read "Love your neighbor as yourself" (Matthew 19:19) and asked, "Who is our neighbor?" The answer the Spirit gave led them to care for the dead and dying. Over time, Chiara says, they asked themselves this particular question: "Is there a word of the Gospel that is particularly pleasing to God? To make him happy, we would like to put that into practice before we die, at least in the last moments of our life."[3] Chiara says the word that God gave them was the new commandment of Jesus (John 13:34–35, 15:12, 15).

Here is Chiara's testimony in her own words, given at the Ecumenical Institute at Bossey in Switzerland, in October 2002:

> Struck by the beauty, by the challenging commitment, and by the radicality of these words, we looked at one another and declared ... we really believe, [in] an altogether special grace: "I am ready to give my life for you. And I for you. And I for you. ..." Every one of us for each of the others. It was a solemn pact which would become the foundation of the entire Movement, whose members would later open up to universal brotherhood with men and women in the whole world.[4]

Chiara Lubich was not an academic theologian, yet she stands as a remarkable witness to the power of Spirit-given divine love centered in Jesus. She said even when those young women were not required to die physically, their little group lived by this pact and died to themselves in order to live out Christ's love for one another. There is more deep theology in this act of love than in a stack of well-written books! Though still a young schoolteacher in war-torn Trent, Chiara was saying she and her companions *experienced* the radical reality of the new commandment. She understood with her whole heart that *mutual love* among Christians is the true measure of giving one's life to what Christ commanded.

Jesus' Central Command

Jesus' *central commandment* for his people is this: "Love one another, just as I have loved you" (John 13:34; 15:12, 17). If this command is central to following Jesus, then the root problem the church faces today is clear: *We do not truly love one another.* Mutual love does not mark our churches, our prayer gatherings or the many programs we undertake in Jesus' name. Chiara discovered that Jesus called this specific command *his own.* (Jesus said, "*I* give you.") She understood because this new commandment was central, everything else followed. This recalls a saying I heard as a young teen: "Jesus said it, I believe, that settles it." Chiara believed Jesus said it, so it was settled for her. She chose to live it and called others into a way of gospel life that later emerged into a lay ecclesial movement that still seeks to practice this love in every way possible.

This story of Chiara and her friends demonstrates powerfully that the only *true* Christian identity is costly love. The first Christians understood that they were called to love in this way. This is why *mutual* love marked their experience of life together in every way. Christians are still called to live with one another in this same love. This is why no denominational barriers, or other humanly defined standards, should be walls that hinder our active, intentional, costly love.[5]

New-Commandment Transformation

The monumental multi-volume work A *History of Christianity* by Kenneth Scott Latourette (1884–1968) provides a moving witness of the development of the postapostolic church. Latourette observed that over time Christianity fell short of its ideals and compromised its moral integrity. But there is more.

During the first five centuries of the Christian era, most people reached by the gospel lived within the Roman Empire. The church had moved east and developed within the Byzantine Empire, but Rome remained the center. Further, the main forms of Christian expression were forged during these first two or three centuries. Basic principles of the faith were grasped and the most formative creeds were formulated orally. The church went from a "sect of Judaism" to an empire-changing social and religious force. Yet Christianity was always threatened more from within than without. Divisions threatened the mission of Christ even while the apostles were still alive (see Acts 15). By the end of the second century, several intense struggles within the church had become prominent. When Constantine ended the legal persecution of the church (AD 313), the power of the state and church were co-mingled, creating more problems. As the empire declined, the church began to embrace state functions. This created *Christendom*.[6] Augustine addressed this problem in *The City of God*, in which he developed the idea of two great cities, one earthly, the other heavenly. Augustine realized these two cities were profoundly intermingled; thus, he believed, this struggle would continue until these two cities are separated at the final judgment.

So the question every modern Christian should ask is this: What happened to the powerful impact of the new commandment inside the Christian church? Jesus clearly designed the church to follow a particular way of life that was to be shaped by God-Love. Living out his new commandment was the means for their life together, and this life together was their God-given way of overcoming pagan culture. Latourette thus concludes the power of Jesus' death and resurrection was "displayed primarily in the transformation of those men and women who became followers of Christ, who put their trust in him." He adds, "The proof that they [the early Christians] had experienced this new birth, this resurrection to a new life, was to be seen in their 'fruits,' in the 'fruits of the Spirit.' These fruits were described in one place as 'love' (the Greek word is *agape*, namely, the kind of love displayed by God in Christ and by Christ in his self-giving)."[7] Jesus, speaking of the difference between true and false teachers, said plainly, "You will know them by their fruits" (Matthew 7:20). The core truth that distinguishes us is not our denomination or creed, but God-Love.

New life in the Spirit was birthed in God's love. This love worked itself out in the lives of Christians sharing in the practice of the new commandment. Tenderness, love, and mercy flowed like a mighty river through the life of the early church so long as love remained costly and Christ-centered.

But how did the church lose the powerful influence of the new commandment and follow a different course, especially by the middle of the fourth century?

The Loss of the New Commandment

The early church faced numerous heresies and trials. False and confusing notions about who Jesus was, as both God and man, and how believers should understand God, as both merciful and just, created disagreements that affected the health of the church. Add to these debates a multitude of ideas about the material and spiritual world, and you have a snapshot of the context in which a strong emphasis on the new commandment appears to have waned after the first several generations. The many debates Christians waged, especially with one another, seem so far from the letter and spirit of the New Testament that they would be virtually unthinkable if history did not tell us they really happened. Some context might help at this point.

Faithful bishops and teachers were required to defend the faith (see 1 and 2 Timothy). Initially the struggle took place primarily *inside* the church. This was true both ethically and philosophically. But by the beginning of the second century, shortly after the death of the last apostle, John, the church embraced what was eventually called the *regula fide* (Latin for "rule of faith"). This was one of several expressions used to indicate the common core of teaching that churches everywhere embraced, even though there were still some differences. *This teaching summarized the essential truths of the Jesus story in a positive way.* The mainstream church, as opposed to sectarian groups such as the Gnostics (who professed a "private" knowledge of God), saw the need to hold on to the *essence* of Jesus' teaching in a confessional way. Almost every historian concurs with this portrait, although there are differences in how they interpret it.

Converts who wanted to unite with an early Christian congregation were catechized (taught) in the way of Jesus, then baptized. The more this new faith in the Jewish Messiah spread beyond Judaism, especially after A.D. 70, the more effort was required of the church leaders to catechize and form these new members (many of whom were Gentiles) into this "once for all" system of belief. After the fall of Jerusalem, Jews and Christians experienced a painful separation that in the second century culminated in an even greater division.[8] This second division led to a virulent strain of anti-Semitism that has hampered the church's witness ever since. This unfortunate divide between those who accepted only the older (Hebrew) covenant and those who also accepted the new covenant led to what is called replacement theology, or supersessionism. This eventually became mainstream in the Christian church and holds that the church *completely replaced Israel* as God's covenant people. It's also why some Christians have held the view that the continued existence of Jews, especially those who did not accept Jesus as the Messiah, was a form of dissent and rebellion against Christ. Replacement theology (supersessionism) became a tenet in some parts of the church and in many cases, whether understood or not, remains so. The Holocaust forced a reevaluation of this unbiblical theology and has led many modern Christian theologians, especially within the Catholic Church, to reject this teaching as heretical and dangerous. The historical realities of this shift are being worked out in the twenty-first century as many theologians, as well as churches, now come to grips with this dark side of our history.[9]

We must never forget Jesus commanded the church to share the Good News with both Jews and Gentiles. This Good News involved teaching and baptizing all those who believed (Matthew 28:18–20). Christianity was, and still is, a deeply missionary religion. If we indeed follow Christ, Christians have no option about this. We must share the gospel. The Lausanne Movement's Cape Town Commitment says this well: "The heart of God longs that all people should have access to the knowledge of God's love and of his saving work through Jesus Christ."[10] Note this statement says the church is to give people "access to the knowledge of God's love." *We do not coerce people into conversion.* We give "access" to God's love. This missionary mandate does not require us to reject the Jews, nor does it require us to view other religious people as our enemies. When the church moved into the global mission context, it often followed the path of a more-developed marriage of church and state in what has been called Christendom. Only centuries later did the church recover the vision of making disciples in all nations. When it did, the church often carried with that vision a virulent, hostile reaction to the faith claims of non-Christians. In our modern Western context, perhaps nothing has more hindered the church from being and living costly love among our neighbors than this pattern of religious intolerance.

Furthermore, Christianity was never meant to be a private "insider" cult but a public faith with implications for all people. The gospel is great news for the whole world (John 3:16). This explains why the early church avoided imperial debates within Rome while continuing to live godly and faithful lives in public and private. Thus, the more the church defined the faith and faced fierce external opposition, the more challenging it became to practice the new commandment.

These problems remain with us today, though they often take different forms. C. S. Lewis explained this when he said atheism is "too simple." But he pointed out another approach that was even worse than atheism. He called this approach "Christianity-and-water." I'd call it "watered-down Christianity" or "Christianity Lite." Lewis added, "This is the idea that simply says there is a good God in Heaven and everything is all right—leaving out all the difficult and terrible doctrines about sin and hell and the devil, and the redemption." Lewis derided such thinking as "boys' philosophies."[11] He focused his apologetic emphasis upon helping the church understand the core teaching and practice of true Christianity, what he called "mere Christianity." This vision of Christianity was never meant to become "doctrine lite"! It was a vision of deep faith rooted in the essential truths that all true Christians everywhere accept. Like his predecessors Søren Kierkegaard in the nineteenth century and Dietrich Bonhoeffer in the twentieth, C. S. Lewis wanted to show that Christianity is a radical faith that requires serious effort to be properly understood. This leads to my main point: *Disagreements are not our central problem*. If we embrace "mere Christianity," we can work on our differences within Christ's love while we carefully maintain the vital center of core faith. This way of thinking may not be the last word, but I believe love requires it be the first.

Having acknowledged the unity of the church, expressed in the core teaching of the apostles and in historical developments like the *regula fidei*, I believe it is equally important to balance this "pattern of truth" with what has been called the "emergence of diversity." Alister McGrath concludes there are reasons for acknowledging diversity from the beginning of the early church, even if later developments embraced it in problematic ways. McGrath names several specific factors that contributed to diversity, such as (1) different interpretations of aspects of faith that would later be gathered into the New Testament itself, (2) a great diversity in patterns of worship, (3) different understanding within the early churches of core aspects of the faith, and (4) an inability to enforce uniformity. Remember, Christianity was a tiny minority group living on the fringes of society.[12]

In the fourth century another misfortune beset the church. In one sense it was necessary to hold church councils and to debate. But these councils were also highly political. The unity of the Roman Empire was at stake, since it now represented Christendom. Bishops kept this in mind as they made decisions. Again, I am not arguing the results were all mistaken, but a search of the Canons and Dogmatic Decrees from the Seven Councils,[13] a compendium of doctrinal developments from the fourth through the eighth centuries, reveals the sinister evolution of anti-Semitism. These developments fostered major errors embraced by the church's expanding definitions of orthodoxy after the earliest church councils. *Sadly, the theological statements in these various decrees never mentioned the new commandment.*

Save for the writings of a few church fathers, following the death of the apostles the new commandment seems to have disappeared from the confessions of the church. Even though writers such as Cyprian and Augustine condemned schism and disunity, such developments became commonplace. The church in Rome sought to maintain Christian unity, even by force, but eventually lost the battle. The Great Schism in 1054 split Christianity into Eastern and Western churches. (Most agree that even before the formal eleventh-century schism this de facto division had existed for centuries.) During the early decades of the sixteenth century the door to reform and renewal remained closed, even though the Catholic Church had been facing new movements and challenges long before Luther. But in 1517 the church suffered another cataclysmic division, a schism over issues as much social and political as religious. This division, the Protestant Reformation, released centuries of conflict and pain that still plague Christians to the present time. Only in the last hundred years or so, through various movements called ecumenism, has there been serious movement toward healing the separation and animosity the Reformation brought about. Without doubt, schism and disunity have thwarted the mission of Christ, perhaps more than any other catastrophe in all of Christian history.

Concept Fabrication

The gospel is clearly God's greatest revelation. This story is our salvation. Yet in addition to our painful divisions, another intellectual development has thwarted love and unity—our tendency to reduce the Good News to concepts. Even the best-intentioned Christians try to reduce the gospel to "simple" words. Others, with equally valid concerns, want to explain it in terms of rigid doctrinal concepts. Both approaches lead the church into ditches that can prove dangerous, if not deadly.

Though it may be upsetting to discuss frankly the way we interpret the gospel, doing so often opens a door for deeper conversation in love. Remember, the context for what Jesus taught about love was rooted not in concepts but in action. The goal is always the well-being of the other person. This action requires care, support, effort, and personal expenditure; it is costly. As we've seen, neither the Hebrew words for love and lovingkindness nor the singular Greek word agape reduce divine love to "warm feelings." Applying Jesus' teaching means everything—*everything*—we believe and practice stands under this commandment of love. We can have our Scripture texts down pat, grasp brilliant and insightful theology, and serve the work of Christ with all our ability yet still fail to love. So here's an honest question: Do we use our insights to manipulate and shame others? If so, we fail the Savior. Do we embrace economic, political, and social views, yet take advantage of others? Do we see those who hold ideologies different from our own as "troublesome liberals" or "opinionated conservatives"? If so, we fail the test. After two thousand years, Christians still fail this test of love. The clearest commandment remains. We can follow the new commandment again if we have the will to do so. But it will cost us. We will be required to die first before we can be raised to God-Love in Jesus! This ultimately begins with you and me responding to God's call.

We all have methods for thinking, feeling, analyzing, measuring, judging, accepting, and rejecting. We want to know if something is true, right, and good. But what has costly love to do with all this? I believe the problem lies in the methods we commonly use for determining the truth, which are rooted in our common (fallen) humanity. We learn these methods from our parents, our religious teachers, our culture and our personal experience. It is hard for us to see and understand how profoundly these methods keep us from accepting and loving the other.

My friend George Koch illustrates this idea with an analogy of two doors, one marked "God" and the other marked "Lectures about God." George says that everyone tends to line up at the second door because it is far easier to enter than it is to engage in the demanding struggle required to enter the first. But this is where love and truth actually meet. We must go through the door marked "God." This is what the mystics and pietists understood. This is the door that prompted some of the church's greatest minds to doubt that a complete system of theology could ever be developed. (You can see this doubt in such great thinkers as Augustine, Aquinas, Kierkegaard, Barth, Calvin, and Luther.) This is what ordinary, everyday Christians instinctively know when they walk with Christ and humbly read the Scriptures. They are seeking Truth not in propositions and formulas, but in the person of Christ. Koch concludes, "What is most insidious among those who claim belief in God is the idolatry of religious doctrine, worship, polity and culture, and the use of disagreement as an excuse to mistreat others."[14] This insight explains how I lost the love commandment in my own life.

Jesus had reason when he was asked about the greatest commandment to answer by speaking about *two* commandments. Had he said the greatest commandment is to love God only, then love for God could have been used as an excuse for all manner of behavior. Sadly, this is what many religious people do. In the name of love for God they have destroyed others, whether in actual persecution or with their words and attitudes. But the second commandment is "like" the first. Jesus closes up any loopholes by which we might seek to embrace sound doctrine without loving our neighbors. In the new commandment he underscores this even more powerfully by showing us how mutual love for all our brothers and sisters in Christ is at the heart of real faith. This means "love for one another" is the truest standard for behavior in the Christian church.

Ultimately, the new commandment was lost when the instruction and content of the entire Bible became a platform for debate and disagreement. As a result, we missed the most fundamental message of all: to love God and our neighbors—and our enemies—and then in Christ to love one another deeply. It is easy to extract various themes and messages from the Bible and make those concepts into the sum and substance of true faith. When we do this, we rarely place love at the center. Concepts become "the truth," replacing Jesus who is himself "the way, the truth and the life" (John 14:6). Truth is not a set of ideas; it is the person of Jesus.

We can also explore the cultural sources of tension between intellectual concepts and the new commandment. In the Greco-Roman world, the culture and methods of the time influenced the church. How do we use the culture and methods of our time to communicate the gospel without compromising the core of our faith? This tension is unavoidable. For example, within this tension there developed the Christian theology of two natures (one fully divine, one fully human) in the one person of Jesus. I believe this doctrine is in the New Testament, but clearly it is not as fully expressed there as in the creeds. The doctrine was developed within a Greek framework. The problem isn't with the doctrinal conclusion but with how these Greek methods were used to analyze texts and extract ideas. These ideas then became even more abstracted into categories and concepts. This is still happening in powerful ways that destroy love and unity.

What's wrong with this picture? George Koch offers an explanation:

> Once a doctrine gains sufficient prominence, it tends to draw not just advocates, but worshipers. Instead of worshiping God alone, we worship doctrines about God, and promote and defend them passionately. They are easier to understand and control than a Being Who is Holy, Wholly Other, Omnipotent and Omniscient.[15]

If we truly believe God loves us, Koch concludes, then God's power and otherness likely will frighten us. But turning doctrines into concepts is only a short step away from their becoming idols. Doctrines, ideologies, ecclesial positions, nations, and races become idols for which we give our lives, and sometimes take the lives of others. But idolatry is our real problem. If love defines us, we will we cherish unity. If we cherish unity, we will not allow these concepts to become idolatrous forms. This is what healthy theology does, all in the service of love for Christ and the church.

Conclusion

Peter Meiderlin, a seventeenth-century Lutheran, sums up my argument: "We would be in the best shape if we kept in essentials, unity; in non-essentials, liberty; and in both, charity."[16] Interestingly enough, this statement about unity is taken from a tract written during one of the bloodiest eras in Christian history, the Thirty Years' War (1618–48). It began as a Catholic-Protestant conflict, but over time devolved into a great struggle between the powers of Europe. Estimates say it reduced the population of the Germanic states by 25 to 40 percent. It also brought about a new way of solving state conflicts that was more secular than religious.

Let's define Meiderlin's three terms.

First, an *essential* is something truly necessary, something required for the faith to remain anchored in Jesus Christ. In mathematics we say "if and only if." This means the premise must be true in order to reach the correct conclusion.

Second, a *non-essential* can be profoundly important—even something taught in Scripture—but it is not necessary for being a faithful disciple. It may shed light on the faith "once for all given," but it is not required for living faith.

Third, *charity* means love. This is how we should treat one another even if we disagree. We should speak with edifying words, act with kindness, and refer to the other person in the way we want to be spoken about. Even when we disagree about essentials (as the church rightly did with the Arians, who denied an essential truth about the person of Christ), we have no excuse for a lack of love. The challenge is clear. We need to learn how to engage in serious dialogue about important ideas while still loving one another. Paul left us instruction about how to do this (see 2 Corinthians 10:1–6). He said we can do this when our weapons are not merely human words but Spirit-directed words. These words destroy prideful arguments that have become strongholds against the knowledge of God. Our goal should be to "take every thought captive to obey Christ" (verse 5). All of Paul's references here transcend the worldly way we argue, when we attack people and motives. Before long we equate true worship with gaining advocates for our understanding. When this happens, the new commandment is lost and love is trampled down. The next several chapters of 2 Corinthians are some of the most deeply personal and autobiographical of all Paul's letters. What he desires is that believers obey Christ, the one who redeemed them through his costly love. The obedience he seeks is plain; thus, our love for God and for one another should triumph over human words and heated debates.

CHAPTER ELEVEN

THE WAY OF THE NEW COVENANT

> The church is the fellowship of those who have
> been loved to the limit and who are called to
> love in the same kind of way.
>
> George Beasley Murray

IN THE PREVIOUS CHAPTER I shared the story of how
Chiara Lubich discovered God-Love. She said there were
at least three wondrous gifts Jesus "held hidden in his
heart." He openly revealed all three of them on his last night
with his disciples.

*First, Jesus revealed the meaning and power of the Lord's
Supper, the Eucharist.* The synoptic Gospels present accounts
of this meal (Matthew 26:17; Mark 14:12–16; Luke 22:15).
John does not record the celebration of the Eucharist, but it
clearly fits into the context of John 13–17. (Recall the words
of Jesus in John 6 as well.) During Jesus' final evening with
his disciples he broke the bread and blessed the cup. These
acts became the memorial to his death for the salvation of
the world. Regardless of our belief about what God does in
this meal, Jesus surely gave it to Christians out of deep love
so all his people would be fed the food of divine life "until he
comes" (1 Corinthians 11:26).

*Second, in washing his disciples' feet, Jesus gave them a
clear vocation: They were to be like him in giving pure, unself-
ish service to one another* (John 13:13–17). "If you *know* these
things, you are blessed if you *do* them" (verse 17, emphasis

added). Whether or not you literally wash the feet of others, this act of humble service portrays immense power. The entire scene is filled with profound symbolism. Jesus "washed" their feet (13:5–8, 12, 14), yet when Peter heard what this amazing act meant, he asked for a bath. Jesus replied that this request was redundant (13:10) because all the disciples (except for the betrayer) had already been made "clean" (13:10) by receiving the word/teaching of Jesus (15:3). Jesus would finish this work of cleansing through his death and resurrection. This is the same truth John underscores when he writes, "if we walk in the light as he himself is in the light, we have fellowship with one another, and the blood of Jesus his Son cleanses us from all sin" (1 John 1:7).

The third gift Jesus revealed is "the new commandment" (John 13:34). Bill Hartnett says Chiara Lubich "recognized that these three gifts were equally new but found something *completely unprecedented* in the new commandment" (italics added). She believed Christians had all but "forgotten" this commandment.[1]

The Covenant Joined with a Commandment

John's account shows a new covenant being enacted in these final hours—in the meal, the cross, and the resurrection that followed. The Spirit-empowered connection between the new covenant and the new commandment underscores the nature of costly love.

Before we proceed we should briefly consider the meaning of the word *covenant*. A covenant is an agreement between two parties that mutually binds them to undertake certain actions on behalf of each other. A covenant between God and us is best understood as a *gracious agreement freely entered into by God for the benefit and blessing of humanity.* Such a covenant has *specific* promises for those who receive God's promises by faith and commit themselves to honor them through what Paul calls "the obedience of faith" (Romans 1:5; 16:25–27). The prophet Jeremiah spoke of this new covenant (Jeremiah 31:31–34) bringing the final work of salvation into the world in "the last days" (Acts 2:17; Hebrews

1:1–2). Thus the new covenant is at the *center* of God's revelation of love.

I missed this connection between love and the covenant until 1991, when I began to reflect on it deeply as I preached through John 13–17. I now see a profound union between the new covenant and the new commandment. This union is central to an authentic, life-changing Christianity. Could it be that some of our most profound problems in the church lie in a better understanding of the relationship of the new covenant and new commandment?

Consider the relationship of the Ten Commandments to the covenant God made with Israel at Mount Sinai. A simple reading of Deuteronomy 30 reveals that the law of Moses was intimately connected with this Mosaic covenant. The same pattern is followed here. Jesus, the greater Moses (Hebrews 3), inaugurates a *new* covenant and gives a *new* commandment. But there's even more.

There are many *new* elements within this covenant. (In every text and comment that follows, observe that I use the plural "we," rather than "me" or "I." I do this because these new covenant realities are designed to be experienced corporately.) We have been given *new* birth (1 Peter 1:3). We have become a *new* creation (2 Corinthians 5:17; Galatians 6:15). We have *newness* of life (Romans 6:4) and we constitute a *new* humanity (Ephesians 2:15–16). We have put on the *new* self (Ephesians 4:24) and we've been given a *new* life in the Spirit (Romans 7:6). And Jesus says one commandment ties all of these together in the new covenant: "Love one another." This *new* covenant is now written on our hearts (Jeremiah 31:31–33). These words convey the content the Spirit writes indelibly on our hearts. It can be summarized in the richness and beauty of the love of God.

Just before he departed, Jesus promised to give "the Advocate" (literally the Helper) *when* he completed the work of establishing this new covenant. The triune God would come to indwell the followers of Jesus permanently and turn their sadness into joy. This God-given joy would become paramount evidence of God's indwelling love (John 16:5–28). Pope Francis captured this in a 2013 Angelus address:

> Love is the greatest power for the transformation of reality because it pulls down the walls of selfishness and fills the ditches that keep us apart. This is the love that comes from a mutated heart, from a heart of stone that has been turned into a heart of flesh, a human heart.[2]

Through this covenant, written on "tablets of human hearts" (2 Corinthians 3:3), the world can now see God's love because his joy and love are in us (John 17:21–23). Pope Francis reiterates this when he says our hearts will "light up" with a joy that spreads to everyone around us when we are truly in love with Jesus. As important as doctrine is—and it would prove tremendously important in the few centuries that followed—this covenant and this commandment must become *primary* if we desire to be close to the witness of Jesus. Paul understood this life-sustaining connection when he wrote, "We don't need to write to you about the importance of loving each other, for God himself has taught you to love one another" (1 Thessalonians 4:9, NLT). Note the tense: "God himself *has taught* you." Paul also wrote that believers become "living letters" *because* "God himself has taught [us] to love one another" (2 Corinthians 3:3).

The Spirituality of Communion

In the early years of her life Chiara Lubich began to experience what can only be called mystical insights. *What I find remarkable is these experiences actually came about as she and her friends sought to live out the new commandment faithfully.* Key words we've been considering from John's Gospel gripped their souls. Words like: "As I have loved you," "emptied himself," and "became nothing" were woven together in their shared lives. Chiara and her friends understood it was Jesus alone who gave this unity. They had this experience and received this insight because they had been "with Jesus." They truly believed they had been "in the bosom of the Father." Because of their mystical union with the Father,

Son, and Holy Spirit, these twentieth-century Italian believers practiced a *new* (yet ancient) form of spiritual life. Chiara called it "collective spirituality," or "a spirituality of communion." They believed those who live this spirituality place the new commandment at the center of everything. The whole of their lives was governed by this one commandment. In community they discovered how people could live in vital unity even when they had serious differences and problems. They came to realize they were called to live out Christ's self-emptying love by taking on one another's joys and sorrows. They sought to become empty in order to become one!

This "spirituality of community" is not new! It is central to Jesus' teaching in John 13–17 and directly connected to the new covenant. This is nothing other than trinitarian spirituality, a spirituality virtually lost to many in the West.[3] In the midst of suffering, Christians are again discovering the power and spirituality of communion. Pope Francis has called this "the ecumenism of blood."

The philosopher Alfred North Whitehead once said religions commit suicide when they find their inspiration in dogma. While I do not endorse his process theology, a philosophy that stresses the liberty of becoming *over* being in the nature of God, I could not agree more on this point. Our true inspiration does not come from an idea (or dogma) but a spirituality that keeps love at the center of everything.

I discovered the power of this Spirit-given spirituality several years ago when I spent three days with Brother Yun, an exiled Chinese house-church leader who had spent almost twenty years in prison. He taught me the power and spirituality of communion. He radiated joy and deep love. I felt privileged to have experienced this newness of life in this little man. He made me long for much more. I discovered there really was no secret at all. *He lived each moment in the power of the new covenant and the new commandment.* Even though some Christians were fiercely attacking him, he did not attack them in response. He prayed much and loved deeply, thereby living in abiding joy.[4]

Another man who lived in the joy of this "Spirit-given spirituality" was François-Xavier Nguyễn Văn Thuận (1928–2002), the former archbishop of Ho Chi Minh City (previously Saigon), Vietnam. In 1975, just a few weeks after he had been nominated bishop, Văn Thuân was arrested. He spent the next thirteen years of his life in a Hanoi prison, nine of them in solitary confinement. Every two weeks the warden would change the guards assigned to him because if they spent more than that they became, in Văn Thuân's words, "contaminated" by his Christianity. In his book *Five Loaves and Two Fish*, he tells one story of "contaminating" his guards:

> It was very difficult for my guards to understand how one can forgive, can love one's enemies, reconcile oneself with them.
>
> "Do you really love us?"
>
> "Yes, I sincerely love you."
>
> "Even when we treat you so badly? When you suffer because you have been in prison for so many years without a trial?"
>
> "Think about the years we have lived together. I really love you!"
>
> "When you are free, you won't send your people to take revenge on us and our families?"
>
> "No, I will continue to love you, even if you want to kill me."
>
> "But why?"
>
> "Because Jesus has taught me how to love you. If I do not, I am no longer worthy to be called a Christian."[206]

Our Fundamental Problem

If Chiara Lubich is right, we should ask: What is the fundamental problem behind the dysfunction of the modern church? The simple answer is that *we have blocked the flow of God-Love, and in so doing, have thwarted God's purpose for the church.* I fear our poor reputation with the world is warranted because we have not practiced "a spirituality of community." We are not joyful lovers of one another or our neighbors.

I want to be clear. We should not seek to become a loving community in order to "build" the church or grow our ministries numerically. A spirituality rooted in the new commandment is *not* a method. Pastor Gregory Boyd says we must not engage in mutual love to "get a reputation."[6] We must "live outrageous love." Only when our love is costly will we change the world. If we make love into a program, we quickly reduce it to a *means* to an end. The difference is obvious: We must live in the fullness of Christ's love and joy with one another so we display God's love without trying to create outcomes. This is commanded of us three times in John 13:34 and 15:12, 17. We get our reputation from the world in response to our influence. If we live "the spirituality of community," the world will notice. Boyd correctly concludes,

> Our one need is to simply be people who are loved for free, who are filled with love for free, and who therefore love all other people for free. Our need is to join in the dance of the triune God, to celebrate in God's triune self-celebration, and thus to live and love in the fullness of triune love.[7]

The New Covenant: "Grace and Truth"

Jesus said his new covenant would fulfill the old covenant in a radical way. Paul spoke of this, as did the writer of Hebrews. But John only uses the word *covenant* once in the entirety of his writing (Revelation 11:19). This puzzled me until I realized that John had a different purpose than other biblical writers. He makes a point of showing how Christ inaugurated the new order in *continuity* with the promises God made with Israel. This requires explanation, but it solves a host of problems created by our nagging misperceptions about radical disconnections between the covenant, law, grace and love.

Before we proceed, we must understand the centrality of the covenant to the biblical narrative. God established the covenant as the sole basis of his gracious love for Israel (Deuteronomy 4:37; 7:7–8; Exodus 14:13–14, 31; 19:4). Israel had only to receive the gracious benefits God offered. Yet he configured this covenant so each generation would enjoy the blessings—the land, their progeny, his presence and favor—*if* they walked in his statutes and ordinances. If Israel kept the covenant, being holy as God was holy, they'd become royal priests among the nations (Exodus 19:5; Leviticus 26:3–13; Deuteronomy 28:1–14; 30:15–16; Joshua 23:1–4). But if they disobeyed/broke the covenant, curses would come upon them (Leviticus 26:14–39; Deuteronomy 28:15–68; 30:17–18; Joshua 23:15–16). True faith in God manifests itself in obedience. God promised unilaterally to bless Abraham and his descendants (Genesis 12:1; 17:1–2, 9–14; 18:19; 22:15–18; 26:1–5). In another covenant he gave the same blessing to the house of King David (2 Samuel 7:14; Psalm 89:30–32; 132:12).

The nation and the people were continually reminded to obey God's law, through which he revealed his love. Most of Israel's story, at least from Judges to 2 Kings, shows how the nation proved unfaithful. The result was a long captivity in Babylon. Yet out of this story emerged a theme in the writings of the prophets. God would once again undertake to bless his people. In "the last days" he would purify them and put his Spirit within them so they would have a deep inward motivation to love and obey (Isaiah 59:20–12; Jeremiah 31:31–34; Ezekiel 36:24–31).

In this new covenant God said repentance, faith, and obedience would still be necessary; thus, the new covenant would not be *radically* different (Leviticus 26:41; Deuteronomy 30:10). But it would be *new*: "Then you shall remember your evil ways, and your dealings that were not good; and you shall loathe yourselves for your iniquities and your abominable deeds" (Ezekiel 36:31). What *distinguishes* the old and new covenants? Many have made the mistake of saying the new covenant is a covenant *without* law.

John plainly describes the contrast between the old and new covenant: "The law indeed was given through Moses;

grace and truth came through Jesus Christ" (John 1:17). By no means is he denying that grace and truth were revealed in the Torah. We must grasp the entirety of John's idea:

> The Word became flesh and lived among us, and we have seen his glory, the glory as of a father's only son, full of grace and truth. (John testified to him and cried out, "This was he of whom I said, 'He who comes after me ranks ahead of me because he was before me.'") From his fullness we have all received, grace upon grace. The law indeed was given through Moses; grace and truth came through Jesus Christ. No one has ever seen God. It is God the only Son, who is close to the Father's heart, who has made him known (John 1:14–18).

John is saying grace did come through Moses, but *in Christ the new covenant takes this earlier expression of grace to a whole new realm.* The new covenant is a *qualitative advance* because now, "grace and truth [have come] through Jesus Christ." If we compare John with Paul, the closest parallel is in 2 Corinthians 3:9–11, where the apostle contrasts the splendor of the old covenant with the *unsurpassing* and *permanent* splendor of the new. We should be careful not to force into John the antithesis Paul articulates between law and gospel. The two are writing about different concerns. Without going into complicated matters of biblical theology, I concur with Paul Rainbow, who writes, "Paul's negative view of the law is a corollary of his associating it with the history of an unbelieving nation still in solidarity with Adam."[8] Paul views the old covenant (law) from the standpoint of the mass of Israelites who broke it. John views it from the standpoint of the "faithful remnant in Israel, who found in it the grace of God that led to life" (Ps 119:92–93).[9] The contrast between these perspectives is clear if we compare Paul's words in Romans 8:7, "[T]he mind that is set on the flesh is hostile to God; it does not submit to God's law," with John's words in 1 John 5:1: "For the love of God is this, that we obey his commandments. And his commandments are not burdensome." Before his conversion, Paul was a Jew who had believed his own righteousness was based on his accomplishments in

173

Judaism. John, so far as we can tell, possessed a deep and true faith in the God of Israel that was rooted in grace even before he personally met Jesus. But by being with Jesus, and seeing in him the hope of Israel firsthand, John had embraced this exceedingly marvelous and superior "grace and truth" *in the person of the Messiah.* If we lose these distinctions, through incongruent interpretation, we lose the entire structure of the Bible's story.

So what is *the fundamental characteristic* that makes the new covenant genuinely *new?* John answers, "grace and truth." What Isaiah, Jeremiah and Ezekiel prophesied has come. God has broken into human history and "taken away the sin of the world" (John 1:29). The writer of Hebrews sums this up succinctly: "Long ago God spoke to our ancestors in many and various ways by the prophets, but in these last days he has spoken to us by a Son, whom he appointed heir of all things, through whom he also created the worlds" (Hebrews 1:1–2). The contrast between the old and the new is *not* between working for salvation (works) *and* trusting God for salvation (faith). The contrast is *internal.* It is the difference between emphasizing obedience to God's *promises* and emphasizing obedience to the *Promised One* who *is* the ultimate revelation of his divine love. This brings us full-circle to the eternal, relational love of the Trinity.

Two statements in John's Gospel demonstrate this point. Some Jews asked Jesus what they must do to meet their religious obligations. In the first statement, Jesus replied, "This is the work of God, that you believe in him whom he has sent" (John 6:29). Jesus sums up the covenantal duties of human persons to God, defined under the old covenant by the Torah, in *one* basic requirement: *to believe in Jesus as the Christ.* But is that all there is? Yes, it really is! But we must understand that living faith in the new covenant brings with it forgiveness, new birth and the power of Spirit-given joy and love. If we are in union with Christ, our lives are internally transformed. Paul expresses it thus: "So if you have been raised with Christ, seek the things that are above, where Christ is, seated at the right hand of God. Set your minds on things that are above, not on things that are on earth, for you have died, and your life is hidden with Christ in God" (Colossians 3:1–3). If we live apart from Jesus Christ, we remain in bondage to sin. All our human attempts to please God will fail (John 8:24, 34). But in Christ, Paul says, "I can do all things through him who strengthens me" (Philippians 4:13). This is true liberty, the freedom to live faithfully in "grace and truth" through deep relationship with the Messiah who in his life, death and resurrection saves us and puts the Spirit (Helper) within us.

John underscores this a second time in John 3:16, though we must read the whole context (3:16–21) to understand the power of love. Here the final judgment is in plain view. Note the last verse: "But those who do what is true come to the light...their deeds have been done in God." The believer who knows Christ through faith produces "deeds" that will be counted as "true" (worthy) because they were "done in God" through faith in Christ. There is, therefore, no sharp division between faith and works, or law and grace. We do the deeds of faith because we are loved and accepted. God's love and joy is in us; thus, we love him *because* he first loved us (1 John 4:19).

What should we conclude about the *new* covenant and its relationship to the *new* commandment? Paul Rainbow says that God does not put the "burden of performing his stipulations on his human partner unaided. A redeemed human being is no independent subject capable of acting without God's moving. God performs God's works in and through the human agent."[10] God requires the removal of our sins. He does this "once for all" in Christ's death (Hebrews 7:27; 9:12, 26). He gives the Spirit to us who believe so that now we participate in the divine nature and accomplish his will. We walk in the light because he *is* the light. We have fellowship with other believers because we are together in his love. This is the "spirituality of communion."

We must go to God together. I have stressed going to him in private. I do not challenge this practice when it retains its proper place. But going to him in private can never fulfill the new commandment; it can only be practiced within the spirituality of the new covenant. This is why we must practice a "spirituality of communion."

Let me emphasize again that we do not *earn* union with God. We receive it, and we are changed by it (John 14:25–31; 15:1–11; 16:4–15). This is how we should read the *new commandment* within the biblical context of the *new covenant*. John makes this plain:

> As the Father has loved me, so I have loved you; abide in my love. If you keep my commandments, you will abide in my love, just as I have kept my Father's commandments and abide in his love. I have said these things to you so that my joy may be in you, and that your joy may be complete. This is my commandment, that you love one another as I have loved you. No one has greater love than this, to lay down one's life for one's friends. You are my friends if you do what I command you. (John 15:9–14)

The new covenant is rooted in God's love. As participants in the work of the Spirit we respond to his love, then "love one another." When this happens, we rightly understand what I referred to as the *qualitative newness* of the covenant *and* the commandment.

What Is Your Deepest Desire?

A conversation that united the ministries of Francis and Clare of Assisi has stirred believers for centuries. The story beautifully captures the way the new commandment works within the new covenant.

"What is your desire?" Francis asked the teenage girl. "God," she answered.

This brief exchange, says Brendan Leahy, "launched Clare into a new life. The beautiful eighteen-year-old, full of hopes and dreams, knew how to envelop the desires of her heart in the one Being truly worthy of our love: God who is Love."

Leahy says Clare's simple answer poses a more precise question, which I believe is the *only* one that matters in our modern, fast-paced world: Is there a summary commandment that pleases God so much that we can discover the invisible but real presence of Jesus among us? Answer: "I give you a new commandment, that you love one another. Just as I have loved you, you also should love one another. By this everyone will know that you are my disciples, if you have love for one another" (John 13:34–35). Leahy adds, "I too am called to envelop the desires of my heart in God, a love expressed ... in love for one another."[11]

The Beloved Apostle

John has been called "the beloved apostle." Traditionally, paintings of the Last Supper depict him as the man leaning on his Lord's chest. Several centuries after John's death, Jerome related how shortly before John died in his ninth decade of life, others would lift him up to speak in a service of worship. And he would say, "Little children, love one another, love one another, love one another." With a little imagination I can picture someone in the crowd who remembered John as one of the "sons of thunder" (Mark 9:33–41). Just think, the son of thunder and fire is now the aged and beloved apostle of love. This gives me hope. When I look back on my own life, I see too much thunder and lightning. I agree with the person who said the best thing about youth is we likely have a lot of time to repent. This has certainly been true for me.

But obviously seeing great potential in John, Jesus invited this young man into his innermost circle. Along with Peter and James, he became one of the three most intimate followers of Jesus. Yet the Gospels of Matthew, Mark, and Luke present three unflattering incidents in John's life, revealing him as ambitious, having a temper that bordered on explosive, and possessing an intolerant heart (Luke 9:51–56; Mark 10:34–45; Mark 9: 33–41).

I sometimes wonder if my mother foresaw something like this in naming me John, especially after watching me struggle in my early years with my passions, desires, and my intellectual orientation toward intolerance. Mark 9:38 captures the point. In my words I can hear John saying something like this: "Lord, I see someone who says he is a Christian but he does not believe what I do, nor does he act like he should, so he cannot be one of yours. This guy is not only wrong but he is not nearly as spiritual as I am." Jesus answered John with strength and kindness (Mark 9:39–40), which gives me hope.

Conclusion

At the beginning of the millennium John Paul II wrote an apostolic letter urging Christians to yearn for a deeper faithfulness to God's plan: "Before making practical plans, we need to promote a spirituality of communion."

> A spirituality of communion also means an ability to think of our brothers and sisters as "those who are a part of me." This makes us able to share their joys and sufferings, to sense their desires and attend to their needs, to offer them deep and genuine friendship.[12]

This spirituality of communion makes all my brothers and sisters God's "gift for me."

Thérèse of Lisieux reasoned that under the old covenant God clearly told his people to love their neighbors. *Under the new he actually came down to earth to reveal this love in human flesh.* Thus, she concluded, we have a "new commandment, his own commandment." Christ did much more than ask us to love our neighbors. *He told us to love one another as he loved us.* Thérèse prayed, "You have given me a new commandment. How I cherish it, for it assures me that it is your will to love in me all those whom you command me to love." When feeling loved and acting with love, she concluded, "I feel it is Jesus who works within me."[13] The closer she came into union with Christ, the more she loved those within her community. (She had more than a few difficulties in loving others, some of whom were not really very loving toward her!)

All genuine love is rooted in God because "God is love." Classic descriptions of spirituality underscore that love for others flows directly out of love for God. This is true. But Chiara Lubich offers a simple insight that radically altered how I understood the way this love works.

> Our inner life is fed by our outer life. The more I enter into the soul of my brother or sister, the more I enter into God within me. The more I enter into God within me, the more I enter into my brother or sister. God—myself—my brother or sister: it is all one world, all one kingdom.[14]

She is saying when I *enter* by love into the soul of another, I experience the new commandment within the deepest bonds of God-Love created by the Holy Spirit through the new covenant. Since we have entered into a new age where a new covenant has been sealed with Christ's blood, we are now truly free to love one another. God pours his Spirit into us and bids us follow him into a unique love for the whole family of God. This is why costly love is the only way to experience unity with all the followers of Jesus. John expresses this with great clarity in 1 John 4:21: "The commandment we have from him is this: those who love God must love their brothers and sisters also."

PART FIVE

WHAT MAKES OUR LOVE SO COSTLY?

"If you love me, you will keep my commandments. And I will ask the Father, and he will give you another Advocate, to be with you forever. This is the Spirit of truth, whom the world cannot receive, because it neither sees him nor knows him. You know him, because he abides with you, and he will be in you.

"I will not leave you orphaned; I am coming to you. In a little while the world will no longer see me, but you will see me; because I live, you also will live. On that day you will know that I am in my Father, and you in me, and I in you. They who have my commandments and keep them are those who love me; and those who love me will be loved by my Father, and I will love them and reveal myself to them." Judas (not Iscariot) said to him, "Lord, how is it that you will reveal yourself to us, and not to the world?" Jesus answered him, "Those who love me will keep my word, and my Father will love them, and we will come to them and make our home with them. Whoever does not love me does not keep my words; and the word that you hear is not mine, but is from the Father who sent me.

"I have said these things to you while I am still with you. But the Advocate, the Holy Spirit, whom the Father will send in my name, will teach you everything, and remind you of all that I have said to you. Peace I leave with you; my peace I give to you. I do not give to you as the world gives. Do not let your hearts be troubled, and do not let them be afraid. You heard me say to you, 'I am going away, and I am coming to you.' If you loved me, you would rejoice that I am going to the Father, because the Father is greater than I. And now I have told you this before it occurs, so that when it does occur, you may believe. I will no longer talk much with you, for the ruler of this world is coming. He has no power over me; but I do as the Father has commanded me, so that the world may know that I love the Father. Rise, let us be on our way."

(John 14:15–31)

CHAPTER TWELVE

COSTLY LOVE IN A HOSTILE WORLD

> For one human being to love another human
> being: that is perhaps the most difficult task
> that has been entrusted to us, the ultimate
> task, the final test and proof, the work for
> which all other work is merely preparation.
>
> Rainer Maria Rilke

T HE STORY OF HOW the earliest Christian churches loved
God, and their neighbors, is nothing short of amazing.
At the center of this small first-century Jewish movement Jesus openly demonstrated love for all people, regardless of their faith and practice. His love became especially
evident in the early Christians' love for one another. A deep
bond of sacrificial fellowship, rooted in the new commandment (John 13:34–35; 15:12, 17; 17:21–23), led them into this
mutual love.

I believe the record of the New Testament, and the additional testimony of early church history, shows us how
this love sustained these believers through dark and difficult
days. I also believe the record shows how Christians eventually overcame their fiercest opposition. We've seen the basis
for this incredible love in the new commandment and the
new covenant. Now I'll focus on *how* the earliest Christian
congregations experienced God-Love within a profoundly
pagan culture. This story is central to my message about the
need to recover a deeper understanding of, and commitment
to, costly love.

The Ideal of the Christian Movement

Kenneth Scott Latourette's aforementioned work contains a summary chapter titled "By Way of Inclusive Retrospect."[1] The famous missionary historian says in the beginning Christianity was "singularly unpromising." Jesus wrote no books. He created no organizational structure to perpetuate his message or ensure his disciples' success. His crucifixion appeared to mark the end of his public ministry before his movement had gained any significant strength. The masses hardly noticed. From the outset, Jesus' followers came from only one of several active Jewish sects. This made the Jesus movement "one of the feeblest of many faiths ... competing in the Graeco-Roman world." And recall the Roman Empire occupied only a relatively small part of the world, thus a small minority of humankind. By the time the Christian faith began to make any significant headway in the wider world, during the first three centuries after Christ, the empire was already in serious decline. So it is crucial to note that *without* Christ this faith movement would never have spread. It was not just another religion or a better philosophy. *Christians believed deeply that when they followed their Lord and Master, they followed the perfect revelation of God's love for all mankind.*

Latourette further notes Jesus stirred "intense intellectual activity," but far more important was that he *transformed* those who embraced the truth of his love. Yet, "Christianity did not save the Roman Empire." Latourette argues the institution we call the church took several forms over the first centuries but what remained most powerful was a *Jesus movement*, not a cultural or religious structure. *Before there was a cultural expression of Christianity, there was a people movement that sought the highest single ideal ever imagined.* This ideal was rooted in the life and teaching of Jesus. This ideal is *the kingdom of God*, and this kingdom is focused on the truth that the individual person can "know the love of Christ which passes knowledge." But this ideal was never alone. It was vitally joined with a specific goal that could never be attained "in isolation, but only in community." This goal was rooted "in Christ's teaching, in love for God, as the duty and privilege of man, [and] is inseparably joined with love for one's neighbor."[2] Latourette concludes that both the ideal and the goal *together* have determined the character of all subsequent movements that bear the mark of Christ.

Here's Latourette's central point: When Christians, in any place or time, seek the ideal of the kingdom and the costly love of God for neighbor and one another, they will have a direct impact on the world. The fruit of the Jesus movement is no accident. The absence of this fruit in the early twenty-first century requires that we ask: *What has happened to the ideal and goal of the Christian movement?*

If you read a newspaper (especially the "Letters to the Editor"), blog and Facebook posts, listen to your neighbors (especially younger ones), and observe the most basic data from any serious polling, you can readily see the world does not believe that Christians are people of love.[3]

But when you read the New Testament and the literature of the first three Christian centuries, it becomes evident that love characterized Jesus' earliest disciples. For the first Christians, love was *the* sign they were God's children (1 John 4:7). They even believed it was the evidence they'd passed from death to life (1 John 3:14). In other words, *love was the mark of the Christian church.* Failure to love was seen as a *blatant denial* of Christ.

Further, the New Testament puts tremendous stress on unity (John 17:21–24; Ephesians 4:1–6; Romans 12:16, 15:5; 2 Corinthians 13:11; Philippians 2:2, 4:2; 1 Peter 3:8). The scandal of division was treated with utmost seriousness (1 Corinthians 1:10–17, 3:3–9, 11:17–22) because it revealed a lack of love. The first Christians expected love to thrive within their communities. Their shared meals, often eaten in connection with social gatherings before they took the Lord's Supper, were called Love Feasts! In the accounts we have, it's clear these various expressions of love empowered the church to demonstrate Christ's love to the world both by their attitudes and their deeds. In Christians' relational unity with

Christ and one another, the world could see the Father had sent Jesus, the Son, and the Father loved the disciples even as God had loved Jesus (see John 17:23). Canonical (New Testament) and non-canonical accounts (both Christian and non-Christian) make it clear that for several centuries love remained *the mark* of Christianity.

From Jesus' Small Circle to a Growing Church

Consider Jesus, a first-century Jewish rabbi who created a fair share of controversy through his astounding claims about himself. After he died an ignominious death on a Roman torture stake, his followers testified to seeing him alive. Still, for several generations, the number of his followers was never large. We are told 120 gathered in the upper room to pray after his ascension, prior to the Day of Pentecost (Acts 1:15). Paul adds that besides his own post-resurrection experience with Jesus on the road to Damascus, Jesus appeared to the Twelve, and later to more than 500 brothers and sisters (1 Corinthians 15:6). The day of Pentecost saw a dramatic increase in the number of Christians, when three thousand Jews received the gospel and were baptized (Acts 2:41). But even this immediate and dramatic increase in membership did not lead to increased growth of the church in the ensuing decades. It was almost a century before this small Jesus movement would increase significantly. Although scholars have debated the actual number of Christians in the Roman Empire at the end of the first century, it seems the number was as low as 10,000 and certainly no higher than 25,000 to 35,000. Some contemporary Christians argue for massive and immediate growth in order to demonstrate the *supernatural* power of the faith. This question is worth considering, especially in an age when we have placed so much stress upon the numerical size of our missions and congregations. But one thing is clear in the historical record: The first Christians and churches did *not* rapidly grow in numbers, and their size was largely irrelevant to the world around them. My point is simple. If fruitfulness in God-Love is measured by the number of people who came into the church then the first Christians failed.

Given these observations, I ask: How did a tiny, insignificant sect of the Jews, who believed an obscure rabbi was actually the risen Jewish Messiah, become an empire-transforming movement that eventually changed religion, culture, and law? In other words, how did this little band of Jesus followers become the largest religion in the world? No matter how you frame this question, or who asks it (friend or foe), it has created more than its fair share of interest.

The Mission of the First Christians

Maybe this is a better way to pose the question: Was the love of Christ the first Christians experienced so distinctive, so life-changing, that their acts of personal sacrifice eventually overcame the fiercest opposition aimed directly at them? Could the way these first Christians lived out the love of Christ speak to our modern world, where Christendom is collapsing?

When we read accounts of how the first Christians actually cared for their neighbors, we should note a distinct priority in their practice—the spiritual *always* precedes the theological. These first Christians *knew* someone risen from the dead and believed he was truly present with them when they came together. This sense of believing he was really still present with them when they gathered was the "how" of resurrection power in their congregations. Men and women, Jews and Gentiles, rich and poor—all joined their hearts and hands in the bond of his love, a love not easily broken. In contrast to their neighbors, they shared life together in an exemplary way.

> To read the early Christians in their own words is to be confronted with a primal boldness and clarity that sweeps the horizon clean and forces us to take a new look at our own situation. What idols confront us as we strive to follow Christ? What powers vie for our allegiance? The first believers were a threat to the social system, the power

structure, the very moral basis for the society in which they lived. Are we? They sacrificed everything, even their lives—for the sake of the Truth that burned in their hearts. Do we? They sold all they had and gave it to the poor, then banded together in close-knit communities where they took care of the weak and sick, and fed the poor. Can this be said of us?[4]

Consider this: The only Scriptures the early church possessed were the writings of the Old Testament. (It is doubtful every congregation actually possessed a copy.) This inconsequential Jewish movement found hope in the martyr, John the Baptist, a man full of the Holy Spirit. They found even greater hope in the witness Jesus passed on to them through a handful of his disciples. But that was it. Except for a few "first-person" accounts, these early Christians had much less than we have—only the good news of Christ in oral form, joined with the Spirit's transcendent power. They gathered for prayer and worshiped God in Jesus Christ. They regularly remembered his death through the sacred meal he instituted (Matthew 26:26–30; Mark 14:22–25; Luke 22:14–23). They baptized those who joined their community. They taught every member what Jesus had commanded them (Matthew 28:16–20; Acts 2:41–42). The original Jerusalem church became the center of the movement. After the Roman destruction of Jerusalem in A.D. 70 things shifted dramatically.

These first Christians believed Jesus had risen from the dead and his kingdom would soon break into the world in fullness and power to end the present age. (It seems they lived *expecting* him to come very soon.) The first martyr, Stephen, revealed the power of God's love and the practice of forgiveness (Acts 7). He was the evangelist who took the gospel from Jerusalem to Antioch and thus began the first mission to the Gentile world. This mission led to the conversion of Saul of Tarsus (later renamed Paul), once a hardcore anti-Christian who became the primary missionary to the non-Jews. It was in Antioch these followers of the Jewish Messiah were first called "Christians." This appears to have been a simple way of saying they were "the people of Christ"

(Acts 11:26). These early Christians had already been called "followers of the Way" (Acts 9:2), a shorthand way of saying they followed Jesus (John 14:6). Paul and Barnabas were sent from Antioch to proclaim to the Gentiles the message of the cross and Resurrection. Under Paul's leadership the church in Jerusalem eventually instituted a standard of behavior that would preserve the unity of the early church. This came about because they had to face the huge challenge of openly welcoming Gentiles into their community (Acts 15).[5]

Paul summed up his own ministry this way: "May I never boast of anything except the cross of our Lord Jesus Christ, by which the world has been crucified to me, and I to the world" (Galatians 6:14; see also 5:11, 6:12). In Ignatius's *Letter to Polycarp* (Polycarp was an early Christian martyr) we see the church is actually called "the fellowship of the cross." Celsus, a Roman who became one of Christianity's fiercest enemies, said the Christians' beliefs and practices all centered on their conviction that they received life and resurrection from a wooden cross. He wrote, "If Christ had been thrown down a cliff or pushed into a pit, or strangled with a rope...then they would speak of a cliff of life, or a pit of resurrection, or a rope of immortality."[6]

The Romans considered Jews an affront to civil society. Their social separatism and insistence God must be worshiped without images were a serious religious offense to all non-Jews. Christians took this identity a step further by removing the idea of connecting a nation, or nationalism, with their faith and practice. "For the pagans, this explained the repulsively new life the Christians led: It was godless."[7] It is hard to fathom that in the first century, Christians were called atheists because they rejected the various Roman deities and believed that Jesus *alone* was Lord. Early-church scholar Robert L. Wilken notes the first Christians were dismissed as one of the many burial societies that proliferated in the empire. Opposition against them increased in the second, third, and fourth centuries. Men like Galen, Celsus, Porphyry and Julian all *systematically* attacked the Christian faith and its practice.[8]

Regardless of how early Christians experienced the rule of various Roman emperors, they passively resisted the state's attempt to *force* them to deny their faith. This led many to their death, especially at various points during the first several centuries when persecution swept over the church. Many of these trials came about for political reasons. The church was an easy target for Roman leaders who were puzzled by the lives of these foolish lovers.

So how did the witness of the early church finally impact a hostile world? The Romans slowly took notice of their purity of life and displays of amazing love. Their purity can be explained in terms of their love for Jesus joined with their humble desire to follow him. Their moral purity was clearly striking, but even more astounding was their love. Without doubt, these first Christians possessed a love so great it led them to serve one another *and* then their pagan neighbors and enemies. *This love, more than anything else, was their greatest apologetic.*

The Ancient World of the First Christians

An impressive three-volume study of the history of Christian charity, written in the nineteenth century, describes the Greco-Roman context in which early Christianity took root as "a world without love." The author's central point was not to say the Greeks and Romans had no earthly idea of love, but their vision of love could not extend beyond their own circle or status toward the well-being of people in general.[9]

Here's one example: Plautus, a Roman dramatist (ca. 254–184 BCE), considered aid to the poor useless, because it could not elevate the recipients to wealth and thus they could never receive real happiness. He said, "What is given to the poor is lost," and, "He deserves ill of a beggar who gives him food and drink. For that which is given is thrown away, and the life of the beggar is protracted."[10] Even the ideal state Plato presents in *The Republic* had no room for the poor. Beggars were to be expelled. There was no moral or social obligation to care for them. A person who could not work had no intrinsic value and was a drain on the state.

Both the Greeks and the Romans shared a disdain for the "least in society," which included women, the weak, handicapped, poor, and marginalized. A marginal system of charity did exist, expressed by the well-known word *philanthropy* (literally, "love for humanity"). But this word meant a "love of public recognition." Such philanthropy was totally self-serving. The wealthy did not get involved with the poor or give themselves to their personal care. Rather, they gave gifts to their city and became known as benefactors. They often paid for public buildings, including pagan temples. The wealthy built theaters and amphitheaters, sponsored games and shows, and sometimes handed out bread or coins to people who attended these spectacles. But there is little or no evidence their works of "charity" were done out of love or compassion. From what we know, they gave gifts so the people in the city would feel more obliged to the wealthy.[11]

In antiquity, it was assumed the poor were destitute because of their fate. Sometimes the needy were helped, but the truly destitute were almost always left in their misery. Essentially, the wealthy believed people got what they deserved. Some emperors fed the poor (this was called the *dole*), but it was only to keep the poor from rioting. Honor might prompt some to act for the poor, but never pity or compassion.

The Radical Love of the First Christians

What made these first Christians unique was their belief God had granted them a transforming experience of radical love! They believed his love brought them into union with him, thus divine-love sustained them throughout all their days. Loving God and one another was the result of a conscious emergence of an entirely new form of love that flowed out of their inner being. This costly love, grounded in the deep inner reality of God's love, called Christians to surrender their lives within the harsh realities of the wounded world. *If we love God, we will love our neighbor.*

Further, this radical love was sacrificial. It did not put the early Christians in a place of power but rather in the place where they stooped to serve the least. Radical love did not conquer the world by force, politics, or control. It did not sound trumpets to call attention to itself (see Matthew 6:2–4).

Radical God-Love is totally free. It cannot be coerced by religion or the church. It cannot be bought or sold. Adolfo Quezada says, "Radical love simply is. We cannot create favorable conditions for it to grow, but ultimately, radical love comes spontaneously. It comes when we least expect it, and it comes in ordinary times and places in our life."[12] This love is unilateral because it is rooted in *God's* love. It is non-contingent and depends on nothing we find in our neighbors. One of the most amazing conclusions we can make about costly love is this: "It is not that we love the unlovable; rather, because we are of God, we consider no one unlovable."[13]

Finally, radical love shapes our entire character, guides our impulses and quite often softens others' hearts. This doesn't mean we allow others to take advantage of, manipulate, or demean us. It also doesn't mean we ignore injustice when wrong is done. It means that we choose to love our neighbors regardless of what they think of us or our motives or what we think of their lifestyles or choices. We may even loathe their choices and actions. But radical love is about who they really are as image bearers of God. God loves them even though they are his enemies, just as he loved us when we were his enemies (see Romans 5:10; Colossians 1:21). The biblical teaching is clear. Within every one of us God has put a deep hunger for love. This hunger can be satisfied with Christ's love. When we love our neighbors with God's radical love, we will rightly long for them to know divine love, but we will continue to love them whether they come to know that love or not, because our love for them is not a means to an end.

Seeing Others through God's Love

In our modern context we are prone to consider some people sub-human, even referring to some criminals as "monsters." In so doing we try to put distance between us and them. But even the worst criminal who ever lived shared in our common humanity and was loved by God.

God's love is colorblind, without prejudice in any form. It comes from his heart, thus it cannot be other than deeply compassionate. Regardless of what justice might require, God's love includes all people. Regardless of others' socioeconomic backgrounds, state of life, religious faith, sexual orientation and practice, race, or ideology, they all belong to God as their Creator. He loves them! A verse from a familiar children's song says it well:

> Jesus loves me still today,
>
> Walking with me on my way,
>
> *Wanting as a friend to give*
>
> *Light and love to all who live.*

This is why the "spirituality of love" is God's gift to us for all people. Everything and everyone in this universe is intrinsically loved by God, not because they're *inherently* good but because "God is love." He loves us because he is merciful and good, not because we deserve it. Costly God-Love is the only power that can penetrate the hardest heart of evil individuals. Time and again Christian history bears witness to this truth. The church is at its best when it lives costly love in a hostile world.

It's easy to *talk* about loving humanity, but *loving* terrible people is another matter. (In truth, for most of us it's *ordinary people* we find so hard to love.) It seems entirely *unnatural* to love a rude person, a bigot, a sexual predator, or—especially—one who takes the life of a person we love. We talk a great deal about how we should have compassion and love for the whole world. We love to talk about caring for hurting people. We (sometimes) care about the multitudes of refugees fleeing their homes in Africa and the Middle East, especially if they are Christians. But cold-blooded killers? We almost instinctively think: "Are you kidding? They should be judged and spend all eternity in torment paying for their crime." Yet Paul's words stand: "While we were enemies, we were reconciled to God through the death of his Son" (Romans 5:10).

How Radical Love Transforms Our Relationships

Once we see others as fully human persons, we can love them in new and radical ways. Paul says, "Love does no wrong to a neighbor; therefore, love is the fulfilling of the law" (Romans 13:10). And, "Let all that you do be done in love" (1 Corinthians 16:14). Following Jesus' teaching, he concludes "the whole law is summed up in a single commandment, 'You shall love your neighbor as yourself'" (Galatians 5:14). There is no question the early Christians received Jesus' teaching about costly love and put it into practice.

If we have not concluded by now that *without* God-Love transforming us first costly love is impossible, then we're mired in religious *concepts*. Yet the biblical perspective is clear: Our actions will flow freely out of hearts that are deeply moved as, moment-by-moment, God's love transforms us. This love caused pagan society to take note of this small Jewish sect that came to be called Christians.

I have used the term *radical love* a great deal in this chapter. In this instance the addition of the word "radical" is used here as a synonym for the word "costly." The early church lived this radical love in and for the hostile ancient world of Rome. This was true because Christian believers *practiced* this love. Christian psychiatrist Adolfo Quesada says "radical" love is not extreme because "[Jesus'] belief in love was deeply rooted in his own intimate and familiar relationship with God" (John 17).[14] So why stress this word *radical*? The word, from the Latin word *radix*, refers to the "root" or "origin." *Radical* love describes the breadth and depth of the love Jesus showed for all people. The love God had for us in creating us, and the love he has for us in sustaining us every single day, is *radical* because it has its origin in God-Love. It is, by nature, eternal love, thus *costly*.

Radical love seeks nothing for itself. It is grounded in agape; thus, it *surrenders* everything to God, giving and giving, even when it seems there is nothing left to give. Radical love will lead to the passionate love of God flowing from our hearts. "It begets passion, not the other way around."[15]

194

Costly radical love begets passion, but it is never an emotion at first. It is an intentional, prayerful choice to *be who I am* in the Trinity. We've been shown agape in God's mercy and forgiveness. In "Amazing Grace" this is what John Newton meant when he said God's grace "saved a wretch like me." This truth is fundamental to the gospel. But, with Adolfo Quezada, I now believe, if I truly share agape, I will begin to seek union within a relationship, even with a person I once deeply hated. Love tears down walls, reconciles enemies, and builds new relationships. It transcends past differences.

Finally, God-Love, what I have called radical and costly love, can never be cautious. It is always deeply centered on the other and will continually seek to find *new* ways to express itself. The philosopher Bertrand Russell understood this better than many Christians: "Of all the forms of caution, caution in love is perhaps the most fatal to happiness."[16] This is how we live costly love in a hostile world, without caution. Costly love seeks to turn enemies into our neighbors and then into friends. Costly love inherently surrenders a measure of personal freedom but it doesn't see this as a loss because there is much more to be gained. *This is precisely what God has done for us in Jesus Christ.*

Conclusion

Out of the *Shoah* (Holocaust), new insights into life's meaning have developed over the last sixty-plus years. One of the most influential discoveries of meaning comes from Viktor Frankl (1905–1997), an Austrian Jew who survived Auschwitz. Some astounding observations from his classic book *Man's Search for Meaning* provide a fitting conclusion of this chapter: "Everything can be taken from a man but one thing: the last of the human freedoms—to choose one's attitude in any given set of circumstances, to choose one's own way."[17]

According to Anthony Gittins, Viktor Frankl spent his lifetime explaining the meaning of human life. His legacy can be summarized in three neat aphorisms that are Frankl's own: *To live you must choose; to love you must encounter; to grow you must suffer.*[18] Gittins says these statements carry the wisdom of the biblical tradition shared by both Christians and Jews. Here is a legacy worthy of our reflection upon how costly love impacts us and the world we live in.

1. *To Live You Must Choose*

   Despite the suffering of the *Shoah*, in which members of his own family died, Viktor Frankl followed the biblical wisdom and stressed the human capacity for choice (Deuteronomy 30:19). He actively and passionately chose life because he discovered this was the only way to live amid unthinkable evil.

2. *To Love You Must Encounter*

   We all know people in the abstract, especially through the social media. But such knowledge does not produce costly love. Only when we know others personally will we truly love them. If the way we live erects walls between us and others we must tear them down to be transformed by costly love. Here we encounter the only real answer to the indifference I've spoken about. We embrace a genuine and radical hospitality that builds bridges of love by which we can know and care for the other.

3. *To Grow You Must Suffer*

   At first glance this statement seems almost perverse. Yet it is the heart of costly love. When we encounter our own suffering we can choose to *not* be overwhelmed. Our choice to love amid our suffering can turn that suffering "inside out." We all know people who have made this choice. Gittins says, "This type of experience ... is one of the strongest faces of the human spirit." Appropriate acceptance of what we cannot change gives us strength so we can become a gift of hope for the entire community.

Tony Gittins concludes:

Christianity, like its sibling, Judaism, does not produce complacency, but complicity or participation with others....[Disciples] must not only have a felt presence that disturbs; to be true disciples they must actually become a presence that disturbs. This disruption is the cost of discipleship. Every disciple is called to practice justice [because of costly love]. That call is bound to be disturbing to some people.[19]

Costly love will always lead us into deep, personal participation with others because we walk in the way of Jesus!

CHAPTER THIRTEEN

FOLLOWERS OF THE WAY

Our unity does not come from agreeing to propositions, but from following his commands and his example—acting with the love he taught and lived.

George Koch

C HAPTER TWELVE RECOUNTED HOW the early Christian church was marked by the love of Christ freely experienced within small congregations of believers who shared corporate life. The new commandment, "that you love one another just as I have loved you," shaped everything about their shared life. But this Christian love was not limited to "one another." These Christians freely shared with their neighbors. We can see this in the way agape became associated with our English word *charity* (Latin *caritas*, "love"). Christianity's earliest critics called its religious teaching strange and foolish. Their criticism was similar to the way modern people speak about ritualistic cults. But there was one mark of Christian identity even the harshest critics could not deny: These believers genuinely loved one another.

Thus, these first Christians provide a powerful model of how love can transform life in the church. We've seen how in the New Testament this *original model is evident in many forms*. We've also observed how this original model of love seems missing in much of Christianity in the West. Yet this is the model of love the Spirit has used over the ensuing centuries to renew Christian practice.

Following the Way

The first believers were not called "Christians" until the gospel had taken root in Antioch (Acts 11:26). Because they followed Jesus as their rabbinic teacher, they referred to themselves as followers of "the Way."

In the Upper Room Discourse (John 13–17) Thomas asked Jesus how his disciples could really follow him if he was going away (14:5). Jesus' response is one of the best-known verses in the Bible: "I am the way, and the truth, and the life. No one comes to the Father except through me" (14:6). In effect, Jesus told his disciples they were to *continue* in "the Way" he'd lived and taught. He would be with them when he went away because he would send his Spirit (14:15–31). The Spirit would "teach you [the disciples] everything, and remind you of all that I have said to you" (14:26). This promise of the sending of the Spirit is introduced in the discourse by the repetition of the command to love one another: "*If you love me, you will keep my commandments*" (14:15).

The book of Acts tells us the early church was threatened by various internal and external trials. In the unfolding story of the growth and development of early Christianity none is more important than the conversion of Saul of Tarsus.

> Meanwhile Saul, still breathing threats and murder against the disciples of the Lord, went to the high priest and asked him for letters to the synagogues at Damascus, so that if he found any who belonged to the Way, men or women, he might bring them bound to Jerusalem. (Acts 9:1–2)

Saul of Tarsus, the great persecutor of this nascent messianic movement, was determined to bring these disciples of Jesus before the Jewish authorities to judge them for their heresies. Yet Saul, who becomes Paul, does not cease to be Jewish when he encounters Jesus on the road to Damascus. His conversion was not from Judaism to Christianity so much as it was a conversion to "the Way." The author of Acts calls these first Christian believers people "who belonged to the Way." This designation has deep rabbinic roots that are rich with meaning. If we recover a Jewish understanding of "the Way" we will better understand this designation of the new covenant community. For example, "the Way" likely refers to *following a divinely appointed path of life* (see Deuteronomy 5:33; 10:12; 30:16; Isaiah 42:24; Zechariah 3:7). This path of life was believed to include brilliant *encounters with the divine*, falling to the ground *prostrate* in worship (see Ezekiel 1:28; Daniel 10:9), a *double-naming* (see Genesis 22:11; 46:2; 1 Samuel 3:4, 1) and a *divine commissioning* (see Genesis 12:1; 22:2). Trustworthy disciples, who make it their aim to live out Jesus' costly love, need this Jewish perspective. There are at least two ways we can apply these insights from Jewish understanding and practice.

First, *Jewish rabbis, over the centuries and at the time of Jesus, all had dedicated followers. These followers were their disciples.* When disciples agreed to follow a particular rabbi, they "took up his yoke." Thus Rabbi Jesus said, "Come to me, all you that are weary and are carrying heavy burdens, and I will give you rest. Take my yoke upon you, and learn from me; for I am gentle and humble in heart, and you will find rest for your souls. For my *yoke* is easy, and my burden is light" (Matthew 11:28–30). This reference clearly defines the disciple's relationship to Jesus as his teacher (rabbi). Any disciple who chose to follow a particular rabbi entered into a unique commitment that *defined* all their relationships. Jesus is calling those who believe in him to follow him and be defined by *his way of life*. His disciples were thus "yoked" to him, but he says his, in contrast to all other yokes, is "easy."

Second, *Jewish rabbis determined who was a disciple by use and practice.* Disciples did not merely say or profess certain things in order to join a religious cause or embrace philosophical ideas. They were humble "learners" who *emulated their rabbi's behavior.* Following a rabbi meant embracing his *halakha.* This Hebrew word is often translated "instruction," "judgment," or "law." The *halakha* referred to following your teacher in the "walk," or the way. This walking in the way of your rabbi included several actions: (1) Hearing how your rabbi interprets the Torah (the written teachings of Moses in the first five books of the Bible), which told religious Jews what to do. (2) Hearing how your rabbi interprets the oral tradition of the Torah and then following in the way that he taught you to practice the Torah in specific contexts. It was believed this oral tradition began after the giving of the Ten Commandments. (3) Hearing how your rabbi taught you what to do in your relationships with others and with the surrounding world. (4) Watching how your rabbi acted and imitating him. In sum, disciples do what their rabbi tells them to do *and* follow the actions and ways of their teacher.[1]

How the First Christians Heard and Followed Jesus

If we are to recover costly love, we must understand how these first Christians followed Jesus in "the Way." The pattern we see in the Gospels is striking, so much so that most of what we call discipleship today seems foreign to the teaching and actions of the Jesus.

One of the first ways to understand how the earliest (i.e., Jewish) believers heard and followed Jesus is by considering the clear New Testament examples. These reveal Jesus' core teaching and daily practice. We've already seen the heart of this teaching in passages such as Matthew 5:43–48, 7:12, 22:34–40; Mark 12:28–34; Luke 10:25–28; and John 13:34–35; 15:12, 17. All these primary texts are about love. Because they present the clearest commandments we have from Jesus, they constitute *the most basic way of following Jesus.*

But even as a good rabbi, Jesus was not content to teach his ideal of love. He illustrated what love means through a great many stories and actions. Consider again the story of the Good Samaritan (Luke 10:25–37). Jesus concludes by asking his hearers a common rabbinic question: "Which of these three [the priest, Levite, or Samaritan], was a true *neighbor* to the man who fell into the hands of the robbers?" The expert in the law said, "The one who showed him mercy." Notice Jesus does not say, "You pass my exam and join my team. Answer a few specific questions about religion and you're in." No, he says, "Go and do likewise." In other words, be like the Samaritan in the story. Jesus told such stories to teach the meaning of the kingdom, and lived the kingdom of God in his actions of mercy and love. And, yes, the same love led him to rebuke some religious leaders harshly. These stories and actions pointed people to him as the one rabbi who fulfilled all the law and the prophets; i.e., the Messiah!

Now, according to first-century Jewish teaching, the Samaritans were not only the arch-enemies of Israel but also a people who misunderstood the nature of God and the Torah. Their theology (beliefs) and tradition (worship, liturgy) offended religious Jews, who would have nothing to do with them. In turn, Samaritans despised the Jews. But the point is clear. The Samaritan in Jesus' story acted with love and mercy, and thus he *actually fulfilled* the second commandment. He lived costly love in an active and faithful way.

Let's take this further. Jesus healed a man who was blind from birth, raised people from the dead, invited himself to dinner with the hated Zacchaeus, forgave a woman of immoral reputation, healed and forgave a crippled man, and spoke with a scandalous Samaritan woman in broad daylight. In all of these actions he continuously demonstrated to his inner circle, and to all who heard him speak, how a disciple of his should *act* in relationships.

Here's the bottom line: *The followers of "the Way" followed Jesus in loving God and their neighbors.*

So What Happened?

As the church moved away from its Jewish roots, reaching out to non-Jews in the surrounding culture, its missionary impulse drew in leaders who became more and more Gentile. Before his ascension Jesus told his followers to "disciple the nations" (Matthew 28:18–20). Paul, a great Jewish teacher himself, led the way in this expansive missionary work. He showed the church how to live the unity Christ had created by his death and resurrection, which saved *both* Jew *and* Gentile. This is why Paul's letters are filled with appeals to remain together in love and unity. While Paul understood the need to take the gospel to the Gentiles, he also knew the unity of the church was threatened as it received people from non-Jewish backgrounds. Paul's letter to the Galatians, one of his most important theological treatises, underscores the need for *both* unity and diversity: "There is no longer Jew or Greek, there is no longer slave or free, there is no longer male and female; for all of you are one in Christ Jesus" (3:28).

It seems as the church grew beyond its Judaic roots, people did not always understand what it meant to follow in "the Way." A transition, with clearly mixed results, followed when the church moved from a deeply rabbinic model of discipleship to one rooted in Greek analysis. This led to the *development* of Christian doctrine in the centuries that followed. We see this beginning in Acts 17 as Paul preaches in Athens, skillfully contextualizing the gospel for Greek philosophers. Later the church would express the Christian faith in "Greek-like" doctrinal propositions, thus leading to the creeds. The Nicene, Athanasian and Apostles' Creeds all illustrate this point.

The Proper Role of Doctrine

Doctrine has great worth. It provides a human method that helps us understand some of the most basic ideas we discover in Scripture. Two striking illustrations can be seen in the development of the doctrines of the incarnation and the trinity. Both were systematic attempts to explain what can be discovered by reading the New Testament. At the same time they helped early Christians by underscoring the content of their faith. These doctrines, which became clearly expressed in the most ancient creeds, showed disciples *how* to answer the teaching of those who opposed the core of Christian teaching. When used well, sound doctrine can nourish faith, expand our sense of divine mystery, and help us to worship God faithfully.

In early Christianity doctrine and dogma are virtually synonymous; doxologies, creeds, and conciliar decrees are all instances of dogma. Vincent of Lérins (d. 450) specified the concept of dogma with precision, defining it as *the truths beyond reason that were accepted because of their Christological origin.* Thomas Aquinas said dogmas were articles of faith.[2] Dogma differs markedly from private opinion. In the original Greek, "dogma" conveys the idea of an established tenet of belief. Today, dogmas are generally understood as the church's expression of revealed mystery. *Dogma refers to an enduring truth expressed in the words and categories of a particular age and culture.* So the way we articulate and teach dogma can and does change. Many Christians do not understand this distinction. But across contemporary Christian thought one thing is almost universally agreed upon: dogma, or doctrine, can never take the place of loving God, loving our neighbors, and loving one another.

How ironic then that Protestant reformer Martin Luther became so fixed on *right* doctrine. This fixation led him to speak of the canonical letter of James as a "strawy epistle." James says, "Someone will say, 'You have faith and I have works.' Show me your faith apart from your works, and I by my works will show you my faith. You believe that God is one; you do well. Even the demons believe—and shudder" (James 2:18–19). The point James makes in this passage illustrates my thesis. Demons believe sound doctrine and experience the awe of truth so profoundly that they shudder—but they *do not* love and faithfully follow Jesus.

James underscores that in the early decades some within the church were already following a dangerous pathway. He calls attention to those who believe right teaching but do not practice a living (loving) faith, a kind of faith with no deep value. *Right beliefs without right actions always fails the test of true discipleship.* Love will always be "the more excellent way" (1 Corinthians 12:31).

The apostles followed their Master (rabbi) by "teaching" his way everywhere they went (see Acts 5:28; Colossians 1:28; 1 Timothy 4:6, 13; 6:3). Texts like these demonstrate that in almost every instance *the purpose of apostolic teaching was to lead Christians to embrace faithful obedience to Jesus' life and teaching.* Paul says, "Sound teaching [is] based on Christ's own words and leads to Christ-like living" (1 Timothy 6:3, J.

B. Phillips). "Sound teaching" is the equivalent of sound doctrine. So the first test of all doctrine is: "Does this teaching lead people to follow the sound words of Jesus and to be genuinely godly in a Christlike way?" If we follow in "the Way," we must restore this simple test to all our use of doctrine.

It seems that the author of James may well be the same individual called "the brother of Jesus" (Acts 15:13–21). After the Resurrection, James became a disciple of Jesus (1 Corinthians 15:7). He then became a leader in the Jerusalem church (Acts 15:13–22). Paul and James were *not* doctrinal opponents. James understood doctrine alone is not enough. (We've already seen that when read correctly, Paul understood the same.) We have to make faith and doctrine relationally real by love. I can confess a host of great beliefs, orthodox and sound beliefs, but if I speak and act hurtfully toward others or ignore real human needs my faith is empty:

> What good is it, my brothers and sisters, if you say you have faith but do not have works? Can faith save you? If a brother or sister is naked and lacks daily food, and one of you says to them, "Go in peace; keep warm and eat your fill," and yet you do not supply their bodily needs, what is the good of that? So faith by itself, if it has no works, is dead. (James 2:14–17)

James sums up the entire letter in one beautiful statement: "You do well if you really fulfill the royal law according to the scripture, 'You shall love your neighbor as yourself'" (2:8).

When the church moved away from its Jewish roots, it began to lose its understanding of "the Way." The Jewish understanding of discipleship slowly gave way to intellectual analysis and creeds. Over time the focus moved from behaving like one's teacher to believing the right doctrines in the book (and creeds) that told the story of the Messiah. Over more time, faith itself became implicit, and multitudes believed the church without much reference to Jesus as their teacher. The idea of *halakha* was lost, and the results have deeply damaged Christianity.

When we move away from following Jesus as "the Way" in a deeply personal experience of love, and settle for affirming a set of logical beliefs as faith, we easily move from *acting* to *asserting*. At first this pattern may seem innocent, but in the end it allows Christians to explain their faith but not live it. The great danger is that we turn these explanations into a faith that does not grow out of relational love. Consequently, Christians come to believe that "defending the faith" is best done by argument, condescension, and dismissal. If I disdain you because I think you are wrong, I have lost the *halakha*, that is, I am no longer following Jesus in "the Way."

Early Christian Practice

Initially Christian practice was joined together in the Pauline triad: faith, hope and love (1 Corinthians 13:13). In this triad Paul was not saying love is all that matters. *Without great faith we will never believe God is good or that he loves us.* True faith, the kind that lays hold of God's promises in Jesus Christ, is the gift of God. It leads us to "strive first for the kingdom of God" (Matthew 6:33). Real hope, a divinely born outlook that seeks eternal things, is also essential. When we have hope, we gladly yield ourselves to God in all things and embrace his gracious work in us even in the midst of great trials and suffering. But love is the greatest of these three because *it will last forever.* It is unequaled in all spiritual writing and remains the goal of true spiritual life. Love may seem a seldom-realized ideal, but costly love can still be found in those who are faithful. It will uplift, inspire, and empower us all to be the people of God who live in "the Way." This is why love is preeminent in Paul's Corinthian Epistles. He is seeking to heal a congregation that was splintered by the misuse of spiritual gifts and by factions rooted in human personality. This context demonstrates why, if we are to learn how to make love our primary aim, we must recover "the Way." In the process we must never separate what God has joined together: faith, hope and love.

In a 1954 lecture Carlton J. H. Hayes concluded, "From the wellsprings of Christian compassion our Western civilization has drawn its inspiration, and its sense of duty, for feeding the hungry, giving drink to the thirsty, looking after the homeless, clothing the naked, tending the sick, and visiting the prisoner."[3] At this point in history we face a vexing question: Can modern society retain these precious values and practices *without* a distinctly Christian motivation to sustain them? Some secularists believe it is possible, but I have doubts. Historians recognize that Christianity has powerfully shaped our Western understanding of law, freedom, moral responsibility, personal ethics, and charity. And all of this came about because a tiny group of faithful followers of "the Way" lived quiet lives in costly love. We will see what the future brings, but without costly love the verdict of history is unsettled!

The Early Church Reversed the Ancient World's Ideas

The ancient world saw moral values in terms of the wealthy and lower classes, the weak and the poor. The wealthy were good. The poor were unworthy, unimportant, wretched. For philosopher and orator Cicero, property rights were far more important than human rights.[4] Carter Lindberg says, "The early church ... reversed the Greco-Roman view of wealth."[5] If that is so, then the greatest reversal in antiquity did not come about through politics, ideologies, philosophies, or power. It came about *through love*.

Theologian and church historian Adolf von Harnack (1851–1930) wrote a great deal about the spread of early Christianity, whose spread he attributed to its being *a faith that was active in love*. Faith, hope, and love were received from God and then lived out in relationship with others. In Lindberg's words, "The Christians not only had a new vocabulary of love, they lived it."[6] The gospel produced a social movement that was deeply and intentionally rooted in faith, hope, and love.

An Apostate's View of the Church's Love

The story of Julian the Apostate (332–363) has always interested students of Christian history. Julian had believed in

Christ, but renounced that faith—hence his title. He set out to reinstate the worship of the old gods of the decaying empire. He rejected persecution of the church, choosing rather to co-opt the Christians' social concerns for the purpose of the wider empire. By the fourth century early Christians had spread their culture so widely that Julian recognized *the Christian principle of indiscriminate love for one's neighbor was a virtue to be preserved.* What Julian attempted is quite revealing. He strongly rejected Christ but approved of Christian social (public) practices. *He wanted to remove the ethical practice of Christianity from Christian doctrine.* That is, he saw the value of Christian love in action.[7]

In one of his letters Julian expressed his belief that Christianity was spreading because of the distinct idea of love:

> I think the impious Galileans [Christians] have observed this fact [pagan neglect of the poor] and devoted themselves to philanthropy. And they have gained ascendancy in the worst of their deeds through the credit they win for such practices.... [T]he Galileans also begin their so-called love feast ["the *agape*"], or hospitality, or service of tables—for they have many ways of carrying it out, and hence call it by many names—and the result is that they have led many into atheism [i.e., disbelief in the Hellenistic gods].[8]

Julian, as the Pontifex Maximus, High Priest of the Empire, wrote to the high priest of the province of Galatia:

> The godless Galileans see that the [pagan] priests neglect the poor, and then immediately take the opportunity for charity. For it is disgraceful, when there is not a beggar among the Jews, and when the godless Galileans support our poor as well as their own, that our people should be without our support.[9]

These words are astoundingly frank. Today the enemies of Christian faith rarely attack the church along these lines. I fear our love is so small, we are mocked and attacked for *not* being people of love who live like Jesus. We are most often attacked for *how* we engage with political and social concerns rather than because we've lived as faithful Christ followers in faith, hope, and love. Somehow we've associated the meaning of Christian love with our moral and political views. Then we believe because we're "right" in such views we're being persecuted. While there is charity left in the church at large, a sweeping, culture-altering stance of corporate Christian love has decreased noticeably over the course of my own lifetime. More and more our churches and Christian missions have left charity to secular authorities alone. Then we claim that state-sponsored welfare is depersonalizing and creates the budgetary waste of more "big government." It's not hard to see why the world despises our witness. Perhaps if we were investing our lives deeply in the weak, the poor, the powerless, and those who hate our faith convictions (doctrines) about Jesus, they would actually notice our real love, just as Julian the Apostate did.

Conclusion

The stories I've shared reveal how early Christians *practiced* the love of Christ, even *after* the church lost direct contact with the rabbinic nature of following in "the Way." These stories should challenge the modern church to make costly love our aim. This is not a sentimental appeal for flabby or poor thinking. *It is a powerful, robust, intellectually rigorous appeal for costly love* (Luke 10:27).

For several decades, publicly and privately, I worshiped doctrinal ideas. I argued passionately for evangelical and Reformed propositions. I believed I was engaging in important kingdom work. For more than a decade I even made particular truths the goal of my life. Only after a deep encounter with the living God, rooted in the character of God's nature as love, did I consciously choose to not substitute dogma for the love of Christ. When I first made this choice, more than two decades ago, the cost was far greater than I ever could have imagined. Solid Christians rejected me. Some even warned me I would lose my orthodoxy. As a result, conferences and churches canceled me as their speaker. Our mission lost hundreds of thousands of dollars. We finally shut down our office and laid off our staff.

During this extremely painful transition, what did not change was my belief in historic confessing Christianity. Today I remain deeply committed to Christian orthodoxy. But the love God gave me now includes Christians I once held in suspicion. My previous response was rooted in the sense I was rightly contending for "the faith once for all delivered to the saints." When I moved away from this mindset, I was rejected. If I remain faithful to my calling, I must not respond in fear or reciprocal rejection. I believe my former allies are real Christians. I also believe they have a deep desire to do what is right. And I have no regrets over my painful transition because, as John says, "Fully-developed love expels every particle of fear" (1 John 4:18, J. B. Phillips). In Christ I am truly free, free to love God and others no matter what anyone else says or does.

CHAPTER FOURTEEN

FINDING DIVINE LIFE
IN COSTLY LOVE

[The] New Testament letters are like a thick
forest of application about how to love one
another. These writings are brimming with
insights concerning what is and what is not
loving behavior.

Gaylord Enns

AS WE SAW IN chapter 12, the new covenant and the
new commandment emerge historically from the
older covenant and the law of Moses. The new covenant replaces the old, but not in the sense of throwing it away.
The new replaces the old by *fulfilling* it (Matthew 5:17–20).
This word *fulfill* has the sense of bringing something to its
completeness so it produces the full fruit that in potential
was there all along.

So, what created the strong reaction against Jesus' teaching seen in the Gospels? I believe it was his *boldness*. Erasmo
Leiva-Merikakis says Jesus' boldness in Matthew 5 "is so
shocking that it could be only the foolhardiness of a de-
ranged, self-appointed prophet or ... the intimate truth concerning the incarnate Son of God."[1] Christians believe it was
the latter; thus, they see his incarnation as a "the one-time,
unique, metaphysical, and historical descent from the Father,
the coming of the divine Word, source of the Torah."[2]

In this way the new commandment also replaces the old commandments, not by dispensing with them but by going beyond the ethics of the Old Testament into a new and deeper way of living in the Spirit. We get a clear sense of what this means when we realize the apostles used the Hebrew Scriptures to teach this new faith. Any idea that the Jews with their law and promises were somehow brushed aside is foreign to the apostles. Paul puts it this way:

> For Christ himself has brought peace to us. He united Jews and Gentiles into one people when, in his own body on the cross, he broke down the wall of hostility that separated us. He did this by ending the system of law with its commandments and regulations. He made peace between Jews and Gentiles by creating in himself one new people from the two groups. Together as one body, Christ reconciled both groups to God by means of his death on the cross, and our hostility toward each other was put to death. He brought this Good News of peace to you Gentiles who were far away from him, and peace to the Jews who were near. Now all of us can come to the *Father* through the same *Holy Spirit* because of what *Christ* has done for us. (Ephesians 2:14–18, NLT, italics added)

One New People

The new covenant (notice again the trinity is clearly present in Paul's language above) "broke down the wall of hostility" between Jews and Gentiles through Christ's "body on the cross." A wall had been placed around Israel to protect God's people culturally and religiously from pagan practice. The new covenant took down this socio-religious wall so Gentiles could easily come to the God of Abraham, Isaac, and Jacob through the Savior. God's intention all along was "to bless the nations" through Israel (Genesis 13:3; 18:18; 22:18; 26:4; Psalm 72:17; Isaiah 61:9; Jeremiah 4:2; Ezekiel 28:25). But Israel rarely remembered this promise, even though some Gentiles had come into the old covenant by becoming proselyte Jews. Thus the new covenant, sealed by Christ's blood, brings together people "near" (Jews) and "far away"

(Gentiles). It also has dispensed with all the rituals and ceremonies of the old covenant, so now all can come to the Father through the same Holy Spirit on the basis of God's love for us (John 3:16).

Through the new covenant, Gentiles now share freely with Jews in God's promises to Abraham. All can enter into this "one new people" through faith in the same Messiah. This new and better covenant creates a *new community* that transcends race, ethnicity, education, gender, and status: "As many of you as were baptized into Christ have clothed yourselves with Christ. There is no longer Jew or Greek, there is no longer slave or free, there is no longer male and female; for all of you are one in Christ Jesus" (Galatians 3:27–28). The two—Jews and Gentiles—have now become "one flock" with "one shepherd."

Here's the vital point: the new covenant binds love *and* obedience together in Jesus Christ. Only eternal love is strong enough to do this, so God rejoices when he sees our "work of faith and labor of love" (1 Thessalonians 1:3), because we are becoming "what he has made us, created in Christ Jesus for good works, which God prepared beforehand to be our way of life" (Ephesians 2:10).

Because the nature of both God *and* the covenants are easily misunderstood, some have developed the mistaken idea Jesus came to save us from an angry God. Jesus came not to condemn but to reveal God's love to all the world (John 3:16–17). *That is to say, he does not placate an angry God.* Jesus reconciles the world to God, not the other way around (Romans 5:10; 2 Corinthians 5:18; Ephesians 2:16; Colossians 1:20–22).

Gaylord Enns conveys the powerful significance of this:

> This was a seismic change. Now all who believed the message that Jesus brought would be members of God's household. Paul affirmed this when he said, "I'm not ashamed of the gospel, because it is the power of God for the salvation of everyone who believes: first for the Jew, then for the Gentile" (Romans 1:16). Jesus' One Command was

an indispensable part of that message. It was imperative that they love one another as Jesus had loved them for the wonders of the New Covenant to be demonstrated![3]

In the first century, Jews and Gentiles considered each other mortal enemies. The Jews had longed for their Messiah to deliver them from the oppression of their Roman (Gentile) overlords. The Romans generally saw the Jews as opponents of the empire because of their faith and practices. God sent his Son to liberate his people, but not by striking down the Romans as many had hoped. He had always planned to pour out his Spirit on all flesh and create one new community (Joel 2:28; Acts 2:17). To first-century Jews nothing could have been more staggering. The new covenant *sounded* like a call to renounce their nationalism, even their distinct ethnicity. They were being called to love their fiercest enemies and to accept and worship God along with Gentiles who accepted the new covenant established through the sacrifice and resurrection of Jesus. This was too much for many Jews to embrace. But *this will not always be the case*, according to the prophets and Paul (Isaiah 27:6–12; Romans 11). Many in Israel were like branches that had been "broken off" from a tree (Romans 11:19) and many Gentiles were now being "grafted" into the tree (Romans 11:11–21). The purpose in these different responses is stated by Paul this way:

> Note then the kindness and the severity of God: severity toward those who have fallen, but God's kindness toward you, provided you continue in his kindness; otherwise you also will be cut off. And even those of Israel, if they do not persist in unbelief, will be grafted in, for God has the power to graft them in again. For if you have been cut from what is by nature a wild olive tree and, contrary to nature, grafted into a cultivated olive tree, how much more will these natural branches be grafted back into their own olive tree (Romans 11:22–24).

The words "cut off" in this Pauline argument could mean "dislocated" or "bent but not severed." If this is the case the natural branches of Israel could be healed when "the full number of the Gentiles" (Romans 11:25) comes to faith. Does the "olive tree" metaphor signify *ethnic* Israel or does it represent *the whole family of God*, both Israelite and non-Israelite? Scholars offer different conclusions. But two things are certain. First, Paul is warning the Gentiles who accept the new covenant to never take their position for granted. They can "stand only through faith. So do not become proud, but stand in awe" (Romans 11:20). Second, Paul argues that God has not finally rejected his people; God has kept him and others throughout redemptive history because of their faithfulness to the covenant. He begins Romans 11 with these words: "I ask, then, has God rejected his people? By no means! I myself am an Israelite, a descendant of Abraham, a member of the tribe of Benjamin. God has not rejected his people whom he foreknew" (11:1–2a). Paul ends his argument saying: "so all Israel will be saved" (11:26). Whatever this means, and there has been considerable debate, it demonstrates my primary point: God has not *replaced* Israel. He still loves her and will keep his gracious promises.

Finally, God has always intended that "all the families of the earth" will be blessed in the promises he made to Abraham in calling Israel to be his people (see Genesis 12:1–3). But those who have received God's mercy often forget that God loves all and will never approve the barriers we use to reject others who are unlike ourselves. This is a major reason for carefully keeping the new commandment and the new covenant together. Without the power and clarity of the new commandment the new community could never have survived: only through the gift of God-Love could Jews and Gentiles come together. But unity is not something we work to create—it is something God gives. Our inherent unity will never be realized until we recover the new commandment and obey it. Unity thrives where radical and resilient love prevails. If we become narrow and sectarian, we will continue to divide what God has united. We do this primarily because of our failure to love.

The Church of Jesus Christ

There are many ways to express the meaning and reality of the Christian church within Scripture. Paul calls the congregation in Corinth "the church of God" (2 Corinthians 1:1). The New Testament abounds with these kinds of metaphors. The following are just a few:

- "God's family" (Galatians 1:2) and "the family of believers" (1 Peter 1:2).

- The church is "the body of Christ" (Ephesians 1:22–23) and "God's building" (1 Corinthians 3:9).

- It is "God's field" (1 Corinthians 3:9) and "the temple of the Holy Spirit" (1 Corinthians 6:19).

- In more Jewish terms it is "the Jerusalem that is above" (Galatians 4:26), "the Israel of God" (Galatians 6:16), and a "holy temple" (Ephesians 2:21).

- Paul calls it "the bride of Christ" (Ephesians 5:25–26), one of his more powerful and endearing metaphors.

- Peter calls the church "a chosen people," "a royal priesthood," "a holy nation" and "God's special possession" (1 Peter 2:9). He also says it is "the flock of God" (1 Peter 5:2) and John calls it "the wife of the Lamb" (Revelation 21:9–10).

This family, saved by the blood of Christ, held regular meetings for worship where they shared in the sacraments (signs) of baptism and Eucharist. The meetings of the church were not a secret society (1 Corinthians 14:24), though it does appear that much of what they did corporately was not aimed at guests. The first Christians shared fellowship, helped one another, told others the story of Jesus, recognized minimal levels of leadership, faced serious problems together, and exercised forms of discipline.

All of this underscores why unity was so important. If the infant church lost unity, they would lose love, and vice versa—and they would destroy their witness to the world. Love and unity were twin truths, unmistakably linked in apostolic faith and practice.

George Beasley-Murray said the new commandment added "a more profound dimension" to the commandment that Christians love their neighbor. "As the commands of the Mosaic law were given to Israel as their part in the covenant by which they became God's people, so the 'new command' is the obligation of the people of the new covenant in response to the redemption of Christ."[4] *This command is unique because of its standard of love: Jesus Christ.*

Definitions of the church abound. Some are simple and many are complex. Some of the metaphors above have been preferred. I've personally wrestled for decades with the doctrine of the church. I once thought I could explain the church with clarity. I tried, for a time, to identify one denominational perspective with the New Testament. After decades of work among Christians from our many traditions of faith I now have what I believe is a more robust and inclusive understanding of the church. This has come about by deep listening within receptive, life-changing relationships. Now when I think about the church, my starting point is simple yet profound: It is Christ's community growing out of the new commandment *and* the new covenant in the Spirit. *The church is the fellowship of the baptized who have been united to Christ in his death and resurrection, through the power of the Spirit, in the gift of the Father's love.*

This statement has a clear benefit: *It is simple.* It allows that there is more, but it starts with the clear and obvious. *It avoids immediate disagreement.* It also resonates with "mere Christianity" without asserting that this definition is the *final word.* It also invites us to *learn together in deeper humility* while we experience what Paul calls "the one body and one Spirit, just as you [plural *you*] were called to the one hope of your calling, one Lord, one faith, one baptism, one God and Father of all, who is above all and through all and in all" (Ephesians 4:4–6).

I am deeply involved in the work of ecumenism (from Greek *oikoumenē*, "the whole inhabited earth"), a global renewal movement that encourages the unity of the church. I have found that ecumenism is hard work. It seeks for a closer relationship with other believers in the love of Christ. Without denying our considerable differences, it includes the global church in all its various denominational, ethnic, and geographic diversity. I believe ecumenism is vital to Christ's mission. In John 17:20–23 our Lord prayed for visible and relational unity. The apostles valued unity highly and focused upon it during the first church council (see Acts 15). Since the late nineteenth century, unity has been important to missions. And since the last great global Catholic council, Vatican II, the interest of the worldwide church in this work has grown more and more.

Let me repeat: *The church is the fellowship of those who have been united to Christ in his death and resurrection, through the power of the Spirit, in the gift of the Father's love.*

They Will Know We Are Christians by Our Love

Some time ago I took a train ride into Chicago, then walked to the lakefront. It was a glorious, sunny August day so I strolled along a magnificent stretch of the city where for miles you can look out over Lake Michigan. I pondered my personal history with this great city that began in 1969 when I came here from the Deep South. One of my stops that day was the Chicago Historical Society Museum. Many things caught my attention, but the portion dedicated to the events of the summer of 1968 reminded me powerfully of the social tensions in the city when I arrived in January the next year. Riots that surrounded the Democratic National Convention rocked the city and the nation. The Vietnam War and demands for civil rights were both at tipping points. I recalled that in 1968 Fr. Peter R. Scholtes, a young parish priest, was serving at St. Brendan's Church on the South Side. Scholtes was looking for a song his youth group could sing at ecumenical, interracial, and interfaith events. In a single day, Fr. Peter wrote his first (and only) hymn, based on Jesus' words in John 13:35: "By this, everyone will know that you are my disciples, if you have love for one another." "They Will Know We Are Christians by Our Love" became renowned, by Christians worldwide. I remember first singing it as a student at Wheaton College.

The story behind Fr. Scholtes's song underscores what was going on in the late '60s as young Christians sought deeper unity in Christ. The music is lyrical, but most memorable are the simple, biblical words and their expression of a powerful Christ-centered desire:

1. We are one in the Spirit, we are one in the Lord.
   We are one in the Spirit, we are one in the Lord.
   And we pray that all unity may one day be restored.

Refrain

> And they'll know we are Christians by our love, by our love
> Yes, they'll know we are Christians by our love.

2. We will walk with each other, we will walk hand in hand.
   We will walk with each other, we will walk hand in hand.
   And together we'll spread the news that God is in our land.

3. We will work with each other, we will work side by side
   We will work with each other, we will work side by side.
   And we'll guard each one's dignity and save each one's pride.

4. All praise to the Father, from whom all things come.
   And all praise to Christ Jesus, his only Son.
   And all praise to the Spirit, who makes us one.

While researching the song's history I discovered an online obituary for Peter Raymond Scholtes. Throughout his life—whether as priest, musician-composer, social worker, teacher, community organizer, therapist, author, or consultant—Peter possessed what his friends called a "genius for making complex and important ideas easy to grasp and put to use." *He was described as confident in his convictions, yet openly embracing differences.* Scholtes's family and friends say he cherished friendships that bridged cultures and countries. Eventually he left the priesthood, married, and became a business consultant. He authored what has become a classic, *The Leader's Handbook* (1998), in which he made a definitive case *against performance appraisal in leadership evaluation.* He argued such appraisals were demoralizing and wrong. When I read his obituary and the tributes of his many friends, I discovered something that did not entirely surprise me: The man behind this well-known song practiced a form of servant leadership that sought the unity of the church in the love of Christ.

The Relationship of Love to Unity

We've established the new commandment is intimately connected to the new covenant, and the two *create* a new community. This new community gathers for worship to express love for Christ, to hear him speak to them as his people and to receive his sacred gifts. Jesus designed this new community to "become completely one, so that the world may know that you have sent me and have loved them even as you have loved me" (John 17:23).

But if one thing describes the new community in the third millennium, it is *dis*unity. We are marked by a continual tendency toward schism. We reach out to the world, yet even as Christianity is growing rapidly in Asia, Africa, and parts of Latin America, the church in the West is declining. The "center" of Christianity clearly is moving away from centuries of European expression. But the danger of disunity and schism still remains strong. Sadly, in both the East and the West the church has maintained its historic division over doctrinal controversies. This scandal of disunity is now being exported to these fast-growing churches beyond the West. We must face this problem head-on if we are to follow Jesus into costly "love (for) one another," the love that leads us into true unity. In so doing we will remain deeply connected to the new commandment and the new covenant as the Spirit's way into unity.

In John 17:10, Jesus prayed that the love the Father had for him, and thus the glory he had *in* the Father, would now extend *beyond* the Father and Son to his beloved disciples "so that they may be one, as we are one." *This is a prayer for deeply relational unity between persons.* The Father, Son, and Holy Spirit are in an eternal relationship of love. And this unity in trinity is being extended to those who are in the Son so we may be one with God and one another.

We must pause to note the great danger of taking *unity* to be the same as *uniformity.* The highly regarded twentieth-century biblical scholar Oscar Cullman referred to our need to pursue "reconciled diversity." (Pope Francis has invoked Cullman's language to describe his own vision for unity.) Our goal is *not* uniformity. *Uniformity is an external, superficial substitute for unity.* Uniformity makes the people in a group look alike, dress alike, and sound alike. But uniformity is *not* an internal, God-given, relational unity rooted in costly love. In some contexts, uniformity is easy, but *relational unity will always demand costly love.*

I have shared the most intimate human relationship in my life with Anita, my wife of forty-six plus years. Our unity often amazes us. We interrupt each other because we know what is coming next. We anticipate each other's moves and respond to our diversity with a great deal of emotion and passion. But our continued pursuit of peace and love leads us, two very different personalities, to pursue deeper unity. *We are very different, but we are one.*

Another great danger for Christians seeking unity is to settle for *an easy religious and cultural uniformity* based on rules, rituals, and religious ceremonies. This is one of the major causes of cheap love inside the church. We must not settle for uniformity, or cultural homogeneity, even in a single congregation.

It is also critical we see that the unity Jesus asked his Father to give to his disciples is the *result* of God's life in them. One of the most important words in this prayer is the word *as* (verse 11). The same word occurs in verses 21–23. "*As*" reveals the basis for the unity Jesus prays we will experience together: the unity *he already enjoys* with his Father! Because we understand and experience God as a community of persons, all our subsequent beliefs and actions must be rooted in relationships. This is why love cannot be known until it is practiced, which explains again the first and second great commandments. Love is not a theory but a deep internal reality.

True Christian unity is the result of Jesus' giving us the same love for one another that he has in the Trinity; thus, it is his costly love that leads us to become our unique (true) selves in love. How do I know this? Because Jesus asked his Father to give *all* Christians *the same kind of unity* that he enjoyed with his Father. The substance of God's love is found in a personal relationship with Jesus, given to us through another person, the Holy Spirit.

This truth is also clear in 1 Corinthians 12. In the body of Christ, true unity emerges when "destructive competition is abandoned and is replaced by loving concern for others.[5] This analogy in 1 Corinthians 12 of how the body of Christ works together precedes the best-known passage in Paul's letters. The whole point of 1 Corinthians 13, the "Love Chapter," is that the unity of the body comes about when *mutual* love is put into action. True mutual love always occurs in the context of true diversity.

Deep Ecumenism

John 17:21 led me to embrace what I now call *deep ecumenism*. This does not mean I deny vital aspects of Christian truth in order to find a lowest-common-denominator expression of faith. As we saw earlier, John's statement about Jesus coming into the world "full of grace and truth" (John 1:14) reveals an important tension that arises from pursuing truth *and* vigorously working to maintain deep unity in grace. Paul expressed this tension between "grace and truth" beautifully when he appealed to the churches in Ephesus "to make every effort to maintain the unity of the Spirit in the bond of peace" (Ephesians 4:3).

"Deep ecumenism" is another way of naming how the union of the new commandment, with the reality of life together in the new community, demands we go to every length possible to seek and preserve unity with one another. I find it helpful to call it *receptive ecumenism*. Our responsibility is not to ask, "What do other traditions first need to learn from us?" We should rather ask, "What do we first need to learn from other traditions?"[6] The assumption is if we ask this question, we can be drawn into a more receptive relationship.

One obvious proponent of these ideas is biblical scholar N. T. Wright. In early 2014 during a lecture in King's College Chapel, London, he said, "The visible tangible thing [to Paul] is the *ecclesia* [church], the united and holy community. Unity is easy if you don't care about holiness. Holiness is quite easy if you don't care about community. It's doing the two of them together that's the real trick."[7]

The tangible tension we often feel is between holiness and unity. Earlier I called it a tension between "grace and truth." But if we opt for a "least-common-denominator" form of Christianity, we will dismiss disagreements, both theological and ethical. The result will weaken the whole church, because we need all the parts of the body thinking, praying and responding to one another. I once heard a leader say, "If everyone is thinking the same thing, someone is not thinking." But when we let go of unity, we will question the legitimacy of anyone who doesn't agree with us. So which is *more* important? Grace or truth? Which reflects the character and nature of God? We can find the answer only in Jesus, who is completely and totally "full of grace and truth." Was Jesus a prophet or a reconciler? He was both—and *at the same time*. He is our model. He is our love.

Another way to consider this is to recall that holiness is prophetic while being unreconciled is unholy (Matthew 5:23–24). As I mentioned earlier, growing up in the Deep South, *the* prophetic issue of my childhood and college years was civil rights. Speaking about it and working for change created tension and provoked division inside the church, yet both speaking clearly and living faithfully were necessary. Justice and truth demanded it. But if we long for justice alone, we will often lose sight of grace. I've learned that this tension will never go away as long as we struggle to do what is right *and* love one another. The answer does not lie in an idealistic "third way." It lies in following Jesus *in* "the Way." We must be true disciples!

In my own journey, I've discovered theological and ethical debates generally lead us to take sides. Once we take a side, we tend to believe we are right. It then follows that if we're right, others must be wrong. This very easily degenerates into an expression of posturing rooted in power and personality. What is the alternative? To live together in the new community, to become those who are "making every effort to maintain the unity of the Spirit in the bond of peace" (Ephesians 4:3).[8]

One thing about pursuing costly love has become clear to me: Purposefully seeking it will create profound tension. We can embrace it, and work from within it for unity with "all humility and gentleness, with patience, bearing with one another in love" (Ephesians 4:2). Or we can compromise costly love and miss this divine call to live in this tension of *both* "grace and truth." When we maintain that tension we can learn to live so "They'll Know We Are Christians by Our Love." The choices we make from within this emotional and intellectual dynamic will determine the future of Christianity—a future that promises to be very different from our recent past.

Conclusion

Chiara Lubich possessed what her companions called a "fundamental intuition" about unity. She described her understanding of God's "primary mode of seeing" as *true unity*. She concluded: "If two minds unite in Christ in their midst, it may seem that in doing so they mortify themselves, but instead they are empowered, because they become closer to the mind of God."[9] She believed unity was *not* a mixture composed through compromise, but a combination achieved when every component is present within the flame of divine love. She further believed a person who is fused into this unity loses everything, but this loss results in true gain. We lose not our personalities (true selves) but our independent selves. *Because God lives in unity and God is oneness, we can empty ourselves and be made one in triune love.* We can rediscover ourselves in Christ. Deep within ourselves we learn that "living is Christ and dying is gain" (Philippians 1:21). *This is costly love.* Anything else is *not* the love of Christ. Such love requires us to "die every day" (1 Corinthians 15:31) so that we may live as "the new creation" (2 Corinthians 5:17). This is *how* we grow into divine oneness and so become the new community that lives out the new commandment in the gracious context of the new covenant.

CHAPTER FIFTEEN

THIS IS MY BODY, BROKEN BY YOU

> Any concern for fresh spiritual life that is in
> accordance with the teaching of the New Tes-
> tament must also lead to a concern for unity
> of the church. Our search is not for unifor-
> mity. But it is only when we can pray together,
> work together, worship together, break bread
> together, and truly love and trust one another,
> that we can begin to speak of a united church,
> however varied its form of expression and
> worship continue to be.
>
> David Watson

MORE THAN A DECADE ago I served as interim minister in a badly divided church. During this time,
for four successive weeks I preached from a text in
Paul's letter to the churches in Ephesus:

I therefore, the prisoner in the Lord, beg you to lead a life
worthy of the calling to which you have been called, with
all humility and gentleness, with patience, bearing with
one another in love, *making every effort to maintain the
unity of the Spirit in the bond of peace.*" (Ephesians 4:1–3,
emphasis added)

I have italicized the words I stressed in my four sermons.
I wanted to do everything I could to plant this divine principle in the hearts of these dear people. One of them asked
me, "When are you going to preach from another text?" (I

was tempted to answer, "When I see you practicing the text I preached from last week.") I explained as clearly as I knew how that I was seeking a *realized unity* in their fellowship, one that involved the Spirit's working in them through love. This unity was far more than intellectual assent to common doctrine, worship, preaching, and prayer. (They thought they were divided by doctrine, but the truth was they were divided by personality, and as much as anything by the loss of love.) I longed to see this church share in Christ's work of mercy and charity as one flock. I explained how God's love, experienced within a reconciled diversity, would lead them into a growing relational unity. This unity would then heal them and allow the world to see and hear their common witness. I further explained how this unity could come about only if they worked together as one, "seeking first his kingdom" (Matthew 6:33). Then they would practice the new commandment within the life of the new community.

God Loves the Whole World

In John 17:9, Jesus enlarged his prayer circle to include his own disciples: "I am not asking on behalf of the world, but on behalf of those whom you gave me." He plainly says he is asking on behalf of his brothers. Does this mean Jesus does not love the world? Only an understanding of the use of the word *world* in the fourth Gospel can provide a solid answer.

I don't believe Jesus is excluding anyone from his love. Here, he is praying *specifically* for his disciples because he loves the world. It may seem that his love excludes some, but numerous texts in this same Gospel say otherwise. The most prominent is John 3:16, which says God "gave" his only Son *because* he loved the world. So what does the word *world* mean here in John 17?

In John, *world* carries a variety of meanings. It can be expansive and positive, the very object of God's universal creativity and love (see John 1:10; 3:16). It can express the sphere of his redemptive intention (12:47). Elsewhere it refers to the place where Jesus does *not* belong (18:36) or to what is hostile to Jesus and his people (14:17; 17:14–15; 19:17). The Johannine church seems to have faced hostility because it was made up of a minority of Christians living among a minority community of hated Jews. Thus it seems apparent that in this context, *world* refers to the "hostile" and unbelieving world; i.e., those who walk in darkness and oppose the light. "[Jesus] cannot pray for their success as long as they remain part of the hostile world. Rather, he prays that the world, understood as a good creation gone bad, should simply cease to exist."[1] In other words, he prays that those in the hostile world would turn to him and believe the Good News. If they believe this joyful message, they will hear his prayer for them in 17:21–24 and (one hopes) apply it to themselves. "The world beyond the disciples may indeed represent opposition to Jesus, but he is well aware that it is the Father's intention that all creation should belong to him."[2]

Jesus would soon leave the physical, earthly world. His disciples would spread the good news of God's love and grace. Their mission would arouse hostility, just as Jesus experienced. The evil one would not stop his attack on Jesus, and thus would unleash his fury against those who followed him. Therefore Jesus asks his Father to *protect* his disciples: "Holy Father, *protect* them in your name that you have given me, so that they may be one, as we are one" (John 17:11). John is writing these words so that particular early communities would keep this truth alive.

Nowhere else in the Fourth Gospel does Jesus use the term *Holy Father* in prayer. Here *holy* is used as his most familiar way of addressing his Father. Through Jesus, who referred to his Father as *Abba*, we can now address God as *our* Holy Father. We are protected "in" the name of our Holy Father. This is an acknowledgment of *both* God's love and his holiness. We have come right back to "grace and truth" incarnated in Jesus.

Does Jesus address this prayer to the authority and power of God's name so that we use it as a holy title? Yes. But what's being said here is specific to this particular context. Jesus is speaking of a *relationship* between believers *and* himself. He's not just saying, "Holy Father, use the power connected with your name to keep my disciples." He *is* saying, "Holy Father, keep these disciples intimately connected with yourself as (*in the same way*) I am in intimate union with you." His request is remarkable because *Jesus prays that his disciples will experience a perfect relational unity patterned after that of the Father and Son.* He is praying that all his followers in "the Way" experience his intimate presence, just as he did with his Father.

Jesus' words clearly mean God wants us to have a unified desire and purpose in serving and glorifying him. Jesus prayed we would be one (17:21–23), *just as* the Father and the Son are one. Or, just as the Father, Son, and Holy Spirit are *united in the bond of eternal love*, so all believers should be united in this same glorious relational and eternal love. Only then can we experience what is promised, namely *the love of God in our relationships with one another.* When we think about it for long, we can't help but conclude this holy, relational, triune love must be costly. This is the costly love that leads us to die so we might live, love that is *the mark of true discipleship.* This love is what it means to follow "in the Way."

Becoming One

When I first began to understand John 17, I realized Jesus most desired for his disciples to live divine oneness together. He wanted them to be united as a powerful witness to the reality of the union between the Father and the Son. *His prayer is that our becoming one will be the catalyst for people to come to know God's love.* I had never before seen this clearly. I'd been engaged in evangelism since I was twelve years old, yet I had never known unity had so much to do with evangelism and mission until I was nearly forty years of age. My growing friendships with Christians who were very different from me, my prayer with these other Christians, and the prayer of Jesus in John 17:20–24 coalesced to lead me into a life-transforming vision of unity rooted in costly love. I experienced precisely what Jesus prayed for: "As you, Father, are in me and I am in you, may they also be in us, *so that the world may believe that you have sent me ... so that the world may know that you have sent me and have loved them even as you have loved me*" (John 17:21, 23).

Christian unity in relationships is clearly the divine design for showing the world that God loves them. When people see true love between Christians, they will believe the Father "loves" them. God loves the world and sent his Son into it as the fullest, final expression of his eternal love. Jesus did not come to condemn the world but to save it (John 3:16–17). What does Christian unity have to do with the love of Christ? *Everything.* It provides *the real-life context* in which people can "see" God's love in action. Pope Francis sums up how Christians should face the world: "Behave like Jesus. Always answer with love and with the power of truth."[3]

Meanwhile Back at the Church

Earlier we considered the matter of "essentials" and "non-essentials." I want to return to this subject again in the light of how unity and love reveal God to the world.

Several years ago I experienced full-force this important distinction during an encounter one Saturday afternoon with some evangelists outside Bryant-Denny Stadium in Tuscaloosa, Alabama. (I was a student at the University of Alabama in the 1960s and remain a serious Alabama football fan.) On my way into the stadium I passed some street preachers. One of them said something I considered so ludicrous I stopped in my tracks. Initially I tried to engage him one-to-one. Before long, three more men converged on me. Although I generally do not react, having learned it almost never results in a godly response on my part, several things they said triggered a reaction. The most obvious comment I remember related to their condemnation of other Christians. They asked me, "Do you really know Jesus as your Lord and Savior?" I smiled and said, "Yes, I do." They pressed me and asked why I was going to the game. (I was wearing a shirt with the university's colors and logo.) They said I was an "idolater" and going to hell. *Now* I was upset. The rest of the conversation went something like this:

They asked, "How do you know you are a Christian?"

I answered, "Because of my faith and trust in Christ and my deep love for him."

They responded, "That doesn't make you a real Christian. You have to reject sin and be baptized in the right way and follow the way of holiness that we follow."

I responded, "What is the gospel?"

Their answer included a lot of man-made concepts. So I responded by telling them what the gospel *really* was and how it was good news. After about two minutes I told them that I had taught evangelism at the Billy Graham Center at Wheaton College, which loosed a torrent of angry words. "You are clearly compromised and lost," they responded. "You are a false teacher and are leading many to hell."

After a few more heated exchanges I recalled a simple principle: *walk away.* Nothing good or godly could come from this confrontation. Besides, now I was a pagan headed to a football game, and they had already upset a perfectly lovely afternoon.

I'm sure many of us could share similar stories. They all come down to some people claiming that they know God and you do not. And they all involve a kind of certitude that condemns the other because some claim to "know" what is true and not true.

Now, these guys weren't *entirely* wrong. Sectarians are never *entirely* wrong. Stressing holiness and obedience to God is good. But these evangelists had made non-essential ideas (in most instances, nonbiblical ones) into essential ones. Their *particular list* had nothing to do with the transforming power of true faith in Christ. Their message contained no love.

So what should we do when we face difficult issues in the church, especially about doctrine? We need to ask, "Is this really a salvation issue?" If the answer is no, then the debate is usually about non-essentials. But even if we disagree regarding essentials, we must still show love! Scot McKnight calls this way of thinking and loving *The Jesus Creed*.[4] This best-selling book encourages Christians to recognize a simple, transforming truth: The gospel tells us God seeks us as sinners in order to restore us to wholeness. He not only makes us better individuals but also transforms us into the new community of Jesus, a society in which we strive to be in union with God and one another by the practice of the new commandment. As a result we will live love *together* as our core creedal confession.

Living by the Jesus Creed allows disagreement about non-essentials. In fact, we can disagree about some things we even call essentials, as long as in arrogance and private opinion we don't walk apart from the life-giving fellowship of the church. Remember, the new commandment brings us into the new covenant and the new covenant is situated in the new community, which is the church.

Does Heresy Still Matter?

It's useful to consider briefly the matter of heresy. Among modern Christians the word is hardly ever used properly. Heresy is most often used to *smear* what we consider wrong doctrine, or to label people or churches we believe are wrong. The Greek word *hairesis* occurs in the Scriptures in several places, though modern versions do not always translate it as "heresy." It specifically means "to break into factions, to cause division or schism (another word for division)."[5] Ironically— and sadly—both wrong doctrine *and right doctrine* can create heresy. The church produced creeds for many reasons, but especially to define orthodoxy more carefully in order to preserve catholicity and unity. C. S. Lewis calls this core of confessed truth "mere Christianity." What he refers to with this term is not content-less faith but the robust beliefs of ancient Christianity that over the ages have been common to nearly all Christians.

The first edition of the *New Living Translation* (1996) captures a key idea. It translates the word *divisions* in Galatians 5:19–20 as "the feeling that everyone is wrong except those in your own little group." This really is *the* point.

Heresy occurs when heterodoxies (unconventional or nonstandard approaches to doctrines or ideas) cause factions. Bad doctrine is a problem, for sure. *But the far-greater problem is sowing division and creating disunity in the church by misusing doctrine, even right doctrine.* This whole matter is seen in Paul's counsel: "The whole law can be summed up in this one command: 'Love your neighbor as yourself.' But if you are always biting and devouring one another, watch out! Beware of destroying one another" (Galatians 5:14–15). Heresies over doctrines and ideas destroy brothers and sisters.

Sometimes I hear, "Love can never triumph over bad doctrine, because bad doctrine will always lead people to error, and error will always lead people to hell." When people think this way, they generally have a hard time with any teaching that disagrees with their viewpoint. They may indulge in hostility and dissension, openly causing division. But if *heresy* is taken in its original, apostolic sense (namely, that which "causes division"), maybe we have misunderstood the word. So I am not arguing for heterodoxy in the ancient Christian sense of the word. I'm pointing out how we use doctrines to create our own particular concepts that we then use to judge others and create division.

To summarize, if we get doctrine right but don't follow the Jesus Creed, we'll *always* be wrong. This is so hard for us to grasp, because it seems to allow, even encourage, complete compromise. We think because we follow Christ, we are right about every concept we believe as Christians; indeed, we think this way within Western culture in general. As consumers we become easily offended, bitter and withdrawn. It is precisely here we should run as fast as possible to the Jesus Creed. George Koch puts real life in perspective:

> When someone complains that the debate has become rancorous and mean, the charge is laid that the

peacemakers value being "nice" over being in accord with God's will, that they stick their heads in the sand or are afraid to name aloud what is seriously wrong. Those who do not approve of vicious attack are themselves attacked—accused of being wimps, or quislings, or traitors—apparently in the hope of silencing them, or justifying the hateful attacker's words and methods.[6]

Koch, an Anglican Messianic Jew, says it would be more accurate if we acknowledged that Christianity cut itself off from Judaism and moved to Greece! In Greece we were assimilated. Our collective memory of our Hebrew ancestry was forgotten. In this context, Christian conservatives and liberals now argue and quarrel and further divide the church. We divide primarily over philosophy, schools of thought, and personalities. We accuse others of bad motives, false teaching, and Christ-denying doctrine. What we need, Koch rightly concludes, is "to be married to God, and [to] let him have his way with us. We need to be ravished, not lectured."[7]

Does heresy matter? It surely does. True heresy sows seeds of disruption and dissension and creates the soil in which the enemy of Christ and his kingdom can work *within* the church. Real heresy actually causes us to forget the new commandment, the new covenant, *and* the new community. The result is massive, unchecked, terrible sin.

The Dark Sin of Schism

The church throughout the world faces a massive sin problem. This is especially true in the West, where Christianity is in decline. Paul names this problem with these words:

> Watch the way you talk. Let nothing foul or dirty come out of your mouth. Say only what helps, each word a gift. Don't grieve God. Don't break his heart. His Holy Spirit, moving and breathing in you, is the most intimate part of your life, making you fit for himself. Don't take such a gift for granted. Make a clean break with all cutting, back-biting, profane talk. Be gentle with one another, sensitive. Forgive one another as quickly and thoroughly as God in Christ forgave you. (Ephesians 4:29–32, The Message)

At this point I could pile up many more texts from James, Peter, or John, all of them reminding us that what really matters is to "love one another." In the end every text I could quote says the same thing—if you ignore these exhortations and speak against one another, your words and actions will cause more division. This is grievous and destructive sin. A divisive person is "self-condemned" (Titus 3:11).

It's one thing to talk about the sin of division in the church. It's another to grieve over it and earnestly pray about how we can stop it. I believe the real difference will come only when our words and actions encourage love and healing. It is time that all the faithful—especially our pastors, bishops, elders, deacons, and ministry leaders—confess that we have created this problem! We must all confess in humble weakness that we have contributed to this sinful disunity by refusing to love one another. We must stop our sinning or face loving judgment. One can hazard an educated guess that the *major* cause of the compromised state of the church in the West, and its rapid decline, is not really secularism, atheism, or aggressive cults. It is not even about who preaches the true gospel, although preaching the gospel is vitally important. Our real problem is that our love is no longer costly; thus those who follow Christ do not seek unity among themselves. Sadly, only a handful of Christians realize the depth and nature of this problem. But the evidence from both surveys and new movements for unity is that their number is growing.

What Does Love Have to Do with Unity?

Everything.

When God revealed a whole new understanding of Christian unity to me—what I now call *missional-ecumenism*—I began to share this message as widely as possible. Over time I came to realize two things.

First, *if I teach and practice our Lord's will for unity in Christ's mission I need to love more deeply*. This love needs to be *both* relational and inclusive. My church was genuinely too small. I had limited its borders to those who embraced my theology, culture, doctrinal preferences, and politics. I soon realized I didn't need to transform my *understanding* of the church so much as I needed to have a fresh vision of it. This journey began in the early 1990s and continues today. The mountains and valleys I've passed over and through have revealed to me that my deeper problem is not unity. *It is costly love.* I could not pursue unity until I learned to pursue and live God-Love.

Second, *the obvious point of our Lord's prayer for unity is that we share in his heart.* Remember, the "glory" he speaks of throughout this prayer is revealed through his showing us the "deeper, hidden nature" of his Father's love. This is what I mean by "heart." *God is love, and Jesus is the ultimate revelation of divine love.* To understand God's love, we must gaze more intently at Jesus. Christ must become our center. Whatever else we see in scripture, especially in the darker portions of the Old Testament, we must realize God *is* love because in Jesus we see love totally revealed.

Clearly God loves Israel. He gave Israel the covenant and the law. This gracious gift was for their guidance and protection. This covenant and the law are good. While admittedly there are some hard passages in the Old Testament, in which some Jews found reasons to avoid others, there are also many instances in which foreigners came to know the power of God and his gracious acceptance. A few come to mind immediately: Jethro, father-in-law of Moses; Rahab, the Canaanite prostitute; and Naaman, commander of the Aramean army. Then there are the wicked citizens of ancient Nineveh, whom Jonah first refused to tell of God's impending judgment because he feared God would be merciful to them (Jonah 3:1–5, 4:2). These and numerous other stories reveal how non-Jews became a part of God's people, but they did not stop being who they were—"outsiders." Many of these who came to believe remained people of other national and ethnic groups but their lives were changed, thus they freely proclaimed the power and mercy of the God of Israel.

Of course, the high point in the redemptive storyline occurs in the coming of the Son of God: "grace and truth" came to *all* through Jesus Christ. He is "God the only Son, who is close to the Father's heart... [who] has made him known" (John 1:18). This is truly superior.

If we are to learn just how much we are loved, we must know Jesus far better, because *Jesus alone reveals the Father's heart to the whole world.* And if we learn how much Jesus really loves us, we can love God—and one another—with a love that will never be cheap or diluted.

Augustine once said when we try to comprehend God, or explain him in our feeble words, we are like children trying to empty the ocean by scooping water into a little pond we make on the shore. In the end whatever we understand about God is only a drop from the sea of our vast unknowing. But the one truth we can grasp, by humbling ourselves before the mystery of Christ, is this—God *is* love.[8]

Theologian Karl Barth understood the nature of man and God very well. When he was asked what he had learned from his lifetime of work in Christian theology, he said simply, "Jesus loves me! This I know, for the Bible tells me so."

Conclusion

I hope you can now see the scope of our *massive problem* in the modern church. I further hope you can see the solution is clear. We need a fresh encounter with God-Love. We need to be transformed by the experience of love so we might become a transforming community of Spirit-empowered people.

Yet you must understand that if you grasp this deeply enough, applying the truth of love may cost you everything. *The problem is division, schism, and sectarianism.* This is an egregious sin against Christ's new commandment and it touches everything about the church in our time. It is sin against the purpose of the new covenant. It eats away the joy and power of the new community. I often hear Christians talk about God judging America or the American church.

Lamentably, I have almost never heard an exposition of the real reason why this could be true.

Yet as odd as it might seem, at this point I do not believe the church's first task in the twenty-first century is to seek for love, at least *not* directly. Why? *The love of Christ is already in us.* The gift of his salvation in us is love itself. What we need above all else is to identify the barriers we've erected, knowingly or unknowingly, against God-Love. These barriers stand within each of us personally and are apparent in *all* our communities of faith. We must tear down every human and diabolical barrier that sets itself up against costly love.[9] Then we must build bridges of faith that allow us to enter more deeply into God-Love in relational unity. This is what our Lord prayed for in John 17:21.

Francis de Sales speaks to our problem with utter simplicity: "We learn to study by studying … to dance by dancing, to swim by swimming. So we also learn to love God and our neighbor by *loving* them."[10] We can no longer afford to be indifferent. We must learn to love by loving!

For this reason I conclude with three prayers that express everything I hope you have heard in my words. I have written with the hope you will embrace these prayers as God's will for all of us as Christian believers.

First, consider this amazing text from the *Book of Common Prayer*, "For the Unity of the Church" (see Various Occasions no. 14, and Collect no 6).

> O God the Father of our Lord Jesus Christ, our only Savior, the Prince of Peace: Give us grace seriously to lay to heart the great dangers we are in by our unhappy divisions; take away all hatred and prejudice, and whatever else may hinder us from godly union and concord; that, as there is but one Body and one Spirit, one hope of our calling, one Lord, one Faith, one Baptism, one God and Father of us all, so we may be all of one heart and of one soul, united in one holy bond of truth and peace, of faith and charity, and may with one mind and one mouth, glorify thee; through Jesus Christ our Lord, Amen.

Second, a modern Chinese Christian prayer has influenced me deeply. It was likely written by someone who understood the true nature of oppression and who also saw the need for a unified church to witness against all that is truly evil and under the power of darkness.

> Help each of us, gracious God,
> to live in such magnanimity and restraint
> that the head of the church may never have cause to say to
> any one of us, "This is my body, broken by you."

Third, I share a prayer, inspired by John Henry Cardinal Newman, which has become my daily prayer. It was adapted and used by Mother Teresa each day after she received holy communion.[11]

> Dear Jesus, help me to spread Your fragrance
> wherever I go.
> Flood my soul with Your Spirit and life.
> Penetrate and possess my whole being so utterly,
> that my life may only be a radiance of Yours.
> Shine through me, and be so in me
> that every soul I come in contact with
> may feel Your presence in my soul.
> Let them look up, and see no longer me, but only Jesus!
> Stay with me and then I will begin to shine as You shine,
> So to shine as to be a light to others.
> The light, O Jesus, will be all from You;
> none of it will be mine.
> It will be You, shining on others through me.
> Let me thus praise You in the way which you love best,
> by shining on those around me.
> Let me preach You without preaching,
> not by words but by example,
> by the catching force,
> the sympathetic influence of what I do,
> the evident fullness of the love my heart beats to You.
> Amen.

FOR FURTHER READING

Armstrong, John H. *Your Church Is Too Small: Why Unity in Christ's Mission Is Vital to the Future of the Church.* Grand Rapids, MI: Zondervan, 2010.

Arnold, Eberhard. *The Early Christians in Their Own Words.* Farmington, PA: The Plough Publishing Company, 1970.

Batson, David. *The Treasure Chest of the Early Christians.* Grand Rapids, MI: Eerdmans, 2001.

Benedict XVI. *God Is Love: Deus Caritas Est.* San Francisco, CA: Ignatius Press, 2006.

Bondi, Roberta. *To Love as God Loves: Conversations with the Early Church.* Philadelphia, PA: Fortress, 1987.

Boyd, Gregory A. *Repenting of Religion: Turning from Judgment to the Love of God.* Grand Rapids, MI: Baker, 2004.

Brümmer, Vincent. *The Model of Love.* New York: Cambridge University Press, 1993.

Cairns, Scott. *Love's Immensity: Mystics on the Endless Life.* Brewster, MA: Paraclete Press, 2007.

Cerini, Marissa. *God Who Is Love in the Experience and Thought of Chiara Lubich.* Hyde Park, NY: New City Press, 1992.

Enns, Gaylord. *Love Revolution: Recovering the Lost Command of Jesus.* Chico, CA: Love Revolution Press, 2005.

Forest, Jim. *Loving Our Enemies: Reflections on the Hardest Commandment.* Maryknoll, NY: Orbis Books, 2014.

Pope Francis. *Evangelii Gaudium: The Joy of the Gospel.* New York: Random House, 2013.

Gillet, Florence, trans. Bill Hartnett. *The Choice of Jesus Forsaken in the Theological Perspective of Chiara Lubich.* Hyde Park, NY: New City Press, 2015.

Gittins, Anthony J. *A Presence That Disturbs: A Call to Radical Discipleship.* Ligouri, MO: Ligouri Triumph, 2002.

Green, Michael. *Evangelism in the Early Church.* Grand Rapids, MI: Eerdmans, 1970.

Grenz, Stanley J. *Theology for the Community of God.* Grand Rapids: Eerdmans, 2000.

Harrington, Daniel J. *Jesus the Revelation of the Father's Love: What the New Testament Teaches Us.* Huntingdon, IN: Our Sunday Visitor, 2010.

Jackson, Timothy P. *Love Disconsoled: Reflections on Christian Charity.* New York: Cambridge University Press, 1999.

Jeanrond, Werner G. *A Theology of Love.* New York: T & T Clark, 2010.

Koch, George Byron. *What We Believe and Why.* Northwoods, IL: Byron Arts, 2012.

Kreeft, Peter. *The God Who Loves You.* San Francisco, CA: Ignatius Press, 1988.

Latourette, Kenneth Scott. *A History of Christianity.* Peabody, MA: Hendrickson Press, 2000 reprint.

Lewis, C. S. *Mere Christianity.* San Francisco, CA: HarperOne, 2001.

_____. *The Four Loves.* San Francisco, CA: HarperOne, 1971 reprint.

Lindberg, Carter. *Love: A Brief History Through Western Christianity.* Malden, MA: Blackwell Publishing, 2008.

Loya, John F. and Joseph A. Loya. *Jesus' Love Stories: Scriptural Insights into the Spirituality of Christian Loving.* Mahwah, NJ: Paulist Press, 2007.

Lubich, Chiara. *Essential Writings: Spirituality, Dialogue, Culture.* Hyde Park, NY: New City Press, 2007.

Lubich, Chiara, eds. Donato Falmi and Florence Gillet. *Unity.* Hyde Park, NY: New City Press, 2015.

Quezada, Adolfo. *Radical Love: Following the Way of Jesus.* Mahwah, NJ: Paulist Press, 2010.

Rossé, Gerard. *The Spirituality of Communion: A New Approach to the Johannine Writings.* Hyde Park, NY: New City Press, 1998.

Smith, James K. A. *Desiring the Kingdom: Worship, Worldview, and Cultural Formation.* Grand Rapids, MI: Baker, 2009.

_____. *Imagining the Kingdom: How Worship Works.* Grand Rapids, MI: Baker, 2013.

_____. *You Are What You Love: The Spiritual Power of Habit.* Grand Rapids, MI: Brazos Press, 2016.

Tippett, Krista. *Becoming Wise: An Inquiry into the Mystery and Art of Living.* New York: Penguin Press, 2016.

ENDNOTES

Introduction

1. This quote is from *Catholicism: The Pivotal Players, St. Francis of Assisi*, video series, 2016.

2. Chiara Lubich, *Essential Writings* (Hyde Park, NY: New City Press, 2007), 11.

3. *Kairos* (καιρός) is an ancient Greek term that refers to the right or opportune moment. *Kairos* signifies a time lapse, a moment of indeterminate time in which everything happens. We are living, it seems to me, in a unique moment in which the social structures that have unified us are now breaking down. What will fill this space is yet to be seen, but I am sure that God is doing something both ancient and new.

4. John H. Armstrong, *Your Church Is Too Small* (Grand Rapids, MI: Zondervan, 2010), 11.

5. Anthony C. Thiselton, *Systematic Theology* (Grand Rapids, MI: Eerdmans, 2015), 43.

6. The split between Christians and Jews came about because of many factors, but the tone and posture adopted by Christians in the early second century became increasingly anti-Semitic. This legacy cut the church off from its historical and (broadly speaking) biblical roots.

7. James K. A. Smith, *You Are What You Love: The Spiritual Power of Habit* (Grand Rapids, MI: Brazos Press, 2016), 6–7.

8. Paul Tillich, *The Protestant Era* (Chicago, IL: University of Chicago Press, 1948), xxv.

Chapter One

1. James K. A. Smith, *Desiring the Kingdom: Worship, Worldview, and Cultural Formation* (Grand Rapids, MI: Baker Academic, 2009), 26–27.

2. *Handbook of Religion: A Christian Engagement with Traditions, Teachings, and Practices*, eds. Terry C. Muck, Harold A. Netland, and Gerald R. McDermott (Grand Rapids: Baker Academic, 2014). This is the finest, most accurate, most complete treatment of world religions I've read by modern Christian scholars. The editors say there are two ways to understand the word *religion*: (1) The academic way defines it in terms of given beliefs and practices and then compares this definition with social and psychological phenomena. (2) The experiential method determines what a religion is by how the adherents judge and practice their beliefs. According to this second way, Marxism, for example, is a religion. One scholar of religions, Gordon Melton, says there are over fifteen hundred *new* religious movements in the United States alone, xii.

3. Charles Hodge, *Systematic Theology*, vol. 1 (Grand Rapids: Eerdmans, 1989 [1871–1873]), 204. I do not deny that these attributions apply to God, only that putting them all together in a kind of logical list provides a "statement of the contents of our idea of God." One reviewer asks how such a statement about God can help us in responding to Islam or to the doctrine of the (relational) Trinity, which Hodge did not even mention until he had written 250 pages of dense exposition of the doctrine of God.

4. Karl Barth, *Church Dogmatics*. ed. G. W. Bromiley and T. F. Torrance (Edinburgh, T & T. Clark, 1957–1975), II/1, 179.

5. When I use the word "ideology" here and elsewhere, I am contrasting Jesus and love with human ideology. What do I mean? This term was born in the philosophical and political debates of the French Revolution. I am using it to refer to a *system of abstract meaning* applied to matters like politics, economic views, or the specific ways in which we explain how the world works. If we distinguish between a public and private life we tend to create ideologies. I am also using ideology to refer to any widely accepted vision of how things should be. An ideology is less encompassing than a worldview but many (so-called) worldviews, including some so-called "Christian worldviews," are nothing more than dogmatic ideologies. *An ideologue is a person who adheres to a simplistic ex-*

planation of the world which generally results in uncompromising dogmatism. Holding to rigid ideology will usually result in the inability to hear other viewpoints with respect.

6.   Ernesto Cardenal, trans. Dinah Livingstone, *Love: A Glimpse of Eternity* (Paraclete Press: Brewster, MA, 1970, reprinted 2006), 88.

7.   "Bertrand Russell Speaks His Mind," interview with Woodrow Wyatt, 1959.

8.   Bertrand Russell, *The Impact of Science on Society* (Sydney, Australia: Allen and Unwin, 1952), 114.

9.   Mother Teresa, in Malcolm Muggeridge, *Something Beautiful for God* (New York, NY: Collins, 1972), 73–74.

10.   Carter Lindberg, *Love: A Brief History Through Western Christianity* (Malden, MA: Blackwell, 2008), x.

11.   I plan to write another book that will deal *directly* with the questions surrounding the nature of God as love.

12.   Dianne Bergant, quoted in the *New Living Translation Study Bible* (Carol Stream, IL, 2008), 1300.

Chapter Two

1.   Christa Tippett, *Becoming Wise: An Inquiry into the Mystery and Art of Living* (New York, NY: Penguin Press, 2016), 10.

2.   Lindberg, ix.

3.   Dallas Willard, *Getting Love Right*, Kindle edition. A paper presented at the American Association of Christian Counselors conference in Nashville, Tennessee, on September 15, 2007. Conference Theme: "No Greater Love." Published as an e-book.

4.   David Robson, "There Really Are 50 Eskimo Words for 'Snow,'" *Washington Post*, January 14, 2013.

5.   Tippett, 103.

6.   This is a profound, mysterious truth that Christians often do not perceive. In a subsequent book I hope to unpack this in some depth. All I can do here is state the theological idea of a relational God who is Father, Son and Holy Spirit. The word "relational" has become popular. But it is a *modern term* rooted in sociological ideas. A family, for example, is a web of relationships. In pietism and evangelical spirituality this idea was expressed by the idea of

entering into a "personal relationship" with Jesus. I cannot find this idea in Luther, Calvin or the Catholic Counter-Reformation but it is clearly *prevalent* today, even in some Catholic circles. The modern term "reflexivity" might convey the meaning of "relational" more clearly. As we mature in discipleship we become more reflexive toward each other within relationships centered in God's love.

7. C. S. Lewis, *The Four Loves* (New York, NY: Harcourt, Brace & Company, 1960), 9–12.

8. Walter Hooper, *C. S. Lewis: A Companion & Guide* (San Francisco, CA: Harper, 1996), 368–370.

9. Travis Bott, "The Loving God of the Old Testament," *The Missioner, Pentecost 2015*, vol. 31, no. 4. *The Missioner* is the magazine of Nashotah House Theological Seminary, Nashotah, Wisconsin. The quotes I reference here are all from this article.

10. Ibid.

11. Allan F. Wright, *The Bible's Best Love Stories* (Cincinnati, OH: St. Anthony Messenger Press, 2010), 1–4.

12. Tippett, 104.

13. Ibid.

14. Timothy P. Jackson, *Love Disconsoled: Meditations on Christian Charity* (Cambridge, MA: Cambridge University Press, 1999), 11.

15. Ceslas Spicq, *Theological Lexicon of the New Testament*, three volumes, trans. by Sister Marie Aquinas McNamara, O.P. and Sister Mary Honoraria Richter, O.P. (St. Louis, MO: B. Herder Book Company, 1963), I:8. One reviewer of this now standard work writes: "Spicq's quest is not for morphology, orthography, or even grammar or syntax; rather, he wants to uncover the religious meaning of the language used in the New Testament."

16. Smith, *Desiring the Kingdom*, 51–52. James K.A. Smith concludes that our real problem is *not* our having desire. Our problem is that we desire the wrong thing! To be human is to be shaped by desire. We all have innate drives that push or pull us in certain directions but when pushed in the wrong direction we choose sin. As Augustine says, our innate love has become "disordered." So the love of God draws us in a specific direction, *through our desires*, into God-Love.

17. William Klassen, "Love (NT and Early Jewish Literature)," *The Anchor Bible Dictionary*, Vol. IV (New York, NY: Doubleday, 1992), 384.

18. Peter Kreeft, *The God Who Loves You: Love Divine, All Loves Excelling* (San Francisco, CA: Ignatius Press, 2004), 53. He also notes that God cannot "fall in love, not because he is less loving than we are but because he is more. He cannot fall in love for the same reason that water cannot get wet: it *is* wet. God *is* love, and Love itself cannot receive love as passivity" (53).

19. Ibid., 54.

20. Ibid., 55.

21. Ibid., 56.

22. Jackson, 23. This entire section on "strong" agape, and the points that follow, come from my personal interaction with his insightful book. His chapter "Biblical Keys to Love" is a brilliant treatise on this subject.

23. Marisa Cerini, *God Who Is Love in the Experience and Thought of Chiara Lubich* (Hyde Park: NY, 1992), 18–19.

24. Ibid., 19.

25. John F. Loya and Joseph A. Loya, *Jesus' Love Stories: Scriptural Insights into the Spirituality of Christian Living* (New York, NY: Paulist Press, 2007), 6.

26. Augustine, *Confessions*, trans. Henry Chadwick. Oxford (Oxford University Press, 1991), 1.1.1.

27. Smith, *You Are What You Love*, 8.

Chapter Three

1. Søren Kierkegaard, quoted in David Manning White, *Eternal Quest*, Vol. 2 (New York, NY: Paragon House, 1984), 128.

2. Ibid., 128–29.

3. The Sadducees rejected Oral Law as proposed by the Pharisees. Rather, they saw the Torah (the written law of the Old Testament) as the *only* source of divine authority. According to the first-century historian Josephus, the Sadducees believed the soul was not immortal, thus there was no afterlife, no rewards or penalties after death. Clearly, the Sadducees did not believe in the resurrec-

tion of the dead, a central doctrine in the teaching of Jesus and early Christians. The Sadducees, members of the wealthier class, descended from Solomon's high priest, Zadok. The Pharisees, who arose after the Maccabean Revolt (which Hanukkah celebrates) were, at various times and in different ways, a political party, a social movement and a school of thought that battled with the Sadducees. They stressed personal holiness by obedience to both Torah and Oral Law. After the destruction of the temple in AD 70, the beliefs of the Pharisees became the liturgical and ritualistic basis for Rabbinic Judaism. Today the term *Judaism* almost always refers to Rabbinic Judaism. Though neither sect exists today, the influence of the Pharisees, who Josephus estimates to have only numbered about 6,000, remains stronger because of its reliance on oral teaching alongside the Torah.

4. Erasmo Leiva-Merikakis, *Fire of Mercy, Heart of the Word: Meditations on the Gospel According to Saint Matthew*, vol. 3 (San Francisco, CA: Ignatius Press, 2012), 580.

5. Ibid.

6. Ibid.

7. Ibid.

8. Ibid., 151.

9. Amy-Jill Levine, *The Misunderstood Jew* (New York, NY: HarperOne 2006), 21–22. Levine shows that the response Jesus offers would be commonly understood.

10. Ibid., 23.

11. There have been many attempts to argue that what Jesus says here is *not* unique, that he is only answering a Jewish question. For example, in *Love Revolution: Rediscovering the Lost Command of Jesus* (Chico: CA: Love Revolution Press, 2005), Gaylord Enns tries to show why the new commandment (John 13:34–35) is unique (70–72). While I am sympathetic with his central point, I do not agree with his understanding of what Jesus is doing in the New Covenant. The New Covenant is "new" but this does not put aside the central elements of the old (see Matthew 5:17–20). The "new" *amplifies love and then expands it*, but John 13:34–35 cannot be *separated* from these synoptic accounts unless you adopt a hermeneutic that separates this Gospel from rest of the NT. Jesus underscores how the New Covenant centers love in himself and

in the work of the Spirit. But love for God and others is *not* new. Remember, along with the oral sayings of their Messiah, the Old Testament was *the* Bible of the earliest (Jewish) Christians.

12. Levine, 23.

13. N. T. Wright, *Matthew for Everyone*, Part 2 (Louisville, KY: Westminster John Knox, 2004), 95.

14. Ibid., 96.

15. Ibid.

16. Kreeft, 190.

17. Robert Barron, foreword to Andrew M. Greeley, *The Great Mysteries: Experiencing Catholic Faith from the Inside Out* (New York, NY: Sheed & Ward, 2003), vii.

18. Scott Cairns, *Love's Immensity: Mystics on the Endless Life* (Brewster, MA: Paraclete Press, 2007), xiii.

19. Ibid., xiv.

Chapter Four

1. Katherine Doob Sakenfeld, "Love (OT)," in *The Anchor Bible Commentary*, vol. 4 (New York, NY: Doubleday, 1992), 376.

2. Werner G. Jeanrond, *A Theology of Love* (New York, NY: T & T Clark, 2010), 31.

3. Ibid., 32.

4. Ibid., 35.

5. Roberta C. Bondi, *To Love as God Loves: Conversations with the Early Church* (Philadelphia, PA: Fortress, 1987), 101.

6. John Paul II, *Fides et Ratio* (Faith and Reason), (Boston, MA: Pauline Books and Media, 1998), 44.

7. Loya and Loya, 6.

8. James Martin, S.J., *The Jesuit Guide to (Almost) Everything: A Spirituality for Real Life* (New York, NY: HarperOne, 2010), 159.

9. Richard Foster, *Celebration of Discipline* (New York, HarperCollins, 1988), 1.

10. Smith, *You Are What You Love*, 16–19. No modern author helped me to better understand this issue of virtue and habit as much as James K. A. Smith.

11. This is not a rejection of psychology. It has a positive role in helping us understand how our emotional and mental lives may have been damaged and how we can go about fixing them. But modern psychology has generally missed what I am saying about loving God.

12. Bondi, 7.

13. Martin, 206.

14. This raises a host of questions about *how* we understand depravity and remaining sin in Christians, but it is a massive mistake to place our view of sin in opposition to God's abundant mercy in Christ. This also reminds us that the fallen world is no friend to grace; nevertheless, this world—as John Calvin argued—is still the theater of God's glory.

15. George Aschenbrenner, S.J., *Stretched for Greater Glory* (Chicago, IL: Loyola Press, 2004), 109.

16. Bondi, 33.

17. H. Elliott Wright, *Holy Company: Christian Heroes and Heroines* (New York, NY: Macmillan, 1980), 180–81.

18. Ibid., 181.

19. Martin, 219.

Chapter Five

1. Anthony de Mello, S.J., *Walking on Water* (New York, NY: Crossroad Publishing Company, 1998), 93.

2. Ibid., 96.

3. Leiva-Merikakis, Vol. 3, 585.

4. Loya and Loya, 9–10.

5. Ibid., 11.

6. Taken from a homily cited in Marisa Cerini, *God Who Is Love*, 18.

7. Thomas Masters and Amy Uelmen, *Focolare* (Hyde Park, NY: New City Press, 2011), 113.

8. Cerini, 12.

9. Greg Ogden, *The Essential Commandment* (Downers Grove, IL: InterVarsity Press, 2011), 160–161.

10. Leiva-Merikakis, Vol. 3, 583.

11. T. W. Manson, *The Sayings of Jesus* (Grand Rapids, MI: Eerdmans, 1979), 61.

12. N. T. Wright, *Luke for Everyone* (Louisville, KY: Westminster John Knox, 2001), 128.

13. Ibid., 128–129. Wright notes that at the heart of this confrontation there are two opposing visions of what it means to be *true* Israel; i.e., the people of God. The question about "entering the age to come" (eternal life) was a standard rabbinic question that got standard answers. It would appear that this man was trying to get an answer from Jesus about the definition of true Israel in order to make Jesus appear to be a false teacher.

14. Ogden, 163.

15. Kenneth Bailey, *Jesus Through Middle Eastern Eyes* (Downers Grove, IL: InterVarsity Press, 2008). Many biblical writers have responded to, and disagreed with, aspects of Bailey's interpretation of the Gospels, but the work has stunning overall value to readers.

16. One of the most helpful academic treatments of the relationship between ethics and morality, and love, is Dietrich Bonhoeffer's *Ethics* (trans. N. H. Smith, 1949; reprint, New York, NY: Simon and Schuster, 1995). Bonhoeffer argues *abstract ethics* can never engage with human reality. He believes a "convulsive clinging to the ethical…which takes the form of moralization of life, arises from fear of the fullness of everyday life and from an awareness of incapacity for life; it is a flight into a position which lies outside real life" (264). He concludes we can live in a truly ethical way only by *clinging to Jesus in love, not to a set of abstract rules.*

17. Dallas Willard, *The Divine Conspiracy* (San Francisco, CA: HarperCollins, 1998), 111.

18. Leiva-Merikakis, Vol. 3, 585.

19. Ibid., 585. Leiva-Merikakis develops this idea wonderfully on pages 585–90. His insights have helped me profoundly.

20. Ibid., 586.

21. Cerini, 15.

22. Joseph Lankford, *Mother Teresa's Secret Fire* (Huntington, IN: Our Sunday Visitor, 2008), 21.

Chapter Six

1. Piero Coda, in Florence Gillet, *The Choice of Jesus Forsaken in the Theological Perspective of Chiara Lubich*, trans. Bill Hartnett (Hyde Park, NY: New City Press, 2015), xii. Italics added.

2. Ibid., 121, 132.

3. Mother Teresa, *A Call to Mercy: Hearts to Love, Hands to Serve* (New York, NY: Image, 2016), 25–26).

4. Willard, *Getting Love Right* (2012), Kindle edition, Location 3. A paper given to the American Association of Christian Counselors Conference, September 15, 2007. Subsequent references will refer to the Kindle location.

5. Ibid.

6. Daniel J. Harrington, *Jesus the Revelation of the Father's Love: What the New Testament Teaches Us* (Huntington, IN: Our Sunday Visitor, 2010), 54.

7. Ibid., 70.

8. *The Cape Town Commitment* (Peabody, Massachusetts, 2011), 9. This document can be accessed online at www.lausanne.org.

9. Cited in Tippett, *Becoming Wise*, 104.

10. Cited by Greg Boyd, *Repenting of Religion: Turning from Judgment to the Love of God* (Grand Rapids, MI: Baker, 2004), 47. This phenomenal book can be read alongside this chapter as a rich and full development of my several points.

11. Cited by Boyd, 1.

12. In my own suburban metro-Chicago county, with a population of nearly a million persons, there are many megachurches. Yet fewer than twenty percent of the population attends any church. But even these numbers are suspicious because "attend church" does not necessarily mean weekly attendance.

13. Scot McKnight, *The Jesus Creed: Loving God and Loving Others* (Brewster, MA: Paraclete Press, 2004). McKnight deals skillfully with Jewish teaching and the Old Testament. The book focuses upon Jesus' weightiest teaching: love God and love others as yourself. His overall writing discusses fully the complex issues we lightly touch upon here.

14. Scot McKnight, *The Story of God Bible Commentary: The Sermon on the Mount* (Grand Rapids, MI: Zondervan, 2013), 67.

15. Ibid., 68.

16. Willard, *Getting Love Right*, Location 140.

Chapter Seven

1. Kreeft, 36.

2. Augustine, *Homilies of the First Epistle of John*, trans. Boniface Ramsey (Hyde Park, NY: New City Press, 2008), 107.

3. Everett Ferguson, *Inheriting Wisdom: Readings for Today from Ancient Christian Writers* (Peabody, MA: Hendrickson Publishers, 2004), 119.

4. Ernesto Cardenal, *Love: A Glimpse of Eternity*, 19–20.

5. Mother Teresa, *In the Heart of the World: Thoughts, Stories, & Prayers* (New York, NY: New World Press, 1997), 45.

6. Adolfo Quezada, *Radical Love: Following the Way of Jesus* (Mahwah, NJ: Paulist Press, 2010), v.

7. Bondi, 29.

8. Søren Kierkegaard, ed. and trans. Howard V. Hong and Edna H. Hong. *Works of Love, Kierkegaard's Writings 16* (Princeton, NJ: Princeton University Press, 2009), 22.

9. Mother Teresa, *In the Heart of the World*, 29.

10. Chad Engelland, *The Way of Philosophy* (Eugene, OR: Cascade Books, 2016), 57.

11. Ibid., 60–61.

12. Bondi, 29.

13. F. Dale Bruner, *Matthew, Volume 1: The Christbook* (Grand Rapids, MI: Eerdmans, 2004), 539.

14. Quezada, *Radical Love*, vi.

15. Bondi, 22–23. For me, no book has more opened up this ancient Christian way of understanding God's love and our perfection in it, than this one. Joined with her companion volume, *To Pray and to Love: Conversations on Prayer with the Early Church* (Fortress, 1991), I came to grasp an ancient/future way of relating God's love and Christian discipleship.

16. Ibid. By putting early church writers into conversation, Bondi shows how they understood God's love and our love for God and each other. I draw much of what I write here from this very helpful book.

17. Ibid., 23.

18. Gregory of Nyssa, *The Life of Moses*, trans., intro., and notes by Abraham Melherbe and Everett Ferguson, *Classics of Western Spirituality* (New York, NY: Paulist Press, 1978), 122.

19. Bondi, 23.

20. There is abundant biblical evidence that God may show mercy in ways beyond our comprehension.

21. Steven W. Manaskar, a modern-language version with notes, edited by Kinda Whited and Cindy S. Harris: *A Perfect Love: Understanding John Wesley's A Plain Account of Christian Perfection* (Nashville, TN: Discipleship Resources, 2004), 43.

22. Ibid.

23. Ibid, 41. These are John Wesley's own words.

24. John Wesley, *Explanatory Notes on the New Testament*, 1 John 4:8, http://www.biblestudytools.com/commentaries/wesleys-explanatory-notes/1-john/1-john-4.html.

25. Excerpts from Pascal's parchment from the translation by Emile Cailliet in *Pascal: Genius in the Light of Scripture* (Philadelphia, PA: Westminster Press, 1945), 131–32.

Chapter Eight

1. This same commandment is mentioned in Luke 6:27–36. There are several differences between these two contexts, though the intent is clearly the same.

2. Leiva-Merikakis, Vol. 1, 236.

3. McKnight, *The Story of God*, 140.

4. Pinchas Lapide, *The Sermon on the Mount: Utopia or Program for Action?*, trans. A. Swidler, (Maryknoll, NY: Orbis, 1986), 85–86.

5. McKnight, *The Story of God*, 142.

6. Sinclair B. Ferguson, *The Sermon on the Mount: Kingdom Life in a Fallen World* (Carlisle, PA: The Banner of Truth Trust, 1987), 102.

Notes for Chapter Eight

7. Jim Forest, *Loving Our Enemies: Reflections on the Hardest Commandment* (Maryknoll, NY: Orbis, 2014), 17.

8. Ibid., 17. This is the best book I've read on this issue. In the first page, Forest asks, "How does a conversion of heart take place?" His stories and examples will move you to see how truly costly this commandment is in everyday life. He concludes this commandment addresses our hearts like no other. As with the Great Commandment, we must love God before we can love our neighbor. Forest answers a primary question: "How does active love help me overcome enmity?" He identifies nine biblical disciplines of active love that will help us to love our enemies. By taking each one of these as far as possible, you can find the grace to act courageously. Do this day-by-day and watch what happens. Forest devotes a chapter to each of these disciplines: (1) Pray for your enemies; (2) do good to your enemies; (3) turn the other cheek to your enemies; (4) forgive your enemies; (5) break down the dividing wall(s) of enmity between you and your enemies; (6) refuse to take "an eye for an eye" with your enemies; (7) seek nonviolent alternatives to attacking your enemies; (8) practice holy disobedience (by which he means not following laws and customs that foster violence and killing); and (9) recognize Jesus in others.

9. Aleksandr Solzhenitysn, *The Gulag Archipelago*, Vol. 2, "The Ascent," trans Thomas P. Whitney (New York, NY: Harper & Row, 1974), 168.

10. Forest, *Loving Our Enemies*, 18.

11. William Barclay, *The New Daily Study Bible: The Gospel of Matthew*, Vol. 1 (Louisville, KY: Westminster John Knox Press, 2001), 188.

12. McKnight, *The Story of God*, 143. McKnight's superb treatment of this passage, both the context and the application, informs my direction here significantly.

13. David W. Bercot, ed. *A Dictionary of Early Christian Beliefs* (Peabody, MA: Hendrickson Publishers, 1998). All of the previous quotations from early church writers are taken from this source.

14. Barclay, 190.

15. www.religioustolerance.org/reciproc2.htm.
In Confucianism, which predates Jesus, it is said, "Do not do to others what you do not want them to do to you" (Analects 15:23).

In some cases I think the parallel between Christianity and other religions is stretched a bit thin. Christian teaching clearly has a theological dimension that is deeper and wider than an "ethic of reciprocity."

16. Barclay, 202.

17. McKnight, *The Story of God*, 144.

18. Ibid., 145.

19. Ibid., 145.

20. Forest, 4

21. http://travelingecumenist.blogspot.com/2016/06/what-makes-christian-part-1.html.

Chapter Nine

1. Gerard Rossé, *The Spirituality of Communion: A New Approach to the Johannine Writing* (Hyde Park, NY: New City Press, 1998), 69–70.

2. See also John 15:12–14, 17; Romans 13:8–10; 1 John 3:21–24; 4:16–21; 6:2–3; 2 John 1:5–6.

3. These discourses precede the final part of the Fourth Gospel; i.e., the glorification of Christ in his death and resurrection and several appearances to his disciples before his ascension. The ascension is mentioned in Mark 16:19–20; Luke 24:50–52, and Acts 1:6–11.

4. In his first epistle John often uses this phrase to describe his relationship with fellow Christians as their spiritual leader.

5. Some suggest that the word *new* contains a force which separates this command from all previous commands to love. This thesis, however, has several flaws. First, the context is far more complex. The noun *commandment* appears in the singular four times and in the plural six times. In John 14:15, for example, *commandments* refers to "doing greater works and asking the Father in Jesus' name." In 14:23 the words *love me* and *keep my word* are clearly specified as commandments. Willard M. Swartley says, "Add these four [commandments] to love one another, and we have *five commands Jesus gives his disciples*" (italics added). See *Believers Bible Commentary: John* (Harrisonburg, VA: Herald Press, 2013). Gaylord Enns makes this mistake in his otherwise helpful treatment of this command to "love one another" (see *Love Revolution:*

Rediscovering the Lost Command of Jesus [Chico, CA: Love Revolution Press, 2005]). Enns reduces *all* of Jesus' particular commandments to two: love one another and make disciples. In 1 John the command to "love one another" is put into practical terms where the word *commandment* occurs six times. In 1 John 2:3, 5, "obeying his commandments" and "obeying his word" reveal that God's love has reached perfection within the believer. When this happens, the believer "walks as Jesus walked" (2:6). Thus in John, Jesus' commandments are *clearly* related to the double commandment in the Synoptic Gospels to love God and our neighbor. Paul Minear rightly calls John the *Martyr's Gospel*. Both Jesus and his disciples are called to lay down their lives for one another in an act of sacrificial, relational love. This is the *costly love* of his new commandment to "love one another."

6. Pope Francis, Twitter post, 16 May 2014, https://twitter.com/Pontifex/status/467232036013350912

7. Gérard Rossé, *Community of Believers* (Hyde Park, NY: New City Press, 2009), 70.

8. Gail O'Day, *The New Interpreter's Bible: The Gospel of John* (Nashville, TN: Abingdon Press, 1995), 734.

9. Willard M. Swartley, *Believers Church Bible Commentary* (Harrisonburg, VA: Herald Press, 2013), 327.

10. See my book *Your Church Is Too Small: Why Unity in Christ's Mission Is Vital to the Future of the Church* (Grand Rapids, MA: Zondervan, 2010).

11. Richard B. Hays, *The Moral Vision of the New Testament: A Contemporary Introduction to New Testament Ethics* (San Francisco, CA: HarperCollins, 1996), 145.

12. Pope Francis, Twitter Post, 16 May 2014. https://twitter.com/Pontifex/status/467232036013350912.

13. This story haunted me for years. I thought the man was crazy and wrote him off.

14. This is not the place to engage with this doctrinal idea, but I believe it has never been a mainstream Christian view. Given that,

Origen's position was never clearly and openly denounced in any council or (early) catholic creed. It seems that charity should at least require us to leave the door open to God's unrevealed judgment being the final word on this subject.

15. H. Elliott Wright, *Holy Company: Christian Heroes and Heroines* (New York, NY: Macmillan, 1980), 172.

16. "What Makes a Christian? Part 2," can be found at http://travelingecumenist.blogspot.com/2016/07/what-makes-christian-part-2.html.

Chapter Ten

1. Chiara Lubich, *Living Dialogue: Steps on the Way to Communion among Christians* (Hyde Park, NY: New City Press, 2009), 23.

2. Ibid., 24.

3. Ibid., 27.

4. Ibid., 27–28.

5. Peter J. Leithart, *The End of Protestantism: Pursuing Unity in a Fragmented Church* (Grand Rapids, MI: Brazos Press, 2016).

6. There are several ways to define Christendom. In a cultural sense it refers to all adherents of Christianity. In its historical sense, the term usually refers to the medieval or early modern period of history. The word also refers to the established religion of the state, especially in regard to the relationship states had with the Vatican. In a modern sense it can refer to the Christian majority that influences a culture by being the *dominant influence* within that culture. In this sense, America was different (because of the separation of church and state), yet it was also deeply influenced by Christendom, a fact that is no longer true.

7. Kenneth Scott Latourette, *A History of Christianity*, Vol. 1 (Peabody, MA: Hendrickson Publishers, 1997 reprint), 263.

8. The disastrous revolt of the Jews against the Romans between AD 66 and 70 ended in the destruction of the Temple and the scattering of the Jewish people (diaspora). It also eliminated all the various Jewish factions, leaving the Pharisees and the followers of Jesus as the primary expressions of Judaism. In the beginning the Jews and the followers of Jesus had worshiped together, but this ceased by the end of the first century. The Pharisees saw the

followers of Jesus as blasphemous heretics, while the followers of Jesus condemned the Pharisees for refusing to acknowledge Jesus as the Messiah. From the Pharisees came the rabbinic and Talmudic tradition that became Judaism. By the year 90 the rabbis had excluded Christians from the synagogues. A larger question is whether the New Testament Scriptures are *anti-Judaic*. It seems the biblical texts are not hostile to the Jewish people, especially since the writers were Jewish. It is clear however, that they do seem to oppose certain Jewish factions (including the Sadducees and eventually the Pharisees) that were anti-Christian. We should remember that in that era the terms *Christianity* and *Judaism* did not even exist. The real problem came later, when Christians read these texts *as condemning all Jews*. Although historians have noted that after this early period Jews and Christians got along fairly well until the middle of the eleventh century, some early Christian sermons and theologies did nurture anti-Judaism. This history is complicated and troubling.

9. In 1965 The Second Vatican Council adopted a dogmatic formulation called *Nostra Aetate* ("In Our Times"). This landmark theological statement repudiates replacement theology and the resultant anti-Semitism that charged the Jews with being collectively guilty for the death of Jesus. The entire document, which is very important for modern Christian understanding, is available at www.vatican.va/archive/hist_councils/ii_vatican_council/documents/vat-ii_decl_19651028_nostra-aetate_en.html. Large portions of Christianity have been anti-Semitic (one could say, more accurately, anti-Jewish), but as *Nostra Aetate* makes plain, this was not the teaching of Jesus himself.

10. *The Cape Town Commitment* (Peabody, MA: Hendrickson Publishers, 2011), 53 (II:D.1).

11. C. S. Lewis, *Mere Christianity* (New York, NY: HarperOne, 1952), 40.

12. Ibid., 46.

13. Henry R. Percival, Henry Wace, Philip Schaff, eds. *The Seven Ecumenical Councils of the Undivided Church: Their Canons and Dogmatic Decrees Together with the Canons of All the Local Synods Which Have Received Ecumenical Acceptance. Edited with Notes Gathered from the Writings of the Greatest Scholars* (Oxford: Benediction Classics, 2011).

14. George Byron Koch, *What We Believe and Why* (Northwoods, IL: Byron Arts, 2012), 215.

15. Ibid., 225.

16. Ibid. 255. This idea has been attributed to Augustine, but so far as I can tell, Meiderlin first expressed it in this way.

Chapter Eleven

1. Chiara Lubich, *The Pearl of the Gospel*, foreword and compilation by Bill Hartnett (Hyde Park, NY: New City Press, 2013), 8–9.

2. Carol Kelly-Gangi, ed. *Pope Francis: His Essential Wisdom* (New York, NY: Fall River Press, 2014), 30.

3. In his apostolic letter written at the beginning of the Third Millennium, *Novo Millennio Ineunte*, John Paul II recommended a "spirituality of communion" to the entire church:

> 43. To make the Church *the home and the school of communion*: that is the great challenge facing us in the millennium which is now beginning, if we wish to be faithful to God's plan and respond to the world's deepest yearnings. ...
>
> ...Before making practical plans, we need *to promote a spirituality of communion*, making it the guiding principle of education wherever individuals and Christians are formed, wherever ministers of the altar, consecrated persons, and pastoral workers are trained, wherever families and communities are being built up. A spirituality of communion indicates above all the heart's contemplation of the mystery of the Trinity dwelling in us, and whose light we must also be able to see shining on the face of the brothers and sisters around us. A spirituality of communion also means an ability to think of our brothers and sisters in faith within the profound unity of the Mystical Body, and therefore as "those who are a part of me." This makes us able to share their joys and sufferings, to sense their desires and attend to their needs, to offer them deep and genuine friendship. A spirituality of communion implies also the ability to see what is positive in others, to welcome it and prize it as a gift from God: not only as a gift for the brother or sister who has received it directly, but also as a "gift for me". A spirituality of communion means, finally, to know how to "make room" for our brothers and sisters, bearing "each other's burdens" (*Gal* 6:2) and resisting the selfish temptations which constantly beset us and provoke competition, careerism, distrust and jealousy. Let us have no illusions: unless we follow this spiritual path, external structures of communion will serve very little purpose. They would become mechanisms without a soul, "masks" of communion rather than its means of expression and growth.

https://w2.vatican.va/content/john-paul-ii/en/apost_letters/2001/documents/hf_jp-ii_apl_20010106_novo-millennio-ineunte.html

4. To learn more about this remarkable man, read Brother Yun and Paul Hattaway, *The Heavenly Man: The Remarkable True Story of Chinese Christian Brother Yun*, fourth edition (Grand Rapids, MI: Kregel, 2002). You can also read Brother Yun and Paul Hattaway, *Living Water* (Grand Rapids, MI: Zondervan, 2008), a book of teaching that shows how he grew in his understanding and faith.

5. François-Xavier Nguyễn Văn Thuận, *Five Loaves and Two Fish* (Washington DC: Morley Books, 2000), 60–61. He shares further spiritual reflections in *The Road of Hope: A Gospel from Prison* (Hyde Park, NY: New City Press, 2013).

6. Gregory A. Boyd, *Repenting of Religion: Turning from Judgment to the Love of God* (Grand Rapids, MI: Baker, 2004), 105. This entire book is an amazing help to anyone who wants to deal with the relevant biblical texts and the *big story*. I have drawn freely from Boyd in framing the fundamental problem.

7. Ibid.

8. Paul A. Rainbow, *Johannine Theology: The Gospels, The Epistles and the Apocalypse* (Downers Grove, IL: InterVarsity Press, 2014), 318.

9. Ibid.

10. Ibid., 319.

11. Brendan Leahy, *Going to God Together* (Hyde Park, NY: New City Press, 2013), 11–12.

12. John Paul II, Apostolic Letter at the Beginning of the New Millennium, *Novo Millennio Ineunte* (6 January 2001), n. 43. https://w2.vatican.va/content/john-paul-ii/en/apost_letters/2001/documents/hf_jp-ii_apl_20010106_novo-millennio-ineunte.html.

13. Thérèse of Lisieux, trans. John Beevers, *The Autobiography of St. Thérèse of Lisieux: The Story of a Soul* (New York, NY: Doubleday, 1957), 122–23.

14. Lubich, *Essential Writings*, 65.

Chapter Twelve

1. Latourette, 463–77.

2. Ibid.

3. See David Kinnaman and Gabe Lyons, *UnChristian: What a New Generation Thinks About Christianity... and Why It Matters* (Grand Rapids, MI: Baker, 2012 reprint), and David Kinnaman and Aly Hawkins, *You Lost Me: Why Young Christians Are Leaving Church... and Rethinking Faith* (Grand Rapids, MI: Baker, 2011). Both books contain compelling data and helpful stories of what is happening in the culture and the church.

4. Eberhard Arnold, *The Early Christians in Their Own Words* (Farmington, PA: The Plough Publishing House, 1997), x.

5. According to the Talmud and Leviticus 17, seven precepts marked the way people outside of Abraham should live: obedience to authority; reverence for God's name; abstinence from idolatry, fornication, murder, and robbery; and a prohibition against the consumption of blood. The Talmud said that these precepts applied to "sojourners living within the gates of Israel."

6. Cited by Origen, *Against Celsus*, VI:34.

7. Arnold, *The Early Christians in Their Own Words*, 18.

8. Robert L. Wilkin, *The Christians as the Romans Saw Them* (New Haven, CT: Yale University Press, 1984). See this book's jacket.

9. Lindberg, 36.

10. Ibid., 37.

11. Helen Rhee, *Loving the Poor, Saving the Rich: Wealth, Poverty, and Early Christian Formation* (Grand Rapids, MI: Baker, 2012), 18.

12. Quezada, 32.

13. Ibid., 33.

14. Ibid., vii.

15. Ibid., 2.

16. Russell Kick, ed. *Quotes That Will Change Your Life* (San Francisco, CA: Plum Island Press, 2015), 100.

17. Viktor Frankl, *Man's Search for Meaning, Fourth Edition* (Boston, MA: Beacon Press, 1992), 75.

18. Anthony J. Gittins, *The Presence That Disturbs: A Call to Radical Discipleship* (Ligouri, MO: Ligouri Publications, 2002), xvii).

19. Ibid., xix-xx.

Chapter Thirteen

1. My thinking about *halakha* ("instruction" or "judgment") and the importance of living "in the Way" is influenced by the thinking of my friend George Byron Koch. George is a Jewish follower of Jesus who grasps these ideas as clearly as anyone I know.

2. Orlando O. Espin and James B. Nickoloff, eds. *An Introductory Dictionary of Theology and Religious Studies* (Collegeville, MN: Liturgical Press, 2007), 362.

3. Carlton J. H. Hayes, *Christianity and Western Civilization* (Stanford, CA: Stanford University Press, 1954), 56.

4. Human rights are a modern idea, perhaps the most important of all modern ideas. Human rights came about through a mixing of Enlightenment humanism with nonsectarian, Christian ideals.

5. Lindberg, 39–40. All the quotes and ideas in this paragraph are taken from this source.

6. Ibid., 41.

7. There are some amazing parallels with our own time. Avowed non-Christians, and some former Christians, want to retain Christian values (at least some of them) while they repudiate the doctrinal teaching about Jesus. There really is "nothing new under the sun."

8. Gaetano Baluffi and Denis Gargan, *The Charity of the Church, a Proof of Her Divinity* (Dublin: M. H. Gill and Son, 1885), 16.

9. Ibid.

Chapter Fourteen

1. Leiva-Merikakis, Vol. 1, 211.

2. Ibid.

3. Gaylord Enns, *Love Revolution: Rediscovering the Lost Command of Jesus* (Chico, CA: Love Revolution Press, 2005), 110.

4. George Beasley-Murray, *Gospel of Life: Theology in the Fourth Gospel* (Peabody, MA: Hendrickson Publishers, 1991), 111.

5. Demetrius R. Dumm, *A Mystical Portrait of Jesus: New Perspectives on John's Gospel* (Collegeville, MN: Liturgical Press, 2001), 78.

6. The University of Durham's Centre for Catholic Studies hosts projects in "constructive theology," which include receptive ecumenism. The terms and explanation that I use here come from the Centre's website. See https://www.dur.ac.uk/theology.religion/ccs/constructivetheology/receptiveecumensim/.

7. See https://recapitulareblog.wordpress.com/2015/07/09/unity-v-holiness/.

8. I could name several contemporary "hot-button issues" that divide Christians, including among others immigration, the environment, economics, the death penalty, abortion, euthanasia, drug policies, mental-health concerns, gender issues, and marriage. I appeal for calm heads and loving hearts so we can engage such issues in a living, loving context of "grace and truth." My greatest personal challenge in these matters is not getting people to agree with me but rather listening to and loving all who follow Christ and seeking humbly to hear what they are saying and to understand why.

9. Judith M. Povilus, *United in His Name: Jesus in Our Midst in the Experience and Thought of Chiara Lubich* (Hyde Park, NY: New City Press, 1992), 59.

Chapter Fifteen

1. Dumm, 76.

2. Ibid.

3. Pope Francis, *The Simple Wisdom of Pope Francis: Hold On to Hope* (Washington, D.C.: U. S. Conference of Catholic Bishops, 2013), 27.

4. McKnight, *The Jesus Creed*.

5. Koch, *What We Believe and Why*, 161–64.

6. Ibid., 170.

7. Ibid., 182.

8. Augustine performed what some have called an "internal excavation" of his own mind and heart, thereby discovering his own desire for perfection in love and his deep limitations. Reinhold Niebuhr said that Augustine's study of memory led him to the "understanding that the human spirit in its depth and heights reaches into eternity and this vertical dimension is more impor-

tant for our understanding of man than merely his rational capacity for forming general concepts." (*The Nature and Destiny of Man* [New York, NY: Scribner's, 1996], 157). This underscores what I've said about the idolatry of concepts and how we've used them in the place of robust, costly love.

9. The words "diabolical" and "Satan" (the devil) come from the same root. It means the one who slanders, accuses, and defames. This means that Satan's work against the church is always to divide us (see Ephesians 6:10–20). No being in the entire universe opposes our unity more clearly than Satan and his servants. This is why our true warfare is *not* against one another but against Satan and the unseen forces of division!

10. Cited by Jean-Pierre Camus in *The Spirit of Saint Francis de Sales* (Middlesex, UK: Echo Library, 2007), 41.

11. Mother Teresa, *A Call to Mercy*, 47.

New City Press of the Focolare

New City Press is one of more than 20 publishing houses sponsored by the Focolare, a movement founded by Chiara Lubich to help bring about the realization of Jesus' prayer: "That all may be one" (John 17:21). In view of that goal, New City Press publishes books and resources that enrich the lives of people and help all to strive toward the unity of the entire human family. We are a member of the Association of Catholic Publishers.

202 Comforter Blvd.
Hyde Park, NY 12538
www.newcitypress.com

Periodicals
Living City Magazine
www.livingcitymagazine.com

Scan to join our mailing list for discounts and promotions

or go to

www.newcitypress.com

and click on "join our email list."